PRAISE FOR

The Gate Church

"Why do some local churches have more influence and impact than others? Interesting question. In this book, Frank Damazio examines the combination of qualities that give certain churches a strategic edge. For any leader who wants to see their church fulfill its God-given potential. The Gate Church *is an inspiring read."*

BRIAN HOUSTON Senior Pastor, Hillsong Church, Sydney, Australia

"Frank Damazio never fails to teach about the local church with clarity and insight. He has a message all pastors need to hear."

TED HAGGARD Senior Pastor, New Life Church, Colorado Springs, Colorado

"Frank Damazio has done it again! When it comes to the revelation of the church, it seems that God has ransacked us with symbolic types and pictures of His church. Frank's book on The Gate Church *presents another of those symbolic and prophetic pictures. "Challenging" and "meditative" are words that describe this latest text.Understanding the life and vision of Jacob will be exceedingly helpful, but only as a leader knows the God of Jacob can "Gate Churches" be built. Once again, anything Frank writes is worthy of a place in your library."*

KEVIN J. CONNER Author, *Interpreting the Symbols and Types*

"The 21st century church is very definitely a new wineskin, and in this book he astutely points the direction that today's churches must take if they want to be used by God to transform their communities."

C. PETER WAGNER Chancellor, Wagner Leadership Institute

"This book will relieve a great amount of frustration for the body of Christ. It is prophetically practical. Every pastor, church leader and believer should read it."

DR. CINDY JACOBS CO-Founder, Generals of Intercession

"Years ago God impressed on my heart a coming global awakening led by pillar churches in every geographic region on earth that would make possible the total spiritual transformation of those regions. Now, I've seen a clear-cut guide to help make all this happen in Frank Damazio's, The Gate Church. It's absolutely must reading for leaders with a heart for city transformation!"

DICK EASTMAN International President, Every Home for Christ

"This is an extraordinary exposition on the marks to hit for a church wanting to have an impact on its inner and surrounding community."

PASTOR CHE AHN Senior Pastor, Harvest Rock Church, Pasadena, California

"The Gate Church by Pastor Frank Damazio highlights an area where God is really moving today. In every town and city, God is leading churches to answer that call to gate keeping, that is, being a force in the areas so aptly detailed in this great book. You'll refer back to The Gate Church again and again."

TOMMY BARNETT Pastor, Phoenix First Assembly of God, Phoenix, Arizona

The Gate Church

*Discover the Authority, Power and Results
God Wants for Your Church*

FRANK DAMAZIO

CITYBIBLE
PUBLISHING

PORTLAND, OREGON, U.S.A.

PUBLISHED BY CITY BIBLE PUBLISHING

9200 NE FREMONT, PORTLAND, OREGON 97220

PRINTED IN U.S.A.

City Bible Publishing is a ministry of City Bible Church, and is dedicated to serving the local church and its leaders through the production and distribution of quality restoration materials.

It is our prayer that these materials, proven in the context of the local church, will equip leaders in exalting the Lord and extending His Kingdom.

For a free catalog of resources from City Bible Publishing, please call 1-800-777-6057, or visit our website at www.citybiblepublishing.com.

Library of Congress Cataloging-in-Publication Data

Damazio, Frank.
  The gate church : discover the authority, power, and results God
  wants for your church / Frank Damazio.
    p. cm.
  Includes bibliographical references and index.
  ISBN 1-886849-75-7 (hardcover) -- ISBN 1-886849-77-3 (pbk.)
  1. Church. I. Title.
BV600.2 .D29 2000
253--dc21

                    00-011849

DEDICATION

This book is dedicated to all young pastors and leaders who are seeking to build a model church for their generation—not so simple a pursuit, but one that God will assist. I especially want to dedicate the book to my brother-in-law, Mark Conner, who pastors a model Gate Church in Melbourne, Australia. He is a young pastor who is giving hope to the next generation by building a house of God with an open gate of heaven.

CONTENTS

ACKNOWLEDGMENTS

A big thank you to:

‡ *The City Bible Church congregation for being a people willing to become a Gate Church.*

‡ *All City Bible Church elders and ministries who have given their lives to make it happen.*

‡ *My personal intercessors for always covering me and my family, especially during writing projects.*

‡ *All the other great leaders in our nation and around the globe who are pursuing a church with the gate of heaven opened and the power of God present.*

‡ *My editor, Karen Kaufman, a true gift to me as a writer to perfect and adjust with sensitivity and partnership.*

‡ *Cheryl Bolton, my secretary, for producing sermon notes and power points and endless filing. Without her help this project may well have been post-millennial in its arrival.*

‡ *Alida Little, my personal assistant, who keeps all trains on the right tracks without collisions.*

‡ *My wife and four children who again found me locked up in my office with the ongoing promise of "It's almost finished."*

‡ *Last, but not least, to the Lord and the Spirit of God for allowing me to learn these things and to have the ability to put them down on paper for all who might be helped by them.*

FOREWORD

It was shortly after the turn of the twentieth century, amid the just-rising, young-but-vital Pentecostal movement, that a prophetic voice rose to assert the ongoing nature of "the Reformation." The essence of the message was (and is) that the Church is progressively recovering the full dimensions of the inheritance she lost during the Dark Ages. In a sense, it might be said that the Church was "saved" or "born again" by faith through the restored message of justification by faith, 500 years ago: a living, biblical, dynamic *soteriology* (the doctrine of salvation) was recovered.

If that analogy holds, and I believe it is credible, to my view the global Church is just beginning to recover a living, biblical, dynamic *ecclesiology*—the doctrine of the Church. Just as the twentieth century has been called *The Century of the Holy Spirit* by leaders from all sectors of the Body of Christ, I predict the coming century to be one in which a clear concept of the Church, her mission and her truest, timeless and most effective strategies will be regained. I believe this book is a part of *that* feature of the continuation of the Reformation, into the twenty-first century.

Frank Damazio has provided much more in these pages than simply a clever plan for local church growth or a set of techniques for pastors to pursue in an effort at "success." "The Gate Church" is the term he employs to describe a local church possessed with a Kingdom mind-set and mission—the church that will make a difference, not just "draw a crowd."

He does not write as an analyst or observer: he is a catalyst and participator! His experience is not in the research library, though he is an excellent student and is not unaware of the Church's yesterdays or todays. But the credibility of Frank's message, and its carefully detailed, practical content, is the fact that he is *doing* church this way. He and the family of City Bible Church in Portland are "a Gate Church," not because they label themselves that, but because they love, live and serve that way.

As I look across 40 years of pastoral leading, and then scan the present horizon of the Church in ours and other nations, I perceive "an hour" has arrived. It is an hour of citywide impacting that is beginning to occur in New Testament ways, because New Testament vitality and spiritual penetration is taking place. In the hour the Church as a whole has become *less* enfranchised by society's institutions, she is becoming more effective in her impact. Jesus laid the truth before us long ago: His "Kingdom" will never gain high currency with any contemporary culture in terms of power, control or economic dominance. But, if she is alive and well, His Bride will multiply children everywhere, until the salt flavors the world around it, and the light beams ever more deeply into blinded souls and steadily shines in the face of evil's surrounding darkness.

The Gate Church is the kind of book that points to that kind of Church. It is one of an early-on, defining genre to help us all see more clearly how to lead more precisely toward serving Jesus' ideas about the "people movement" He founded. It is a solid, scriptural, sanely put, spiritually impassioned resource written by a sound and faithful pastor of whom those adjectives could equally be ascribed. Read it. Prayerfully apply it. And thank the Lord for using Frank to share these thoughts of His...because they are *His*. Jesus is still "reforming" the Church–and she's becoming an increasingly more faith-filled and more fruitful Bride as He does.

JACK W. HAYFORD
Chancellor, The King's College and Seminary
Founding Pastor, The Church On The Way

Van Nuys, California
Summer, 2000

INTRODUCTION

Like Solomon of old, I have purposed to build a house for the Lord (see 1 Kings 5:5,6). This house is not made of materials I choose. It is not made according to my mind, my plans, my desires or my ambitions. This is the Lord's house, the house of His heart, His plans, His dreams. As a leader, I must have a clear biblical perspective on the church that Christ is building. Most churched and unchurched people alike, I believe, have never had the opportunity to experience a true, biblically functioning New Testament church.

For many, the idea of church is boring, monotonous, predictable, stale and nonrelevant. A large percentage of our nation does not attend any kind of church, and those who do attend on occasion would never describe the church as an exciting place. And yet, church is to be life changing, wonderful, a great investment of time and money. People should feel that they wouldn't trade the experience for anything—can't wait to go, hate to leave, love the preaching, uplifted by the worship. What would we do without church?!

In Bill Hybel's book *Rediscovering Church*, Dr. Gilbert Bilezikian describes the church as "God's ultimate achievement, a community, a center of warm, effervescent, outreaching of Christian love, a place with all of its components united in order to become a force in this world instead of a farce!"[1]

A Gate Church is not a farce church. It is not a pathetic, lifeless church. It is a life-giving, life-changing, energetic, encounter-with-God kind of a church. It opens a way into the presence and power of a living God. When people visit a Gate Church, they come out saying, "The Lord is in this place. How awesome is this place!" (Gen. 28:17).

Eleven characteristics from Genesis 28:10-22 will be cameos of what will be developed in this book as the vision for a Gate Church. The healthy, functioning Gate Church will have all of them:

1. A prayer-intercession ladder connecting heaven and earth (see Gen. 28:12)

2. A sustained, healthy spiritual atmosphere (see Gen. 28:12,16,17)

3. A wise and balanced assimilation of prophetic truths and trends (see Gen. 28:13,15)

4. A qualitative and quantitative growth with deep relational footings (see Gen. 28:13)

5. A rich environment for building and blessing the family (see Gen. 28:14)

6. A faith in God that opens the doors of divine opportunity (see Gen. 28:15)

7. A sustained, awesome, manifested presence of God (see Gen. 28:16,17)

8. A foundational core of living stones and strong leadership pillars (see Gen. 28:18,19)

9. A Word-driven focus (see Gen. 28:19; 1 Tim. 3:15)

10. A covenantal commitment in giving of the tithe and offerings (see Gen. 28:20-22)

11. An open heaven with healing, miracles and deliverance (see Gen. 28:12; John 1:50,51)

This book is written for leaders who desire to build Gate Churches. Using the Old Testament character of Jacob, this book looks at what Gate-Church leaders go through to become the broken but empowered people who build a Gate Church. It also examines the eleven characteristics of a Gate Church with practical steps for implementation. With Genesis 28:17 as the backdrop, it reveals Jacob's introduction to "the house of God, the gate of heaven" that results in his confession, "How awesome is this place!"

Gate Churches encounter the biblical gate of heaven, establish the house of God and enjoy His awesome presence. Are you hungry for that kind of church? If so, I invite you to journey along with me.

FRANK DAMAZIO
City Bible Church
Portland, Oregon

NOTES

1. Bill Hybels, *Rediscovering Church* (Grand Rapids: Zondervan Publishing, 1995), p. 157.

*The gate church needs to have built into it a
Ministry of Prayer, prophecy + outreach. I want to
do this. This is my passion → to build intercessory
Prayer, prophecy, sign + wonders + outreach into the church.*

CHAPTER ONE

*You cannot have a gate church w/o prayer + outreach
in its core foundation.*

*And he was afraid and said, "How awesome is this place!
This is none other than the house of God, and this is
the gate of heaven!" Genesis 28:17*

*The gate church may not be @ a strategic
geographic place but can be assigned there.*

The Gate-Church Vision

Jacob sees a vision of the house of God and the gate of heaven. Like Jacob, if the church of the twenty-first century is going to become what Christ has envisioned, it will need open heavens, *a gate* that establishes the manifest, powerful presence of God.

THE GATE

The gate in Scripture is a very powerful symbol and is used in connection with a powerful church. Jesus connected the two in Matthew 16:16-18.

The word "gate" in the original language can be defined as a structure closing, or enclosure; a large opening through a wall or a barrier created so that people and things can pass to another area, a new area. A gate opens the way into something. It is a passageway or a channel, an avenue. Gates, because of their function in the Old Testament cities, took on a symbolic meaning. Both the prophets and Christ Himself used this symbolism. The Bible describes four functions of city gates during Old Testament times:

1. A place that controlled access and provided strongly fortified protection (see Josh. 2:7; 7:5; Judg. 16:2,3; 18:16,17; 2 Kings 11:6; 14:13).

2. A place where legal or governmental leaders of the city sat to hand down judicial decisions (see Gen. 19:1; Deut. 25:7; 2 Sam. 19:8; Lam. 5:14).

3. A place where business and social functions occurred and where business contracts were made and witnessed (see Gen. 34:24; Ruth 4:1,11; 2 Sam. 15:2).

4. A place where prophetic messages were brought by the prophets and delivered to the elders of the city (see 1 Kings 22:10; 2 Chron. 18:9; Jer. 7:2; 17:19).

The gates are powerful symbols of God's authority over His people. As we see in the book of Isaiah, God's laws that keep His people and the spiritual health of the nation could be symbolized by the usage of this word "gate" (italics added):

✝ Isa. 26:2: Open the *gates*, that the righteous nation which keeps the truth may enter in.

✝ Isa. 60:11: Therefore your *gates* shall be open continually; they shall not be shut day or night, that men may bring to you the wealth of the Gentiles, and their kings in procession.

✝ Isa. 62:10: Go through, go through the *gates*! Prepare the way for the people; build up, build up the highway! Take out the stones, lift up a banner for the peoples!

The gates are also symbolic of evil powers that war against the souls of people and against the church that Christ is building (italics added):

✝ Isa. 38:10: I said, "In the prime of my life I shall go to the *gates of Sheol*; I am deprived of the remainder of my years."

✝ Isa. 45:2: "I will go before you and make the crooked places straight; I will break in pieces the *gates of bronze* and cut the bars of iron."

✝ Jer. 51:58: Thus says the LORD of hosts: "The broad walls of Babylon shall be utterly broken, and her high *gates* shall be burned with fire; the people will labor in vain, and the nations, because of the fire; and they shall be weary."

✝ Matt. 16:18: "And I also say to you that you are Peter, and on this rock I will build My church, and the *gates of Hades* shall not prevail against it."

The Gate Church is a biblical description of the church that Christ is building. We as Gate-Church leaders must systematically prepare to build the church that is in prophetic seed-form in Genesis 28:10-22 and full bloom in the book of Acts—but in order to build this kind of church, we must have God's dream or vision for what we are to build.

STRETCHING FOR GOD'S DREAM

Vision stretches us into the future; it stretches our abilities, including our ability to dream. Jacob, our model of a Gate-Church dreamer, received a dream from God on his journey of divine surprises. In his dream, Jacob saw several elements that were far beyond his ability to comprehend—he did not understand what these elements represented or how they would affect his future. What he actually saw was a prophetic picture, a word for the future that was not just for him.

The different elements within Jacob's dream are visited in other passages of Scripture as symbols used to describe the glorious church that Christ is building. The terms "open heavens," "stones," "pillars," "oil," "house of God," "presence," "ladder"—all of these are interpreted for us by their use in Scripture.

The first important factor, however, is that Jacob had received a dream, or a vision, that was a word for the future. This vision involved a place where a gate of heaven opened and supernatural activity was taking place. The Gate-Church leader must understand the gate and have a vision.

THE VISION FACTOR

George Barna defines vision in his book *The Power of Vision* by stating that "you might define vision as foresight with insight based on hindsight. This definition underscores the importance of looking to the future, emphasizes the significance of possessing a keen awareness of current circumstances and possibilities, and notes the values of learning from the past." [1]

Vision is seeing the invisible and making it visible. Vision is an informed bridge from the present to the future; vision is a sanctified dream. The vision must be clear, biblical and precise. Rick Warren, pastor of Saddleback Church in California, encourages pastors to ask the right questions in discovering vision.

1. Why does the church exist?

2. What are we to *be* as a church? (Who and what are we?)

3. What are we to *do* as a church? (What does God want done in the world?)

4. How are we to do it?[2]

Rick has put his vision into a concise vision statement:

To bring people to Jesus and *membership* in His family, develop them to Christlike *maturity* and equip them for their *ministry* in the church and life *mission* in the world, in order to *magnify* God's name.[3]

In 1981, I pioneered a church in Eugene, Oregon, and pastored that church for twelve years before returning to Portland, Oregon, where I am now. Establishing a vision with a small leadership team in a church plant is not nearly as complex as establishing a vision within a church that has existed for many years with other pastors and leaders who have been in that church for a long time. When I returned here in Portland, I invested a considerable amount of time with our leadership team discussing our future and writing a very simple vision statement and some vision values. We then gave the vision statement to the congregation so we could all build with the same focus, pursuing the same vision.

The Gate-Church leader must be able to put the vision in writing so that the church may own the vision as well. Visionary pastors are great gifts to their churches. They are motivated—not by self-aggrandizement or ego-gratification —but by a burning desire to see God's purpose accomplished. These leaders catch a vision for the church that will make a difference in today's world.

GLEANING FROM THE GATES OF THE GREATS

A Gate-Church leader recognizes the many blessed, healthy, growing, influential churches of the present and past. Many of the great leaders who have produced great churches have created models with both strong and weak points. To copy any one model entirely is to sacrifice the power of God-given vision for the church you are to build. To ignore these churches—thus receiving or learning nothing from them—is to allow spiritual pride and spiritual blindness to rob you of the tried-and-proven principles for church health and growth.

Most of the great churches flow out of three historical streams: "pietism," which emphasizes holiness and intimacy with God; "revivalism," which emphasizes the sovereign outpouring of God's Spirit upon His hungry people; and "evangelism," which emphasizes winning people to Christ. Great leaders and churches have emerged from all three streams.

Every great church, however, must discover its destiny, its reason for existence and its strengths. Its vision is set around an essential DNA, which becomes the main recognizable characteristic of the church—and that DNA is determined as you wrestle with God in prayer for answers to the following questions:

‡ What are the main ingredients you are to build into your church?

‡ What will you borrow?

‡ What will you create?

‡ What will be the dominant characteristic of your Gate Church?

ENVISIONING AN ATMOSPHERE THAT ENCOUNTERS THE GOD OF JACOB

To build a Gate Church is to build a specific atmosphere that has a specific effect on those who become involved in it. As I have studied Genesis 27 and 28 (our biblical text), I have seen in the Old Testament patriarch Jacob the characteristics of a twenty-first-century emerging pastor or leader and Gate-Church builder.

Jacob was by no means a perfect man, but his life provides a remarkable example of God's grace working through us, even when we stumble and don't have things all worked out. Sin is a real danger that can torpedo a great work of God, and we can thwart our destinies through rebellion; however, when God's hand rests upon us, He uses even our worst flaws to work together for our good (see Rom. 8:28). Jacob's journey of failure and success, his encounters with God, his brokenness and vision, and his character growth from scoundrel to "leader in process" have much to teach us.

Jacob finds a gate that opens up to the heavens. He finds a ladder that connects heaven and earth and a stone that begins as his pillow but becomes an anointed pillar for the house of God. He sees a vision, feels a powerful presence of God, and his life is changed forever!

We are the Jacobs of the twenty-first century. We are on a journey. The road is often crooked and, at times, very lonely—even a little confusing. All the pieces don't fit all the time. We know that, like Jacob, we have weaknesses, but we're hungry for an encounter with a living God, a face-to-face with the God for whom all creation longs. Jacob encounters God and confesses: "How awesome is this place. This is none other than the house of God and this is the gate of heaven!" (Gen. 28:17).

The twenty-first-century person is searching for the gate of heaven, an entry point into the unknown and the supernatural—a place of acceptance and love. The gate of heaven that Jacob saw is not some mystical experience we might stumble into. It's not some new Eastern religion or a new religious experience. The gate of heaven is first Christ, the One who opens the heavens and opens a way into the manifest presence of a real and living God in spite of our imperfections (see John 14:6). The local church is the vehicle we use to preach Christ and establish a gateway to God. The Gate Church is founded upon Christ, preaches Christ, is filled with the manifest presence of Christ, sees the power of Christ at work and creates an atmosphere where Christ is genuinely experienced by all.

The twenty-first-century person is not looking for better church buildings, more creative church programs, shorter services, more relevant music, hot public speakers. No! A thousand times no! This individual is looking for the living presence and person of a living, powerful, loving, life-changing God. The twenty-first-century person will risk visiting a church when he or she hears that there is a presence in that church, a real "life encounter" with the invisible God.

The Gate Church has a different atmosphere, an atmosphere charged by the Holy Spirit's power. It's a joyful, uplifting, hope-filled, mind-changing, bad-habit-delivering church. You don't just attend this church. You don't just pay your dues, fulfill your social obligation and then retire to real life unchanged and untouched. No! That's impossible when you attend a Gate Church! It's not the institution called "church" that draws the twenty-first-century person—it's the gate. It's the possibility of entering into something new, life changing and powerful!

THE JACOB JOURNEY OF PROVIDENCE AND DESTINY

A Gate Church is built by a Gate-Church leader, a transformed Jacob, a person who is pursuing God's destiny. Genesis 27 traces Jacob's steps prior to his encounter with God, which allows him to discover the gate of heaven. The context of Jacob's circumstances plays into the context of God's sovereign visit with him. Jacob's journey provides several points to ponder for all twenty-first-century Jacobs who are seeking to become Gate-Church builders. First, God changes the person into a vessel who can build His house; then He gives the vision, power and will to build.

Let's examine some of the significant markings in Jacob's journey of providence and destiny so that we might learn from his mistakes and know his God.

AN EMOTIONALLY STRESSFUL CIRCUMSTANCE THAT BECOMES SURPRISINGLY COMPLICATED

A quick read through Genesis 27 shows that Jacob desired a holy thing, but had unholy motives and used unholy means to attain it. He longed for the blessing of his father by the laying on of hands before his father's death. The problem: the blessing was not supposed to be his—at least not through his own efforts or in his own timing. The blessing belonged to Esau, his older brother, from whom Jacob had already taken the birthright. Similarly, we pastors and leaders desire the full blessings of God upon our ministries and churches, but how we attain those blessings is important. We like Jacob should not lie, connive or manipulate to gain the desire for blessing that God has placed in our hearts. We must recognize that to be one minute outside of His timetable is to be completely outside of His will.

A few significant Scriptures reveal the deception involved:

‡ Genesis 27:1: Now it came to pass, when Isaac was old and his eyes were so dim that he could not see, that he called Esau his older son and said to him, "My son." And he answered him, "Here I am."

‡ Genesis 27:11,12: And Jacob said to Rebekah his mother, "Look, Esau my brother is a hairy man, and I am a smooth-skinned man. Perhaps my father will feel me, and I shall seem to be a deceiver to him; and I shall bring a curse on myself and not a blessing."

‡ Genesis 27:18,19: So he went to his father and said, "My father." And he said, "Here I am. Who are you, my son?" Jacob said to his father, "I am Esau your firstborn; I have done just as you told me; please arise, sit and eat of my game, that your soul may bless me."

One has to wonder what was going on in the hearts of Jacob's parents? When we walk in the kind of manipulation and deception that we see in Jacob's life, those we are called to bless are also infected and affected by our lies.

If we are not accountable to God and others, we put all of our relationships in jeopardy.

After a particularly strenuous hunting trip, Esau arrived home exhausted and hungry. Too tired to fend for himself, he begged Jacob to share some of the savory-smelling stew that he was making. Jacob offered him some, but with the condition that Esau trade his birthright for it. Esau agreed and sold his birthright for the bowl of stew. Hebrews 12:16 calls Esau a profane man. And though Jacob was ruthless in his bargaining, Esau was reckless and flippant in his response.

The blessings due the firstborn related to the concept that the firstborn was the head of the family and responsible for the spiritual and material well-being of its members. There were advantages as well as responsibilities to being the firstborn. The firstborn received the status of the father and also a double-portion of the inheritance (see Deut. 21:15-17). This meant that considerable prestige, power and property were involved in the birthright.

A Gate-Church leader should desire the blessings of the birthright, but must not use manipulation, cheating or lying to attain those blessings. The birthright belonged to the firstborn and, as believers, we now are the firstborn, the receivers of the birthright through Christ:

+ Israel was the firstborn son (see Exod. 4:22).
+ Christ was also the firstborn son (see Matt. 1:25).
+ We are now the firstborn positionally in Christ (see Rom. 8:29).
+ The church is the firstborn (see Heb. 12:23).
+ We then are receivers of the firstborn birthright of the double-portion (see Deut. 21:17; 2 Kings 2:9).

The Gate Church understands this firstborn birthright as a "now" promise from God for the church and contends for that birthright, but it does so God's way.

The church can learn from Jacob's mistake. We are not to be people committed to our own ends, achieving ministry goals by any and all means irrespective of who might be abused in the process. It was the will of God for Esau to serve Jacob. God had already purposed who would receive the firstborn rights (see Gen. 25:23). Jacob, however, was not willing to wait for God to work out His plan His way. He was not prepared to accept this piece of divine determination.

God has already prepared a blessing for you, your family, your ministry and, if you are pastoring, your church. Do not force the hand of God or manipulate church growth, hype your worship service or pressure the flock to evangelize because you desire a double-portion church or ministry. Be patient. Be a person of faith in God's providence and sovereignty.

A SEVERELY DAMAGED RELATIONSHIP CAUSED BY CARNAL MANIPULATIONS

The relationship between Jacob and Esau was severely damaged by Jacob's crafty resourcefulness. Genesis 27:41,42 says that "Esau hated Jacob because of the blessing with which his father blessed him, and Esau said in his heart, 'The days of mourning for my father are at hand; then I will kill my brother Jacob.' And the words of Esau her older son were told to Rebekah. So she sent and called Jacob her younger son, and said to him, 'Surely your brother Esau comforts himself concerning you by intending to kill you.'" Was this really necessary? Was this the only way Jacob could attain his vision? I think not.

Jacob had gained what he wanted, but at the expense of his own brother, Esau, who lost his birthright and blessing. God would take both brothers on a long journey before their relationship would be healed. Even though he was a vain person, Esau did not deserve to be deceived, treated with disrespect, emotionally drained and wounded.

As we pursue a Gate Church—a church and ministry of influence—let us pursue it with respect for all those around us: family, friends and fellow ministers. Let us not damage relationships to attain ministry status or goals. You never know how your relationship with another person will affect your future and your children's future.

There's a lesson we can learn from the story told of a poor Scottish farmer named Fleming. One day, while eking out a living for his family, he heard a cry for help coming from a nearby bog. He dropped his tools and ran to help. There, mired to his waist in black muck, was a terrified boy screaming and struggling to free himself. Farmer Fleming saved the lad from what could have been a slow and terrifying death.

The next day, a fancy carriage pulled up to the Scotsman's sparse surroundings. An elegantly dressed nobleman stepped out and introduced himself as the father of the boy that Farmer Fleming had saved. "I want to repay you. You saved my son's life," said the nobleman.

> "We must recognize that to be one minute outside of His timetable is to be completely outside of His will."

"No, I can't accept payment for what I did," the Scottish farmer replied, waving off the offer. At that moment, the farmer's own son came to the door of the family hovel.

"Is that your son?" asked the nobleman.

"Yes," the farmer proudly replied.

"I'll make you a deal. Let me take him and give him a good education. If the lad is anything like his father, he'll grow to a man you can be proud of."

And the nobleman did. In time, Farmer Fleming's son graduated from St. Mary's Medical School in London and went on to become known throughout the world as the noted Sir Alexander Fleming, the discoverer of penicillin.

Years afterward, the nobleman's son was stricken with pneumonia. What saved him? Penicillin. The name of the nobleman? Lord Randolph Churchill. His son? Sir Winston Churchill.

Taking a poor Scottish farmer's son into his home did not further the nobleman's ambitions in any way and, in a class-conscious society, could have been a hindrance. But the nobleman did not allow these things to prevent him from forming a relationship that seemed to be of no great benefit to him, yet in time proved to be the very thing that saved his own son.

AN UPHEAVAL OF LIFE'S COMFORT ZONES AND ROUTINES

Jacob had no idea what he had set in motion. He may have thought it would end when he finally obtained the birthright and the blessing. Did he even consider the consequences? Didn't he understand the law of sowing and reaping (see Gal. 6:7-9)?

Jacob had sown to the wind and now reaped a whirlwind of surprises (see Hosea 8:7). The first was having to leave his home and go on a long journey just to save his life from Esau's anger.

In Genesis 27:43,44, Rebekah says, "Now therefore, my son, obey my voice: arise, flee to my brother Laban in Haran. And stay with him a few days, until your brother's fury turns away." Rebekah foolishly thought it would only be for "a few days." And many of God's dealings with us are for a "few days," but they are the few days of God's calendar, not ours. Jacob was to go "for a while" with full intention of finding a wife in his mother Rebekah's homeland so he could quickly return. All would finally be worked out, and Jacob could then enjoy his self-guided destiny. But the Lord had other plans. This little journey would take twenty years, and Jacob would return a changed man.

God used Laban, a man of equally manipulative character flaws, to change Jacob. Laban was the brother of Rebekah and father of Leah and Rachel. Herbert Lockyer explains that "the transactions between Laban and Jacob are well known, and speak of cunning on both sides. After twenty years, Laban was reluctant to part with Jacob, whose presence was an assurance of divine blessing. In character, Laban is not pleasant and seems to reflect in an exaggerated form the more repulsive traits in the character of his nephew Jacob."[4]

THE HIDDEN SOVEREIGNTY OF GOD

Behind the scheming and conniving of man, the sovereign Lord is still at work (see Rom. 8:28). Despite all human efforts to thwart the purposes of God through all manner of mistakes and misdemeanors, Jacob, whom God had chosen to be the next link in the chain of divine purpose, had arrived in the exact position to fulfill destiny. He was now on his way to the family where he would find God, change deeply, mature immeasurably and find a wife through whom the promised line would be extended.

To understand the sovereignty of God is to realize that God is God and that He can do anything He desires, whenever He wishes, to whomever He wants. To me this means that because I love the Lord with all of my heart, He will lead me to do His will, place me in any geographical location He chooses or give me any responsibility that He wishes. He will determine what is best for me at all times, even when the circumstances appear to be a poor choice by my definition of best.

Jacob, like you or me, would not have chosen a trip down to Laban's home that would bring twenty years of life's dealings, disappointments, heart-breaking problems and questions about why Laban would treat him so dishonorably. Jacob was on a journey of destiny, and all the parts were working together for his good—without his awareness. Mundane normal parts of life became sovereign encounters with his destiny. He was quietly and secretly being made into a Gate-Church leader. Had you been present to spy out the Potter's hands that laid upon the vessel on the wheel of destiny, you might not have been able to discern this Gate leader being fashioned. But fashioned he was—though reluctantly—without missing a beat, God was changing this man. Jacob was about to meet

> "To understand the sovereignty of God is to realize that God is God and that He can do anything He desires, whenever He wishes, to whomever He wants."

God on his journey and receive a "gate of heaven" experience.

All of Genesis 28 is very important and foundational as we develop the total vision for a Gate Church. All the pieces from Genesis 28:10 to Genesis 28:22 will be examined and applied to twenty-first-century leaders and church models for the Gate Church.

A CERTAIN PLACE

As Jacob journeys, the Bible says that "he came to a *certain place* and stayed there all night, because the sun had set" (Gen. 28:11, italics added). In other words, he stumbled into God's sovereign design. Jacob struck upon a certain place sixty miles from Beersheba that was situated in the mountains of Ephraim, several days journey by walking. He had no idea that this "accidental place" was a "certain place" in God's sovereign plan for his life. This was a "no big deal place," a "nothing special place"—it was simply a stopping point, a place to rest and sleep. Jacob had no expectations of anything out of the ordinary, just a quiet night's sleep. He was not looking for a revival meeting—he was in a lonely, hurting place. He was by himself, sixty miles from home, no hotels, no people. His mind was crowded with thoughts of what he had done to his father, how his brother hated him and how his mother had used him. He was thinking that his journey would be for a few days; he had no idea that those few days would turn into years.

Have you journeyed to a certain place in life or in ministry, to a city you really didn't think that much about before? You applied for a job, the board hired you because the church needed someone for now. It was just for a while, not very long. It was just a stopping point, a resting place, a place of no real future.

Jack Hayford describes his own journey in his book *The Church On The Way*. He reflects on coming to a small—very small—unknown foursquare church in Van Nuys, California:

> None of us had the remotest dream of what was beginning with my few remarks that evening. I had simply consented to come here on a temporary assignment, feeling led by God to accept Dr. VanCleaves invitation to assist this declining church. It was a help-out-on-the-weekends-and-midweek-services proposition and the challenge it offered seemed exciting, but I did not expect we would do anything more than that for perhaps a year or so.[5]

Pastor Jack Hayford had no idea that he had come to a sovereign place, even though it seemed like just a certain place, a good thing to do for a while. This certain place would become The Church On The Way, one of the most famous churches in the world.

Maybe you are at a certain place right now. Don't miss what God might seek to do through that place.

AN ORDINARY STONE

Jacob "took one of the stones of that place and put it at his head, and he lay down in that place to sleep" (Gen. 28:11). He had no idea that the stone he chose casually—accidentally, without careful selection—was not your usual stone. More than just another ordinary stone, it would become the pillar to the house of God. The stones and pillars in Genesis 28 are symbolic and prophetic of the people who become the building blocks for God's house and the people who become the pillar leaders.

We have no idea which of those people that God has brought into our lives will become life-long partners in the building process. We choose casually what God has chosen sovereignly. We should be aware that ordinary stones, ordinary common people, are the ones God will use to construct His house. Treat all ordinary people with respect; they may be with you all the days of your life and be the key to your future.

When Gary and Steve asked to rent our basement, our choice to do so was merely a casual decision. These were just two young men who were in my college classes and needed a place to live. When they arrived, however, I noticed that they were more than curious about my office, my books, my notes and my sermons, so it was only natural that we strike up a mentoring relationship. There was no plan for the future, I simply gave them what help I could. Then when my wife and I left the college in 1981 to pioneer our first church, who do you think became part of that church-plant team? Gary and Steve. These two men eventually became elders and part of the staff ministry. Steve was sent from that church to plant a church in Toyko, Japan, which is still thriving today. Gary is the pastor who was chosen to replace me at my former church in Eugene, Oregon, so that I could return to Portland to pastor City Bible Church. They were just ordinary college kids who became life-long partners.

> "We choose casually what God has chosen sovereignly."

A SURPRISE DREAM

Jacob was fatigued and emotionally drained when "he dreamed, and behold, a ladder was set up on the earth, and its top reached to heaven; and there the angels of God were ascending and descending on it" (Gen. 28:12).

When Jacob had that dream, he was not in the frame of mind to write out his life-mission statement or his future vision. He was not in the mood to intercede, travail before God or receive a word from the Lord. He was simply bone tired. He needed rest, and any place would do. Jacob had picked a rock for a pillow and settled down for the night to try to get some sleep. This was not exactly the setting for a life-changing visitation of God or a supernatural dream. It was merely a place of rest for a lonely sleeper, fatigued by life, saddened by the thoughts of the past, pondering the great benediction of his aging father. Sound familiar?

Permit me to share my story. I wasn't asking, nor was I ready, for the Lord to speak so forcefully to me about my dreams that day in the car. "Lay down your dreams and serve his." I couldn't believe what I had just perceived as a direct communication from the Holy Spirit. The voice was familiar and unbelievably clear: "Lay down your dreams and serve his." Obeying that directive would become one of the most pivotal decisions of my life. It meant laying down my vision to plant sixty-eight churches in Oregon in order to join my spiritual father in pioneering a new pastors' and ministers' fellowship. I was laying down my desires and—in a way—my chance to build what I felt to be a God-given dream.

I pulled the car over to the side of the road as the tears flowed. God's presence was very real and very tender. I replied, "Yes, I will lay down my vision to serve another. I let go." I let my vision die in my spirit that moment. God's dreams don't always come at the perfect time, and they don't always agree with our ideas or plans. I had no idea that this 15-minute sovereign encounter in my car would seal my destiny in returning to Portland years later to succeed the spiritual father for whom I had previously laid down my vision. The vision I chose to serve came to be part of my own future. I've often pondered what would have happened if I had simply said, "No. This isn't God. God wouldn't ask me to do such a thing." What or whose dream would I have fulfilled?!

The Lord is able and willing to communicate with His servants in the most desolate places, in the most lonely times and in the most emotionally draining seasons of life. Look to the Lord, even if you are on a Jacob journey along a crooked path of destiny. Dreams are coming your way, visions that will change your life. Expect them.

God speaks to His people through God-given dreams:

- ✝ Abraham dreamed (see Gen. 20:6).
- ✝ Jacob dreamed (see Gen. 31:11).
- ✝ Joseph dreamed (see Gen. 37:5).
- ✝ Solomon dreamed (see 1 Kings 3:4,5).
- ✝ Joseph dreamed (see Matt. 1:20).
- ✝ Believers dream (see Acts 2:17).

The dream God desires to give you may not come to you while you are sleeping. It may begin as a slow-rising, inner understanding of what you are to build with your life. It may be evidenced as a new vision for what the church could be, a dream that sees heaven open and a new ladder connecting heaven and earth. It may be a dream that asks, "What if?" What if a true New Testament book-of-Acts community could be established in the twenty-first century?

Bill Hybels caught such a dream:

> We dreamed of a place where the Word of God could be communicated in an irresistibly compelling way. We dreamed of people getting together in informally small groups and meeting in homes and taking meals together and talking about real-life issues. We dreamed of a community in which prayer would unleash the prevailing power of God. We dreamed of a church that would be distinct and counter-cultural, in which affluent members would say, 'Enough is enough,' and would funnel their excess resources back into the local fellowship for distribution to the needy. We dreamed of church members displaying so much love and integrity that good rumors would begin to circulate among the lost, and when unchurched people would come to see what was going on, they would find Christ. We dreamed of a place where there would be a sense of the miraculous, where what was happening couldn't be explained in human terms. [6]

God has a dream for you. Why not start dreaming right now?!

NOTES

1. George Barna, *The Power of Vision* (Ventura, Calif.: Regal Books, 1992), p. 50.

2. Rick Warren, *The Purpose-Driven Church* (Grand Rapids: Zondervan, 1995), p. 98.

3. Ibid., p. 107.

4. Herbert Lockyer, *All the Men of the Bible* (Grand Rapids: Zondervan Publishing, 1958), p. 215.

5. Jack Hayford, *The Church On The Way* (Lincoln, Va.: Chosen Books, 1982), p. 12.

6. Bill Hybels, *Rediscovering Church* (Grand Rapids: Zondervan Publishing, 1995), p. 50.

"Then he dreamed, and behold, a ladder was set up on the earth, and its top reached to heaven; and there the angels of God were ascending and descending on it." Genesis 28:12

The Spiritual Atmosphere of the Gate Church

The dream Jacob had was an actual visitation of God with God revealing His plan, not only for Jacob but also for His people throughout the ages. Jacob saw in symbolic form the elements of a functioning New Testament, apostolic church. The ladder was the connecting force that brought the atmosphere of heaven, God's voice, angelic movement and prophetic promises to earth.

HEAVEN ON EARTH

The Gate Church experiences a supernatural atmosphere, one that is discernibly different from any other. It is alive with God's presence, God's voice, God's promises—it is the atmosphere of heaven on earth.

Every church has its own culture—its own feel, or atmosphere. Church culture is the behavior (rituals), values (beliefs), principles (rules) and atmosphere (felt presence) of a group of people. Atmosphere can be experienced but not always explained. Every person, home, business, church, city and nation has a unique atmosphere. The word "atmosphere" means a pervading or surrounding influence or spirit, a general mood or environment.

The spiritual atmosphere we encounter has a manifold effect upon the mind, will, emotions and spirit. The atmosphere that people submit themselves to has the power to actually change and shape their lives—to bind, to loose, to confuse, to inspire, to make sad or happy, to change opinions. It can cause people to remember past experiences, both good and bad. Obviously, there is both a negatively charged atmosphere that is empowered by the evil powers of hell (see Eph. 6:10-12) and a positively charged atmosphere that finds its source in God, His Word and the Holy Spirit. Discerning different identifiable spiritual atmospheres is part of the believer's responsibility.

Have you ever entered a particular town or city and felt an oppressive spirit of darkness, or entered a home or a certain room in a home and felt the atmosphere of violence, confusion, helplessness or evil? Do you believe that evil can manifest itself in a very real felt presence and that atmosphere, if encountered for a long enough period of time, could actually influence your mind, emotions and will?

Most Americans have been taught that they should only believe in visible things because "seeing is believing." They think, If I can see it, then it must exist. And yet according to Scripture, there is an unseen world with unseen but felt powers, both good and evil (see Eph. 6:12; Heb. 11:27). A Gate-Church leader understands that our homes and churches can be greatly influenced by the unseen powers of hell as well as the unseen powers of God.

THE NEGATIVE POWER OF ATMOSPHERE

The following are six biblical examples of the negative power of atmosphere:

1. **The atmosphere of chaos, emptiness and darkness (see Gen. 1:1,2; Exod. 10:22; Ps. 107:10):** The word "darkness" is *hoshek* in the original Hebrew language and refers to a covering of darkness under which everything is influenced. Our society is blanketed with a darkness that affects every person, every institution, every church and every family in a subtle and consistently invasive manner. *Hoshek* is the kind of darkness the apostle Paul refers to in 2 Timothy 3:2-5 when he describes the character traits of a people overcome by darkness: "lovers of themselves, lovers of money, boasters, proud, blasphemers, disobedient to parents, unthankful, unholy, unloving, unforgiving, slanderers, without self-control, brutal, despisers of good, traitors, headstrong, haughty, lovers of pleasure rather than lovers of God, having a form of godliness but deny-

ing its power." Don't these words sound descriptive of our own culture? This kind of darkness can so overwhelm a people that they become burdened, weary and hopeless about ever changing their way of living.

2. **The atmosphere of a corrupt earth (see Gen. 6:5-8):** Genesis 6 describes not only the condition of Noah's time, but also the twenty-first century in which the wickedness of humanity has become great and seems to be growing increasingly more wicked. Most of us are astonished at the depth of corruption expressed today through media, music, writing and conversation. Our culture appears devoid of embarrassment with regard to immorality, including adultery and homosexuality. Any subject is fair conversational game. No matter how crude the topic, nothing is beyond impropriety. The atmosphere of earth has been insidiously and pervasively corrupted by impurity. Only by the grace of God will we be able to combat a corrupt earth atmosphere.

3. **The atmosphere of a corrupt city (see 2 Pet. 2:6-8):** Not every city in America could be labeled a Sodom and Gomorrah; however, when these words are used to describe a city, we all know exactly what they mean. They depict a place given totally to ungodly, filthy conduct where righteous people are tormented by the daily sights and sounds of the atmosphere. The atmosphere of rebellion, immorality, political corruption, violence, child abuse, spousal abuse, divorce and other degenerative conduct reminds us daily that all cities carry some seeds representative of Sodom and Gomorrah. Living in this atmosphere, our lives will be contaminated unless we daily put on the full armor of God (see Eph. 6:11-17).

4. **The atmosphere of a disorderly, ungodly house (see Prov. 17:4; 18:21; 19:13; 21:19):** We understand from Scripture and other research that the home is the school ground where young people are being trained in the values and virtues of living. When parental authority in the home becomes divisive and unstructured in its disciplines and godly values, an atmosphere is created that breeds confusion, insecurity, sorrow and rebellion. Many children and young people live outside of God's divine order and blessing for their lives. The seeds of their destruction have usually been sown during their years of living in a disorderly, ungodly atmosphere. To restore the atmosphere of the home, the structure of the home must be realigned with God's authority and values.

5. **The atmosphere of accepted demonic activity (see Rev. 18:2-4):** The occult is riddling our society with diabolic messages through media, advertising and other forms of communication. Palm reading, fortune telling and psychics have become an acceptable part of life, affecting millions of people in our nation. New Age and satanic worship centers have peppered our society with demonic activity. Fascination with the paranormal and supernatural are evidenced by the popularity of television shows such as "Sabrina the Teenage Witch" and "Buffy the Vampire Slayer," which are both geared toward our youth. In our syncretistic society, witchcraft, ghosts, angels and demons are blended into an appealing fantasy world that has become a box-office draw for the entertainment industry. We have become just like the great city of Babylon described in the book of Revelation as "a dwelling place of demons, a prison for every foul spirit and a cage for every unclean and hated bird" (v. 2). Our nation has as much demonic activity as any Third World country or non-Christian nation, even though we don't like to admit, or deal with, that fact. Demons don't always look the way we expect them to, so it's time to wake up, identify them and realize that they are influencing the atmosphere of the twenty-first century.

6. **The atmosphere of corrupt individual attitudes (see Prov. 21:24; 22:24; 1 Cor. 15:33):** Every person carries an atmosphere—what we refer to as a personality, aura or vibes. A person's atmosphere may be one of anger, impurity, egotism, righteousness, selflessness or servanthood. The Bible says we are to be aware of the atmosphere of others and not allow them to negatively influence our lives or change our own personal atmosphere. It warns that if you make friends with an angry person, you will become like him or her (see Prov. 22:24). It also says that if you befriend a proud person, you, too, will become proud (see Prov. 21:24). We are all individually responsible for the choices we make and the atmosphere we create. As Christians, our atmosphere should be characterized by love, joy, peace, gentleness, goodness, faith, meekness and temperance.

THE POSITIVE POWER OF ATMOSPHERE

In a biblically based, Holy Spirit-empowered Gate Church, the atmosphere will have excitement, joy, victory, love, encouragement, power, anticipation, faith and a river of life that flows freely and powerfully. Someone once said that it takes five to seven years to build an atmosphere in the church. Building attitudes, faith, right feelings, right perceptions, unified vision and truths takes time. It is easier to construct a building and raise a budget than it is to create or change the culture of atmosphere.

The Gate Church seeks to establish a positive, godly, transforming atmosphere. "Where the Spirit of the Lord is, there is liberty. But we all, with unveiled face, beholding as in a mirror the glory of the Lord, are being transformed into the same image from glory to glory, just as by the Spirit of the Lord" (2 Cor. 3:17,18).

Twelve specific atmospheres need to be cultivated in the Gate Church. They include:

1. **An Atmosphere of Open Heavens:** No spiritual hindrances allowed—thus, breakthrough happens here!

2. **An Atmosphere of Unified Expectancy:** No "business as usual" services.

3. **An Atmosphere of Supernatural Surprises:** He's no common, ordinary God.

4. **An Atmosphere of Everyone Can Receive:** No limitations are allowed to be placed on anyone.

5. **An Atmosphere of People Are Important:** No person is undervalued.

6. **An Atmosphere of Victorious Living Is Possible:** No defeatist spirit —God is able to deliver anyone at anytime.

7. **An Atmosphere of Reaching Our City:** No "hold the fort" philosophy here; we attack and take no prisoners.

8. **An Atmosphere of Financial Blessing:** No excuses or apologies; God is good and He desires to bless and provide for His work.

9. **An Atmosphere of Communion:** The voice of God is heard clearly.

10. **An Atmosphere of Faith:** No pessimism about the future—God is in control.

11. **An Atmosphere of Vision:** People see the invisible and do the impossible.

12. **An Atmosphere of Worship:** The river of God is released in fullness.

THE GATE CHURCH—A HOUSE OF GLORY

The greatest hindrances to a positive, powerful, glory-filled church atmosphere are divisions, discords and unresolved offenses. When people are polarized and fighting among themselves, a thick cloud of oppression hovers over the church. A visitor can quickly sense whether the atmosphere is one of division, or unity—hatred, or love. A Gate Church seeks to establish an atmosphere of harmony and unity that is evidenced by joy and peace. This atmosphere can be described as the glory of the Lord filling the house of God (see Num. 14:21; Isa. 60:3; Hab. 2:14).

The word "glory" is translated from six different Hebrew words:

- *Hadar*: beautiful, excellent, majestic

- *Tohar*: purity and transparency

- *Tsebhi*: denoting that which is prominent and conspicuous

- *Addereth*: something broad, expanding, limitless, able to move beyond the natural realm

- *Hod*: grandeur, awesome, spectacular

- *Kabod*: weighty, to be noteworthy or impressive, to have a reputation as a person in high social position like a king, a person with wealth, authority, power to act or influence

The glory of God revealed in the church speaks of restored reputation and godly influence. The atmosphere of glory is sustained by the flowing together of God's people in a place (see Eph. 3:21; 1 Pet. 5:1; John 17:1-10). The church is called to represent God's glory to the world; it is to be the head and not the tail (see Deut. 28:13).

Several years ago, an article in the U.S. News and World Report magazine ranked the church twenty-sixth among the main factors that influence American society. God wants Gate Churches to restore the spiritual atmosphere and thus restore the church's influence in the world today. The Gate Church is to be a place that beholds the manifested glory of God, a house built on top of the mountain for all to see and respect (see Mic. 4:1,2). It is to be a place where the manifold wisdom of God is revealed (see Eph. 3:10,11)—a place where influence is seen as the salt and light of our decaying world (see Matt. 5:13-16).

THE "DIVIDED HOUSE" PROBLEM

The glory of God will not be manifested in the midst of division. Jesus taught that a "house divided against itself will not stand" (Matt. 12:25). The church must clean up its own atmosphere before the atmosphere in the city will be affected. Discord in the local church will cause discord in the city church, thus hindering the power of God to be released in both the church and the city. Therefore, unity is key to a sustained atmosphere of glory in the Gate Church— and building unity means working relentlessly to remove all unresolved offenses.

In Matthew 24:10 Jesus said, "And then many will be offended, will betray one another, and will hate one another." Notice the progression from offense to betrayal to hatred. Have you ever experienced or witnessed a church atmosphere riddled with hatred because of betrayal, a betrayal that began with small, unresolved offenses and grew into huge unresolved offenses that gave way to disloyalty, betrayal and finally hatred?

This kind of relational digression can happen in friendships, marriages, business partnerships; it can happen among church leadership teams, local churches and city pastors' relationships. The apostle Paul warns us to "note those who cause divisions and offenses, contrary to the doctrine which you learned, and avoid them" (Rom. 16:17). Scripture provides many passages dealing with the subject of offend, offense, offended and stumble (see Prov. 18:19; Matt. 5:29,30; 11:6; 13:21; 15:12; 17:27; 26:31; Rom. 14:13,21; 16:17; 1 Cor. 8:13; 2 Cor. 11:29).

The word "offense" in the original Greek is *scandalizo* (verb form) or *scandalon* (noun form) and comes from the picture of a trap that has been baited with a stick. When the bait was taken, the stick would fall forward and spring the trap shut. Thus the word came to mean "closed in or trapped, to catch something in a trap that has been baited." This Greek word can be expanded to mean:

- ‡ An obstacle on the path over which one falls, stumbles or is hindered
- ‡ The cause of spiritual or moral ruin
- ‡ To suffer injury, to be hurt
- ‡ To cause a person to begin to distrust or desert one whom before was trusted
- ‡ To wound with words or actions, to violate someone
- ‡ To act injuriously or unjustly, to be insensitive

Every church is presented with many occasions for offenses to happen and to grow. Offenses may occur because of disagreements and hurts over people's actions, perspectives, conversations, decisions, standards, politics, budgets, hiring, firing, sermons, bulletins, forgotten announcements, unattended weddings or funerals, forgotten birthdays, insensitivity to a crisis, gossip, backbiting, taking up the offenses of others—the list could go on and on. The point is that we can be offended anytime for almost any reason if we don't guard our hearts and continually cleanse our mind and spirit.

The Gate Church emphasizes mercy rather than judgment (see Jas. 2:13); it establishes an atmosphere where problems can be safely confronted, dealt with and forgiven. We have signs in our cities that read "No smoking here," "No parking here," "No eating here" and "No drinking here." Shouldn't we add a sign for our churches that reads, "No offenses here"?!

IDENTIFYING THE SIGNS OF OFFENSE

Seven sure-fire signs point to unresolved offenses lingering in the atmosphere. Let's examine them here:

1. **Strained relationships:** The Bible says a brother offended is harder to win than a strong city and contentions are like the bars of a castle (see Prov. 18:19).

2. **Resistance to authority:** Those offended will not respond to the leadership of the church. The resistance may not be full-blown rebellion, but it is felt at sensitive times. Counsel is rejected, ideas are ignored, decisions are overturned (see Prov. 19:20; Heb. 13:17).

3. **Detachment and drifting from the church:** Detachment is first detected in an attitude of distancing, withdrawing from the hub of the church, the church at large and its flow. It is not a quick leaving of the church, but a gradual, subtle drifting in the wrong direction (see Prov. 27:17; Ps. 1:1-3; 27:1-10; 1 John 2:19).

We have signs in our cities that read "No smoking here," "No parking here," "No eating here" and "No drinking here." Shouldn't we add a sign for our churches that reads, "No offenses here"?!

4. **Strongholds of vain imaginations:** When the offense is deeply lodged in a person, that individual begins to see everything through the glasses of unresolved offense. The smallest action from the one who has offended will be vainly enlarged into a stronghold

of beliefs about his or her actions, words or attitudes (see 2 Cor. 10:3,4; Phil. 4:1-3).

5. **Opened doors to satanic harassment:** The demonic powers of hell are attracted to unforgiveness, bitterness, resentment, gossip, backbiting, anger, hatred and the like. To carry an offense is to open the door for satanic harassment (see Eph. 4:27). The root of bitterness will spring up, causing trouble and by this many will be defiled (see Heb. 12:15).

6. **Dried up rivers of the Holy Spirit:** The fresh, powerful flow of the Holy Spirit in the believer is likened to a mighty river. When offenses are allowed to lodge inside our spiritual wells, they are like huge stones blocking the river's flow. The loss of spiritual vitality and momentum, joy, and faith can often be traced to unresolved offenses (see John 7:37-39).

7. **An unhealthy conscience:** The conscience is the inner judge or umpire that expresses God's holiness and reproves sin. It is the faculty of the spirit that approves or disapproves of our thoughts, words and actions. When unresolved offenses turn into unforgiveness or bitterness, the conscience becomes weak, wounded, sick, unreliable and troubled (see John 8:9; 1 Tim. 1:19; Titus 1:15; Heb. 10:22). An unhealthy conscience is a hindrance to spiritual life and maturity.

The Gate Church fosters an atmosphere where the offenses hidden deep in people's lives, and ultimately the life of the church, can be easily and continually cleansed. It is one that is offense-free and has nothing for anyone to strike against or to stumble over. Every believer is able to look every other believer in the eye, knowing that no one can point a finger and say, "You wronged me and never tried to make it right" (see Acts 24:16).

The Gate Church atmosphere perpetuates purity. In the Greek *katharos* means to be cleansed or purged free from any admixture that soils, corrupts or defiles (see 1 Tim. 3:9; 2 Tim. 1:3). The Gate Church atmosphere is purged by the blood of Christ (see Heb. 9:14). It is an atmosphere in which people are taught to handle offenses and to remove them (see Matt. 5:23; 18:16-18).

CLEANSING THE ATMOSPHERE BY REMOVING THE OFFENSES

Biblical reconciliation is the first step toward removing offenses. Every believer must accept responsibility for taking the initiative to resolve any and all conflicts. Matthew 18:15 places the responsibility to take the initiative on the one who has been hurt. In Matthew 5:23,24, the responsibility is placed on the one who has done the hurting. Both parties are responsible for taking initiative.

The second step is seeking wisdom to know when, where and how to discern which offenses need to be taken to a full two- or three-party reconciliation (see Col. 3:13; Eph. 4:31). Not all offenses need to be verbalized in an eye-to-eye confrontation. Some immature actions that were done without an intentional desire to hurt need to be released to the Lord, forgiven and forgotten so that we can move on with life and God.

If the offense is an isolated instance that is not likely to be repeated, affects only ourselves and can be sincerely forgiven, then we should forgive and release it to the Lord, never mentioning it again. If the offense affects more than ourselves, is likely to be repeated and could offend others, then we must go to the person and deal with the problem (see Matt. 18:15,16). Some offenses are not really biblical, genuine trespasses against us. We can get offended over things that don't really warrant biblical attention, such as a person's loudness, dress, humor, unmowed lawn, dirty car, inattentiveness or sleeping in church, or outbursts of amen at the wrong time or in too loud a voice. These are not worthy of biblical attention.

The atmosphere of a Gate Church is forgiving, compassionate and longsuffering:

✝ Psalm 86:5: For You, Lord, are good, and ready to forgive, and abundant in mercy to all those who call upon You.

✝ Matthew 6:12-15: And forgive us our debts, as we forgive our debtors. And do not lead us into temptation, but deliver us from the evil one. For Yours is the kingdom and the power and the glory forever. Amen. For if you forgive men their trespasses, your heavenly Father will also forgive you. But if you do not forgive men their trespasses, neither will your Father forgive your trespasses.

✝ 2 Corinthians 2:7: You ought rather to forgive and comfort him, lest perhaps such a one be swallowed up with too much sorrow.

When the Gate Church practices the true biblical order for handling offenses, removing them and forgiving one another quickly and totally, a clear atmosphere is nurtured and God will release His love and power. This atmosphere is built by people who willingly give a sincere apology from a broken and contrite heart, adjusting attitudes and actions in order to prevent further offenses. The atmosphere of unity and harmony grows and becomes a dominant atmosphere.

THE ATMOSPHERE OF COVENANTAL LOVE

God has called us to walk in covenantal love, having a united vision and purpose. In Matthew 18:19 Jesus says, "Again I say to you that if two of you agree on earth." The word "agree" is *sumphoneo* and means "to harmonize as in one accord, to cooperate, bind together as in agreement, to be like a symphony" (see Amos 3:3; Eph. 4:6; 1 Cor. 1:10). Like the Early Church, the Gate Church nurtures a spirit of "one accord" (see Eccles. 4:9-12; Acts 1:14; 2:46; 4:32; 5:12; 15:25; Rom. 12:10; Col. 2:2). In the Greek, *homothymos* means to be unanimous, like-minded, together in vision, unified in purpose. It refers to an atmosphere where people set aside personal ambition and agendas to work together toward the vision and purpose of God, rising to the challenge with one heart.

When the atmosphere of spiritual unity and harmony has been built and sustained, we can expect the following dynamic effects:

‡ Success in spiritual warfare (see Judg. 20:11; Isa. 14:6,7)

‡ Restoration of waste places (see Isa. 52:8,9)

‡ Restoration of broken-down walls (see Neh. 4:16-19)

‡ Answered prayers (see Matt. 18:19; 1 Pet. 3:7)

‡ Continual anointing (see Ps. 133; Zech. 4:6,7)

‡ Fulfillment of God-given visions and dreams (see Gen. 17:5-7; Neh. 4:1-6)

‡ Glory filling the house of God (see 2 Chron. 5:13,14)

‡ An atmosphere where purity is reflected in the corporate church as well as in the hearts of individual believers

A PURE HEART

The Gate-Church leader who has learned to walk in purity of heart will always see the best in every situation. Think about that as you read the following story:

Robert De Vincenzo, the great Argentine golfer, won a tournament. After receiving the check and smiling for the cameras, he went to the clubhouse and prepared to leave. Later, as he walked alone to his car in the parking lot, he was approached by a woman. She congratulated him on his victory, then told him that her child was seriously ill and near death. She explained that she did not know how she could pay the doctor's bills and hospital expenses.

De Vincenzo was touched by her story, and he took out his pen and endorsed his winning check for payment to the woman. "Make some good days for your baby," he said as he pressed the check into her hand.

The next week he was having lunch at a country club when a PGA official came to his table. "Some of the boys in the parking lot last week told me that you met a young woman there after you won the tournament."

De Vincenzo nodded. "Well," said the official, "I have news for you. She's a phony. She has no sick baby. She's not even married. She fleeced you, my friend."

"You mean there is no baby who is dying?" asked De Vincenzo.

"That's right," replied the official.

"That's the best news I've heard all week!" De Vincenzo said.[1]

We are under a magnifying glass and the world is watching to see how we will respond in the most difficult circumstances. Let's make the famous prayer of Saint Frances from Assisi our own so that we can be Gate-Church leaders who bring the atmosphere of heaven to earth:

> Lord, make me an instrument of Your peace;
> where there is hatred, let me sow love;
> where there is injury, pardon;
> where there is discord, unity;
> where there is doubt, faith;
> where there is error, truth;
> where there is despair, hope;
> where there is darkness, light;
> where there is sadness, joy,

O divine Master, grant that I may seek not so much

to be consoled as to console,

to be understood as to understand,

to be loved as to love.

For it is in giving that we receive,

it is in losing ourselves that we find ourselves,

it is in pardoning that we are pardoned,

it is in dying that we are born to eternal life.

Amen!

NOTES

1. Jim Burns and Greg McKinnon, *Illustrations, Stories and Quotes to Hang Your Message On* (Ventura, Calif.: Gospel Light Publications, 1997), p. 161.

"Then he dreamed, and behold, a ladder was set up on the earth, and its top reached to heaven; and there the angels of God were ascending and descending on it." Genesis 28:12

The Gate-Church Prayer-Intercession Ladder

The ladder didn't quite reach high enough for me to hang the Christmas lights on the eaves of our house. What a nuisance! I had to climb down, find another ladder, climb back up, stand on my tiptoes—only to find that the other ladder still wasn't high enough! Reaching the right spot was physically impossible, not to mention the danger involved. I tried but wasn't able to make the stretch. The ladder started to move. Now what?! Great...now I have to get down and start all over again.

Finally my trusty co-laborer wife came to my rescue, "You need a ladder that's high enough to reach the edge of the house. Get down before you kill yourself!" Pulling out the right ladder, she climbed up herself, fixed the lights and gave me one of those "Think of it!" looks as she climbed back down.

THE LADDER OF HEAVEN

Jacob sees in his dream a ladder "reaching" from earth to heaven. There was no problem with his ladder. It was the right size to accomplish the job of reaching.

The Hebrew word used in Genesis 28:12 for "reached" is *nega,* denoting that which pertains when one thing, or person, physically contacts another. It means "to touch." It can refer to a thing touching or contacting another thing (see Isa. 6:7; 16:8; Hos. 4:2), a man contacting a thing (see Exod. 19:12), coming into an area (see Esther 6:14), or God touching a man (see Dan. 8:18; Ps. 144:5). This word *nega* has the idea of touching something to extend one's authority over it or to claim it as one's own.

The ladder Jacob saw reached to heaven; it was a ladder strong enough and tall enough to bridge the gap, a ladder that put man "in touch" with God. Jacob's vision suggests that we are connected to an invisible, real spiritual world where angels freely move and the voice of God can be heard.

God is seeking to touch people of all ages, of all backgrounds, at all times. Our ladders may fall short in their ability to reach, but there is a ladder that does reach all the way and does bridge our spiritual gap. That ladder is Christ. His person, His work, His death and His Resurrection have made the reach from earth to heaven. He bridged the gap. We now have a "ladder" to climb, a reason to reach. God desires to continually touch His people with His awesome love, mercy and presence. Divine communication is readily available to every person who steps onto the first rung, accepting Christ as mediator and ladder.

The ladder that connects heaven and earth is also the prayer ladder that belongs in every person's life, home and church. The Gate Church establishes a prayer-intercession ladder that opens the spiritual door to spiritual activity in the house of God. The Hebrew word for ladder is *sulla*, suggesting the idea of a stairway, a stepping up or onto steps, a connecting to something. The word "intercede" or "intercession" in the Hebrew language is *paga*, meaning "to encounter, meet with, reach or stretch unto, to touch."

As you can see, the Hebrew word for reach, *nega*, and the Hebrew word for intercession, *paga*, are very close in usage and meaning. The prayer ladder is to stretch out and touch God; it is to allow God to touch us. A Gate Church is serious about building a prayer ladder—reaching, stretching and encountering God.

INTERCESSION—EVERY BELIEVER'S PRIMARY RESPONSIBILITY

Scripture clearly indicates that intercession is the primary responsibility of the entire congregation, not just a few select radicals:

‡ Ezekiel 22:30: So I sought for a man among them who would make a wall, and stand in the gap before Me on behalf of the land, that I should not destroy it; but I found no one.

‡ 1 Timothy 2:1: Therefore I exhort first of all that supplications, prayers, intercessions, and giving of thanks be made for all men.

‡ 2 Chronicles 7:14: If My people who are called by My name will humble themselves, and pray and seek My face, and turn from their wicked ways, then I will hear from heaven, and will forgive their sin and heal their land.

Every believer is to be a praying believer, moving up the ladder to encounter God. Prayer is key to the atmosphere of a living, growing, hell-threatening church. Prayer intercession is a vital link to the Gate Church's future; it is the hidden force behind vision fulfillment. Gate Churches are called by God to reach first toward God, then toward their cities. Every believer in the Gate Church is motivated to become a prayer warrior, a member of an occupational force that has one principal purpose—to enforce the victory of Calvary.

Each significant spiritual breakthrough in my life or ministry has occurred because I climbed the ladder of prayer intercession. Prayer is the single most important key to church health, growth and influence. The prayer-ladder connection is a vital principle in the kingdom of God. When heaven's power does not connect to earth, everything is impotent. There are no real miracles, healings or salvations; there is no spiritual life or momentum. When heaven touches earth, the gate of heaven is opened—the ladder is the connecting key.

The prayer-intercession ladder could look something like this:

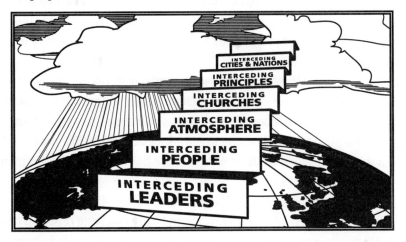

Our church begins each year in the month of January with three days of corporate prayer and fasting, which we call a Solemn Assembly (see Neh. 8:18, KJV). This kind of gathering always changes the entire atmosphere and attitude of the church congregation. It unifies hearts, ignites expectation and allows for corporate cleansing. Seasons of prayer and fasting release spiritual breakthough.

Jacob was promised heaven's blessings, the "dew" of heaven (see Gen. 27:28,39). Like Jacob, we are pursuing the blessings of heaven upon us now, here on earth, in our churches and in our ministries (see Gen. 49:25). We desire to hear God's voice on earth as it is in heaven (see Deut. 4:36-39; 26:15); therefore, it is our responsibility to establish a prayer ladder that will connect all the wealth, resources, power and majesty of heaven to earth.

THE PRAYER LADDER

Sturdy prayer ladders are those that have every rung in place, because a missing rung can mean missing the reach.

INTERCEDING LEADERS

The Lord is searching for leaders who will build a prayer ladder, leaders who will take seriously their responsibility for paving the way to make prayer intercession a reality in all people's lives (see Ezek. 22:30). Like Solomon of old, we must "spread our hands toward heaven" (1 Kings 8:22) with focus, commitment and determination. Leaders, specifically the pastors of the churches, are the key to releasing a prayer spirit upon the congregation. We are the watchmen who must find the Lord in our cities (see Song of Sol. 3:3; 5:7).

The prayer pastor of the church should first be the pastor—not a staff person hired to create a prayer spirit within the congregation. The pastor himself should become a man of prayer. The pastor is called to be an interceding leader, a watchman on the wall who lifts his voice day and night. Isaiah 52:8 says that "your watchmen shall lift up their voices, with their voices they shall sing together; for they shall see eye to eye when the LORD brings back Zion." When the watchman does not intercede with a passionate, on-fire prayer heart, he runs the risk of becoming blind and ignorant (see Isa. 56:10). The desire of the Lord is to "set watchmen on the walls" (see Isa. 62:6) who will cry out continually (see Jer. 31:6; 51:12).

The interceding leader is to keep watch (see Matt. 24:42; Mark 13:33-37; Luke 21:36), which means keeping awake and alert, observing closely in order to guard. The interceding pastor is to be an interceding watchman, keeping the "watch of the Lord." Historically and biblically, "the watch" is a military term used to define segments of time during which the sentries guard their cities from harm, alerting the citizens of approaching enemies (see Isa. 21:6-9,11,12). A praying watchman is responsible to watch over the city, staying on the walls at all times.

The first rung in the prayer ladder is a praying leader! The Lord is calling leaders today. Now, at this moment, as you read these words, He is calling YOU. Can you see the ladder? Do you understand the ramifications of connecting heaven and earth through prayer? Have you started the climb? Have you put your feet on the first rung? This ladder is of vital importance to your church, your city and to all those who might be set free through prayer intercession. Read the following passage from Habakkuk 2:1-3 and let those words rest within your spirit:

> I will stand my watch and set myself on the rampart, and watch to see what He will say to me, and what I will answer when I am corrected. Then the LORD answered me and said: "Write the vision and make it plain on tablets, that he may run who reads it. For the vision is yet for an appointed time; but at the end it will speak, and it will not lie. Though it tarries, wait for it; because it will surely come, it will not tarry."

Will you rise and stand on your wall, set yourself at your station? Will you hear the voice at the top of the ladder? Will you obey? The Gate-Church leader sees clearly the vision and establishes the ladder. Connect through intercessory prayer all the wealth and power of heaven. Do it now!

You are called to be a "breaker" (see Mic. 2:13). Once the ladder is established, it locks in place, firmly planted on earth, firmly established in heaven. Nothing can move it out of place. Intercessory prayer is your key to breakthrough. You could see years of fruitfulness released upon you and your house just by establishing a prayer ladder.

INTERCEDING KEY PEOPLE

The second rung in the prayer ladder is that of raising up key interceding people who will take the burden of intercession and carry it into the heart of the congregation. The pastor initiates the establishment of the prayer ladder, then others pick up the burden and begin to sustain the spirit of prayer, giving the congregation time to absorb it. James 5:16 says to "pray for one another, that you may be healed. The effective, fervent prayer of a righteous man avails much." The key people are usually those who already have a personal prayer life, people who have already developed some level of intercessory prayer, people who are sensitive to the Holy Spirit and know how to work with the pastoral leadership in establishing new and important truth.

When we first began to build a prayer ladder, we were like the farmer. We would sow seed, water the ground and then patiently wait for the harvest. To prepare a whole church to become a prayer-intercession church, you must sow seed liberally and consistently, hoping and praying that some seed will fall on good ground, on people who are ready to hear and obey. The seed that falls on your key people will be the first harvest and the first step in establishing a "whole church" prayer ladder.

Allow me to change metaphors for a moment from ladder to seed. The interceding pastor must understand that it takes a lot of seed sowing before the whole field will bring forth the harvest. Psalm 126:6 says that "he who continually goes forth weeping, bearing seed for sowing, shall doubtless come again with rejoicing, bringing his sheaves with him." Notice the prayer-birthing words in this passage: "goes forth," "weeping," "bearing seed," "sowing," "doubtless," "rejoicing," "bringing sheaves."

The wise pastor-seed-sower understands that there will be some toil, some hard work, some faith testing and a season of time before the prayer seed in the people will bring forth the prayer spirit. The word "seed" means "that from which anything springs, the first principle of the original, that which contains life, to grow to maturity under right conditions." That which grows down is the root and that which grows up is the shoot. The pastor-seed-sower must let the prayer seed go into the ground deeply, giving it time to grow some roots while watering and waiting patiently (see Gen. 1:11,12,29).

> "To prepare a whole church to become a prayer-intercession church, you must sow seed liberally and consistently, hoping and praying that some seed will fall on good ground, on people who are ready to hear and obey."

The interceding pastor or leader should read and meditate on Mark 4:26,27 and Galatians 6:7,8.

A wise interceding pastor understands the principles of sowing the seeds of prayer: right timing, right soil, right depth and the right seed (see Jer. 2:21; Ezek. 17:5). Seeds have an intricate mechanism that determines the right time and the right place for sprouting. Four locks, however, must be opened in the right time and sequence if growth is to occur. If only three conditions are met, three locks open, but not the fourth, the seed will not grow. A seed must be absolutely sure it has arrived at a certain safe and suitable space; thus it will fail to grow if these locks are not opened properly. The four locks are:

1. **The water lock:** When water penetrates the seed, change begins and cannot be stopped; however, the right amount of water is essential. If allowed to dry out, the seed will die. If the seed receives too much water, it will rot. Our water lock is the Word of God, which must be allowed to penetrate our hearts in order to change our attitudes and actions so that God's will can take root in our prayers. A lack of God's Word will cause our spirits to become parched and hardened to God's truth; a deluge of God's Word can cause us to rot without the proper drainage that practical prayer application provides.

2. **The oxygen lock:** The breath of life is in the oxygen. Air mixed with water in the right balance will result in growth. Our oxygen lock is the Holy Spirit. Only when His power is breathed into our prayers can we have the balance needed to unlock our answers to prayer.

3. **The temperature lock:** If the climate is either too cold or too hot, the seed can be destroyed or kept dormant. Balanced warmth opens the seed for growth. Our temperature lock is the spiritual climate that is necessary to pray the Word of God in conjunction with the Holy Spirit's direction and timing. The right climate means coming into agreement with the Word and the Holy Spirit's wisdom so that the prayer-seed is matured at the right time, or in the right season.

4. **The light lock:** Light tells the seed that it is near enough to the soil surface to emerge and break ground. Our light lock is the illumination of God's presence as we see the breakthrough in prayer that causes His will to be done on earth just as it is in heaven.

Sow the seed of prayer liberally into all the people. Some will receive the seed and bring forth thirty- sixty- or a hundredfold. A small seed can yield an enormous harvest (see Matt. 17:20; Luke 8:11; 2 Cor. 9:6-10; 1 Pet. 1:23).

INTERCEDING ATMOSPHERE

The third rung of the ladder is to build an atmosphere in the church of prayer intercession (see Isa. 56:7). Atmosphere is a very powerful shaping influence upon people's souls, more than we usually realize. Businesses, restaurants, schools—all use atmosphere as part of achieving their goals. Every church has an atmosphere, and the most dominant part of every church atmosphere should be prayer.

Establishing a prayer atmosphere in the main corporate gatherings—our Sunday services—is the place to start. Prayer seemingly has been removed from our main public services and pushed off in a corner somewhere. Churches may have prayer on Wednesday night, during a weekday-morning prayer time or at a few prayer meetings that are scantily attended, but what happened to prayer as the main thing, the main course during the Sunday meal?

It was Steven Covey who turned this astoundingly simple statement into a nationwide slogan: "The main thing is to keep the main thing the main thing." [1] Consider the big picture. Connect your vision and mission to your decisions about what you do with your time in church. What is most important? What gives church meaning? What do you want people to touch and receive from in the service? What is the main thing? If you go to McDonalds, you expect McDonalds's hamburgers. When you go to Taco Bell, you expect tacos. If you had your taste buds set for a juicy hamburger with everything on it and headed into McDonalds, you would be a little miffed if they served up two chicken tacos for you! Similarly, when people come to church, they should get prayer, do prayer, hear prayer, say prayer, sing prayer and be in a prayerful atmosphere.

"My house shall be called a house of prayer " (Isa. 56:7). That sounds to me like prayer is the "main thing"—so let's keep it the main thing! Our church has opening-service prayer for everyone during every service on every Sunday, fifty-two weeks a year. We also have several thousand visitors each year. Knowing that we will start with twenty minutes of prayer, people still invite their friends and neighbors. Opening-service prayer is a foundational part of our service. It creates an atmosphere in which everyone has an opportunity to nurture their hearts in communion with God. During this time I ask everyone to stand and pray, visitors and members alike. I've had visitors tell me that they have never prayed before, yet in this atmosphere they begin to pray for the first time in their lives. Those who are uncomfortable praying out loud find a freedom to do so as their voices merge with those of hundreds of others praying with them.

Scripture dictates prayer in church:

✝ Acts 4:31: And when they had prayed, the place where they were assembled together was shaken; and they were all filled with the Holy Spirit, and they spoke the word of God with boldness.

you have to Build a spirit & ministry of prayer

‡ Matt. 21:13: And He said to them, "It is written, 'My house shall be called a house of prayer,' but you have made it a 'den of thieves.'"

An interceding leader who motivates key interceding people to help establish an interceding atmosphere will build an interceding church. Corporate intercession calls for the whole church to assemble together and encourages the lifting of every voice to God in fervent prayer. We must break the bondage of silence in our public corporate services. Let us encourage the sound of voices raised in prayer. The Bible describes praying as "lifting up voices and crying aloud" (see Judg. 21:2; Exod. 2:33). As an interceding pastor or leader, call the whole church into a prayer covenant:

‡ 2 Chron. 15:1,2: Now the Spirit of God came upon Azariah the son of Oded. And he went out to meet Asa, and said to him: "Hear me, Asa, and all Judah and Benjamin. The LORD is with you while you are with Him. If you seek Him, He will be found by you; but if you forsake Him, He will forsake you."

Interceding churches encourage prayer in every age group, every department, at every event and every staff meeting. Interceding churches raise up a prayer leader who can become a prayer pastor to nurture, oversee, create and enlarge the prayer spirit and the prayer vision. If prayer is birthed in specialized intercessors' groups only, without being birthed into the spirit of the entire congregation, then you run the risk of never lifting the church higher in prayer and never finding more people in the congregation to become specialized intercessors.

In his book *Churches That Pray*, Peter Wagner states, "In my guesstimate, I allowed for five churches out of one hundred that might well have a lively, dynamic prayer ministry."[2] Wayman Rodgers of Christian Life Center says, "The ministry of prayer is the most important of all ministries in the church. Prayer creates the atmosphere and binds the powers of darkness so the gospel of Jesus can go forward and the church can prosper. This is the area that the majority of our church talks about the most and practices the least."

> "My house shall be called a house of prayer " (Isa. 56:7). That sounds to me like prayer is the "main thing"—so let's keep it the main thing!

For years, Jack Hayford's church, The Church On The Way, has been a model for thousands of pastors. I have always been greatly impressed by its long-term commitment to being a church that prays. Jack describes the three stages that his church went through to become a dynamic, praying church: "First, how in the beginning we had to confront a decadent habit; second, how the Holy Spirit called and constrained the congregation and inaugurated our intercession; third, how the pattern of our weekly prayer service has emerged from the learning processes." [3] He then describes what happened to that church service, Wednesday-night prayer and the effect upon the entire congregation: "Thus our own corporate action in spiritual warfare and authoritative prayer is not based on shallow promises or parroted slogans. We have accepted God's summons to bold belief on biblical terms that build character. Our prayer meeting has become a continual, mighty, week-after-week act of faith. We build on the foundations of the Cross and commit to ceaseless intercession, and obey the discipline of fasting according to scriptural guidelines."[4]

To become a Gate Church, the Gate Leader must commit to being an interceding leader who motivates intercessors to carry the burden, who creates an atmosphere of prayer for every service, and who teaches, equips and releases the whole church to prayer intercession (see Acts 1:14; 2:42; 12:5; 12:12).

INTERCEDING PRINCIPLES

The next rung of the prayer ladder is the aspect of deepening or maturing the praying church by practicing biblical laws of prayer intercession. In my book *Seasons of Intercession,* I present several functions of prayer intercession that can be nurtured into the heart of the church in order to deepen the spirit of prayer. First is gap-standing, hedge-building and cup-filling prayers (see Ezek. 22:30).

The whole church is responsible for standing in the gap for cities and nations. The power of prayer is released when even one person stands in the gap. The difference one person, one church or one group of praying gap-standers can make is a motivating factor for the praying church (see Gen. 18:25-27; Exod. 32:11-14, 30-34; Ps. 106:23; 2 Chron. 7:14). Praying churches are to stand in the gap and to rebuild the hedge that has been broken down (see Neh. 4:7,8; Ps. 80:12; Eccles. 10:8; Isa. 5:5). Praying churches are to fill the cup of prayers so that God will pour out His Spirit of mercy and not wrath, of revival and not judgment, of healing and not destruction (see Rev. 8:3,4).

Praying churches understand the principle of travail. To give birth to something requires travail, a time of intense labor accompanied by pain (see Isa. 66:7,8; Gal. 4:19). Spiritual travail and intercessory prayer produce the desired results of the Holy Spirit. Travailing intercession claims the promises and does

Travail

battle with the devil, the flesh, unbelief and weariness. It is praying with deep feeling, tears, weeping and wrestling. The church world needs to be equipped for this kind of praying. Supplication with travailing intercession is the kind of prayer that will not take no for an answer—it storms the battlements of heaven and brings confusion and defeat to all the powers of hell, even death itself.

The praying church learns the principle of striking the target. Intercessory prayer is the "spear" (see Josh. 8:18) that focuses with authority on the desired circumstance, event, person or nation with strategic targeting. Intercessory prayer must involve a specific target that is held before the church and focused on, bombarded, proclaimed, agreed upon and prayed for without ceasing (see Acts 12:5).

The prayer-intercession church understands the principle of pushing back the devil's boundary lines. The Holy Spirit has hedged us in according to God's divinely set boundary lines. The devil also seeks to set boundary lines, but his boundary lines are always set to limit God's best, to bind us, to pull us back and to remove from us a spirit of faith and vision. God has, metaphorically speaking, given us a 5,000-acre farm to live on and enjoy. The devil works on shrinking those boundary lines down to one acre. Intercessory prayer pushes the lines back to where God intended them to be (see Ps. 139:5-8; Prov. 18:16; Jer. 29:11). (Refer to *Seasons of Intercession* for further study.)

INTERCEDING FOR CITIES AND NATIONS

This last rung in the ladder is a key that will unlock the harvest in cities and nations. The interceding pastor or leader—who motivates key intercessors, creates a dynamic prayer atmosphere, equips the entire congregation for prayer intercession and teaches the whole church how to use the principles of intercession—will find that moving up one more step to take on cities and nations will not be difficult. Jimmy and Carol Owens state in their book *Heal Our Land*:

> In intercessory prayer we stand between others and God, asking for favor or forgiveness on their behalf. Or we may stand between others and Satan, pleading God's intervention and using spiritual weapons to secure protection and deliverance. [5]

> *"Supplication with travailing intercession is the kind of prayer that will not take no for an answer—it storms the battlements of heaven and brings confusion and defeat to all the powers of hell, even death itself."*

Praying for cities and nations with faith, vision, understanding and passion is a chief mark of a Gate Church. As you read the following passage of Scripture, ask the Lord to deposit seeds of intercession in your heart for your city and nation:

> ‡ 2 Chron. 7:14: "If My people who are called by My name will humble themselves, and pray and seek My face, and turn from their wicked ways, then I will hear from heaven, and will forgive their sin and heal their land." (See also Gen. 18:25-27; Jer. 27:18; 2 Chron. 21:16,17.)

Loren Cunningham, founder of Youth With A Mission, has identified what he calls the seven mind-molders of society: the family, government, media, education, business, religion, arts and entertainment.[6] This would be a great place to begin categorically interceding for your city or your nation. Pray for those in positions of influence who are standing for righteousness. Pray for those who champion ungodly causes, asking that either they will change their ways or be removed from their places of influence.

In his book *Primary Purpose*, Ted Haggard relates how their church was mobilized to pray for their city:

> Then they traveled throughout the city anointing major intersections, spiritual power points and churches. They sprayed oil on the pavement and the grass but showed respect to property owners by not putting it on buildings or windows. They visited fifteen houses that were said to be owned by witches and prayed for them. Within a month, ten of those fifteen houses went up for sale. Our church was praying for the Holy Spirit to bless every person in Colorado Springs. Literally, we cut up the pages of the phone book into little pieces with five names on each piece. Each church member received five names to pray for every week! [7]

A Gate Church is not so absorbed in its own vision, buildings and organization that it misses what God desires to do in the city; instead, it is involved with praying for and reaching out to the city and the nation. Time, money, emotions and some processing will be required to effect change, but it is God's will to reach our cities and nations. Jimmy and Carol Owens have written a great prayer to pray as we intercede for our nations. Please pray it with me:

Father, on behalf of our nation, we confess that we have offended You disgracefully with our ungodliness. We have become thankless, rebellious and unclean. We have ignored Your guidance and spurned Your presence. We have become a hedonistic, violent, greedy people. Our foolishness has led us to the brink of destruction. O God, forgive us and deliver us! We pray earnestly, desperately and expectantly for a massive spiritual awakening and transformation in America.

Father, bless and move upon all the leaders of our nation. Stir and transform their minds and make them righteous and wise. Pull down from power those with inflexible hearts who set their faces against You. Replace them with those who will be led by Your Spirit and Your principles. Give these new leaders wisdom, grace and courage. Protect them and their families from every ungodly influence and attack. Bless and prosper them and bring their righteous plans to fruition.

Establish truth in our educational systems and give us godly teachers and educators who will be righteous role models for our children. Remove those who bring immorality, heresy or occultism into our classrooms.

Give us integrity, fairness, and truth in our news media.

We ask for righteous judgment in our courts, with equal justice for everyone in our society. Particularly in our supreme court, bring Your influence to bear. Give these judges revelation, wisdom and courage to make godly and righteous decisions. Give us righteous attorneys who desire justice and truth more than personal gain.

Move sovereignly in the media and arts and entertainment industries. Pull down the ungodly and raise up men and women of Your choice in this arena of unprecedented influence. Redeem it for Your own; let it encourage righteousness and be a tool for spiritual ingathering.

Heal our homes and cement our family relationships. Help us to "do love" there, above all. Fill our homes with wisdom, fairness, compassion, affection and fun.

Deliver the children who are subjected to abuse and fear and who are led into sin by those who should be their defenders. Protect them with your angels, Father, and heal their wounded hearts.

Help us with wisdom, power and love to take back the liberties the church has lost to those who neither know nor respect you.

Protect and encourage the Christian heroes of our nation, those who face threats and persecution as they confront the viciousness of entrenched depravity in their given arenas of influence.

Heal the soul of America. May it once again truly be "one nation under God," filled with Your glory. Amen. [8]

NOTES

1. Steven Covey, *First Things First* (New York: Simon&Schuster, 1995), p. 3.
2. Peter Wagner, *Churches That Pray* (Ventura, Calif.: Regal Books, 1993), p. 81.
3. Jack Hayford, *The Church On The Way* (Lincoln, Va.: Chosen Books, 1982), p. 11.
4. Ibid., p. 110.
5. Jimmy and Carol Owens, *Heal Our Land* (Grand Rapids: Fleming Revell, 1997), p. 12.
6. Ibid., p. 105.
7. Ted Haggard, *Primary Purpose* (Lake Mary, Fla.: Creation House, 1995), p. 33.
8. Jimmy and Carol Owens, *Heal Our Land*, pp. 106-108.

And behold, the LORD stood above it and said:
"I am the LORD God of Abraham your father and the God of Isaac;
the land on which you lie I will give to you and your descendants.
Behold, I am with you and will keep you wherever you go,
and will bring you back to this land; for I will not leave you
until I have done what I have spoken to you." Genesis 28:13,15

The Gate Church Implements Present Prophetic Truths

Every generation must hear the rhema word of the Lord for its own generation. Hearing God's spoken word, however, does not take the place of studying God's written Word as His highest level of truth and communication. It is out of His written Word that God quickens present truth—a truth in season for a specific day and a specific people to do a specific thing.

The twenty-first-century church must deal with numerous spiritual trends regarding present truths; however, the Gate-Church leader must also handle the pressure point of implementation. Permit me to explain.

THE PRESSURE POINT OF IMPLEMENTATION

Throughout the years, I have attended two Bible colleges, two seminaries, dozens of conferences and seminars and many equipping/training meetings. I have read hundreds of books and studied some of the world's greatest churches. The end result of this learning process has been an awareness of the pressure point of implementation. I have realized that it is not enough to have knowledge of church-growth principles, or dozens of great scriptural ideas for developing a cutting-edge church, or a plethora of great material on reaching your city and changing the world for Christ. Questions still remain unanswered: What do I do with all this stuff? How will I, with some level of wisdom, implement all these newly found truths in a local-church setting? Which idea should I implement first? What should I do next? And so on! The pressure point of implementation is the point where all of the knowledge, study, ideas and research bears down, requiring a decision about what to implement, how to implement it and when.

I believe in the success of the local church. It is God's plan and vehicle for ushering in His Kingdom upon the earth. Jesus said that He would build the church. The apostle Paul gave his life to establishing key churches in key gate cities. The local church becomes the point of implementation for the many truths taught in colleges, seminaries and conferences. Long after the great conventions and conferences are over, local church leaders have to figure out all that has been proclaimed in those meetings and what, if anything, is usable in their churches.

A truth preached is not a truth implemented and bearing fruit. A truth understood is not a truth automatically applied to the church.

I am not on a crusade to negate conferences, seminars or all the easily accessible information available to most church leaders. This is an expression of the information era in which we live as the flood of information changes the way we live and possibly even the way we do church. I love learning and researching. I love being able to find information on the Internet that previously took hours at a library. I love having access to so many great people and churches. The problem is not the information—it is the pressure point of implementation. What do we do with so much revelation, so many insights, principles and cutting-edge ideas? We must take seriously this challenge and, with God-given wisdom, implement truth at a God-given pace.

Not only do we have to deal with many great truths, but we are also confronted with many new trends and new movings of the Holy Spirit upon credible church leaders worldwide. I believe most spiritual leaders in the Body of Christ desire to see an authentic revival sweep through our churches, our cities and our nations. The hunger is real and leaders are sincere in their pursuit of worldwide revival.

As the pastor of a large church in the Northwest, I have embraced several present trends and dealt with the pressure point of implementation. First was revival as a present-truth reality. I have endeavored to lead our church into the rivers of revival with the Word and the Spirit. We have experienced some newness of spirit, a revived passion for God and the lost, a new simplicity of single heartedness, and a reviving of our congregation in many significant scriptural areas. The pressure point of implementation caused me to take a very strategic approach toward ensuring that the truth of revival was assimilated and not just the emotion, or the inspiration of the moment. This journey is recorded in my book *Seasons of Revival*. Within its pages, the teachings, principles and safeguards that ensured a fruitful and sustained revival presence are recorded in detail— 300 pages worth!

The pressure point of implementation did not discourage us from pursuing revival, visiting revival hot spots, reading revival books and having revival meetings. Our pursuit for God changed us and our church, but we maintained our basic spiritual DNA. I believe God respects our spiritual heritage and moves within our own unique spiritual personality and apparent giftings as a church. We never became like what we saw in other revival churches. They have their own unique worship styles, altar ministries, service structures and leadership styles. We realized that these were not the causes for a move of the Spirit, but merely the vehicles to carry out what the Spirit was desiring to do.

The Gate-Church leader must, with wisdom and balance, assimilate present truth along with prophetic emphases. All spiritual truths and trends must be handled with spiritual maturity so that the church prospers. We hear terms such as "city reaching," "spiritual mapping," "deliverance," "apostolic ministries," "prophets" and "prophetic messages." We see new seeker-sensitive church philosophies develop, worship styles change and new healing methods of prayer arise. The Gate-Church leader must hear clearly and loudly the voice at the top of the ladder, the voice of the Lord indicating which truths to develop and what the vision is for the church today. The first step in applying new truths is respecting the principle of balance.

ASSIMILATING TRUTHS BY MAINTAINING BALANCE

The work of the Gate-Church leader is to maintain spiritual balance while moving forward in the things of God. The word "balance" denotes a pair of scales, the weighing of two things, one against the other. Accurate scales were a "delight" (see Prov. 11:1) to God and the ancient Hebrew people; but the wicked person corrupted the scales by changing the weights used for accurate balancing. Spiritually speaking, balance involves accurate analysis and discernment; it is the general harmony brought by the integrating of many parts. Balance is achieved by accurately defining the different parts and harmonizing them to prevent harm to any one part. It is evidenced when wise leadership perceives the result of a contemplated course of action and seeks to produce stability, steadiness and equilibrium.

The synonyms for the word "balance" are "evenness," "poise," "wisdom," "level-headedness," "steadiness," "judgment," "discretion," "stability," "common sense" and "consistency." These are words that describe the healthy Gate Church and its leader. When the Gate-Church leader is weak in direction and vision, is dogmatic or extreme in one truth, or a new truth, the church is vulnerable to spiritual viruses and satanic attacks. A leader who is isolated, independent or lacking spiritual common sense is a detriment to building a Gate Church; that individual's imbalance can weaken and possibly even destroy it.

All new and old truths, spiritual trends and insights carry the potential for being either a blessing or a very real threat to the church. If the pressure point of implementation is not wisely handled, many bad consequences result, such as a continual turnover or loss of stable pillar people. When new trends and truths are continually introduced to a church, people can become frustrated and unable to keep pace with the constant influx of new ideas. The church may then become riddled with discord, division, criticism and loss of faith for the vision. If the imbalanced approach to new prophetic truths is not corrected, people will lose confidence in the leadership and ultimately in the church itself. Some people will be ruined for life, never again seeking out a spiritually forward-moving church.

> "A leader who is isolated, independent or lacking spiritual common sense is a detriment to building a Gate Church; that individual's imbalance can weaken and possibly even destroy it."

POSSIBLE AREAS OF IMBALANCE

Imbalance may appear in several categories. Let's consider some of the possibilities:

‡ **Imbalance of praise and worship** reflected in zeal without true sincerity, loudness without power,

form without the authentic presence of God.

✝ **Imbalance of the use of the gifts of the Spirit** seen in the spectacular without foundational teaching and an emphasis on the Spirit without the Word, inspiration without instruction.

✝ **Imbalance of eschatology** discerned when the church has an extreme future expectation without present practical truths for living, creating a weak church without spiritual reality.

✝ **Imbalance of theology without spiritual life** evidenced in a doctrinal correctness without the life of the Holy Spirit, a letter of the law mentality lacking the grace for doing.

✝ **Imbalance of faith teaching** seen when the people are stretched to believe for things beyond their spiritual capacity and maturity as they make promises that God will do anything and everything only to face the reality and truth that God cannot be cornered and pressured into anything.

The Gate-Church leader must learn how to approach new truths and prophetic trends for today with wisdom, balance and patience. The same water that has the power to bring life can also bring death. The same wind that brings refreshing can also bring destruction. The fire we use to warm ourselves, if out of control, brings devastation. When establishing a new truth regarding city reaching, prophetic ministry, apostleship, deliverance, spiritual warfare, prayers of repentance and the like, the leader must thoroughly be grounded in the Scriptures on that subject.

A biblical foundation must be established by groups of Scriptures and themes seen throughout the written Word, not by one or two isolated passages. The leader should take time to prayerfully and patiently search for the truth, examining books from different teachers and different denominations or movements with different points of view. If you are a leader, don't just study people you agree with. The scales for discovering balance only work when you weigh one thing against another thing. Two opposites cause a tension and help you to discover true balance. Ask yourself the right questions:

✝ Is this truth a major emphasis in Scripture?

✝ Did Jesus and the apostles use this truth?

✝ Did the Early Church in the book of Acts model this truth?

✝ Which respected leaders or what model churches are pursuing this truth?

‡ Where can I study a model that applied this truth and produced healthy spiritual fruit as a result of its implementation?

‡ What direction will this truth bring to our church? Is this the direction I want to go? Where will it lead the church ultimately?

Balanced leaders will not resist the voice of God because His people must hear and discern what the Spirit is saying to the church. The Gate Church is a place where the voice of God is welcomed and the people seek to understand the prophetic truths that the Lord is bringing back to His church. Just as Jacob heard the voice from the top of the ladder, so the Gate Church is eager to hear and respond.

THE PRESENT TRUTH OF PROPHETIC MINISTRIES, A CAREFUL APPROACH

One present truth that the church enjoys is the ministry of the prophets and the prophetic word. A Gate Church is a prophetic church, which consists of a people who believe that God still speaks by His Spirit and through apostles and prophets. For some churches, however, even the mention of apostles, prophets or prophetic ministry can be a stumbling block. A part of the church has theologically dismissed these ministries as being for the Early Church of the first century and not for today. The gifts of the Spirit have been relegated in the same manner—gone and no longer necessary. We have the Bible and need nothing more. This is not my view. I believe the five-fold ascension gift ministries (see Eph. 4:11,12) and the nine gifts of the Spirit (see 1 Cor. 12) are for today and are needed more now than ever. Applying this truth to the local church with vision and balance is necessary—not optional.

Because the prophetic ministry is being spotlighted today through books, conferences and prophetic activity, I will concentrate on this presently quickened truth. Some parts of the church are just now being introduced to this powerful and needed ministry; other groups have believed and functioned for many years in the prophetic. As with most trends, there have been some extremes, some damaging practices, some unbiblical and unprincipled approaches to the function of this important ministry.

As a Gate-Church leader who desires to hear the voice of God, I want to create biblical guidelines for the church so the people can hear the voice of God personally for themselves. Sometimes this voice will be the "still small voice" that registers within as God speaks to the believer's spirit. That voice may come through visions, dreams or through the ministry of prophecy as given from another believer or prophetic ministry. The following verses give credence to the fact that God does want to speak to His people in this way:

‡ Joel 2:28: And it shall come to pass afterward that I will pour out My Spirit on all flesh; your sons and your daughters shall prophesy, your old men shall dream dreams, your young men shall see visions.

‡ Acts 21:11: When he had come to us, he took Paul's belt, bound his own hands and feet, and said, "Thus says the Holy Spirit, 'So shall the Jews at Jerusalem bind the man who owns this belt, and deliver him into the hands of the Gentiles.'"

‡ 1 Corinthians 14:3: But he who prophesies speaks edification and exhortation and comfort to men.

‡ 1 Corinthians 14:29-31: Let two or three prophets speak, and let the others judge. But if anything is revealed to another who sits by, let the first keep silent. For you can all prophesy one by one, that all may learn and all may be encouraged.

To prophesy in the Hebrew is *naba*, meaning to bubble forth, gush out or to pour forth, to boil over. The Greek word *propheteuo* means to say or speak forth, to declare or make known. Prophecy is to build up the local church, to make the great stated truths of Scripture become personalized and real in a given setting.

THE FOUR REALMS OF PROPHECY

There are four discernible realms of prophecy. They include:

1. **The prophecy of scripture:** This realm of prophecy speaks of the declaratory and revelatory elements of God's Word as the highest revelation of God to man. All prophetic utterances must be judged by the prophecy of Scripture. (See 2 Tim. 3:16; Heb. 1:1; 2 Pet. 1:20,21.)

2. **The spirit of prophecy:** Here, we are referring to the anointing of the Holy Spirit that enables men and women who do not possess the gift of prophecy, or the office of a prophet, to speak under

the influence of the spirit of prophecy. (See Rev. 19:10.)

3. The gift of prophecy: C. Peter Wagner said, "The gift of prophecy is the special ability that God gives to certain members of the Body of Christ to receive and to communicate an immediate message of God to His people through a divinely-anointed utterance." (See 1 Cor. 12:4,10.)

4. The office of the prophet: David Hill said, "A Christian prophet is a Christian who functions within the church, occasionally or regularly, as a divinely called and divinely inspired speaker who receives intelligible and authoritative revelations or messages which he is impelled to deliver publicly, in oral or written form, to Christian individuals and/or the Christian community." (See Acts 13:1-5; 21:10; 1 Cor. 14:37; Eph. 2:19,20; 4:11.)

The first realm of prophecy has the greatest level of authority and acceptance, the prophecy of Scripture. The other three realms are becoming more widely accepted today by both charismatics and non-charismatics. I find it encouraging to see so many people open to all five ministries of Ephesians 4:11,12 (apostles, prophets, evangelists, pastors and teachers) and to all the gifts of the Spirit listed in 1 Corinthians 12 and Romans 12. This new openness to the prophetic ministry, however, has also opened people up to misusing, or being misused by, prophecy. The Gate Church puts the prophetic ministry in the right perspective. It also establishes biblical guidelines for safeguarding the people who are affected by this powerful gift and ministry. We must understand the biblical function and biblical limitations of prophecy.

LIMITATIONS OF TODAY'S PROPHETIC MINISTRY

Clearly, the New Testament epistles teach that prophecy was a functioning gift in the first-century church. This instruction is the earliest record in the New Testament concerning prophecy in the Christian community. From the following verses, we can conclude that the apostle Paul is giving guidelines to a very normal activity in the Early Church:

‡ 1 Thess. 5:19,20: Do not quench the Spirit. Do not despise prophecies.

‡ 1 Cor. 14:29: Let two or three prophets speak, and let the others judge.

‡ 1 Cor. 13:9: For we know in part and we prophesy in part.

‡ 1 Cor. 13:12: For now we see in a mirror, dimly, but then face to face. Now I know in part, but then I shall know just as I also am known.

‡ 1 John 4:1: Beloved, do not believe every spirit, but test the spirits, whether they are of God; because many false prophets have gone out into the world.

These instructions provide some basic modern-day guidelines to implement.

PROPHECY MUST BE JUDGED

The word "judged" in the Greek means to separate, make a distinction, to discriminate, to discern. Prophecy can be impure, therefore, it must be judged. Our own thoughts or ideas can get mixed into the message we receive. Whether we receive the words directly or receive only a sense of the message, the possibility for imperfect prophecy is present. Some people refuse to recognize any source of prophetic utterance other than the divine or the satanic. They refuse to see the important place of the human spirit. As a matter of fact, they discount the fact that a whole range of degrees of inspiration can exist, from the very high to the very low. The majority of prophecies that we feel compelled to either reject completely or receive with great reserve do emanate from the human spirit.

For example, when Samuel was seeking to anoint a new king, he called the sons of Jesse together (see 1 Sam. 16:1). He was moved by his human spirit first and did not speak with the word of the Lord in his mouth. First Samuel 16:6,7 explains:

> So it was, when they came, that he [Samuel] looked at Eliab and said, "Surely the LORD's anointed is before Him." But the LORD said to Samuel, "Do not look at his appearance or at the height of his stature, because I have refused him. For the LORD does not see as man sees; for man looks at the outward appearance, but the LORD looks at the heart."

Samuel did not come under the power of a demonic spirit or a false anointing. He was not acting in a wicked way. He was simply moving in and from his human spirit and understanding.

All prophecy must be judged and discerned—whether given by well-known and respected prophets, or by unnamed and unknown prophets. No message should be received without carefully weighing the prophetic utterance. Paul instructs the believer to judge or test all prophecy. Never does Paul indicate that a prophetic word is to be raised to the level of the inspired text. Many contemporary charismatics hold prophecy and prophets in such awe that they almost never test the message, which is in contradiction to the Pauline instruction. Prophecy today—although it may be very helpful and, on occasion, overwhelmingly specific—is not in the category of the revelation given to us by the Holy Bible. A person may hear the voice of the Lord and be compelled to speak, but there is no assurance that what was spoken is pollutant free. A possibility of mixture always exists: flesh, human mind, human spirit and preconceived impressions.

PROPHECY MUST BE PROVEN

First Thessalonians 5:20,21 gives a powerful warning: "Don't suppress the spirit and don't stifle those who have a word from the Master. On the other hand, don't be gullible. Check out everything and keep only what is good. Throw out anything tainted with evil" (The Message Translation).

Paul is giving clear instruction for every believer to follow: Prove all things and hold fast to what is good. To prove is to examine, to put to the test and to recognize the genuine after examining closely. The Old Testament carries instructions given by Yahweh to test the prophets. The judgment upon the false prophet, or false word given, was severe. God knew that presumption could enter in and that we would need to prove the prophecy:

> ✝ Deut. 18:21,22: And if you say in your heart, "How shall we know the word which the LORD has not spoken?"—when a prophet speaks in the name of the LORD, if the thing does not happen or come to pass, that is the thing which the LORD has not spoken; the prophet has spoken it presumptuously; you shall not be afraid of him.

The believer is responsible to prove or test prophecy (see Matt. 7:15,20; 24:11,24; 1 John 4:1). He or she should ask:

> ✝ Does this prophetic word contradict the written Word?
>
> ✝ Does this prophetic word contradict the character of God?
>
> ✝ Does this prophetic word have two or three other confirmations?
>
> ✝ Does this prophetic word come from a proven, trustworthy vessel?
>
> ✝ Does this prophetic word exalt and glorify the Lord Jesus Christ?

Testing

‡ Does this prophetic word work in unity with the letter and spirit of Scripture?

‡ Does this prophetic word have solid theological or doctrinal content?

‡ Does this prophetic word have something worthwhile? Is there substance?

‡ Does this prophetic word have specific predictions that can be judged?

‡ Does the person giving the prophetic word submit to authority? Is he or she connected to and accountable to a local church?

‡ Does this prophetic word seek to control or manipulate?

‡ Does my spirit bear witness to the prophetic word, or do I feel confused, alarmed or checked in my spirit?

The Gate Church seeks to release the voice of God continually through teaching, preaching, prophesying and other means. The misuse of prophecy should not be countered with a no-use mentality. To allow prophecy is to have certain problems surface (see Prov. 14:4), but we can all benefit from this ministry.

BENEFITING FROM PROPHETIC TRUTHS AND PROPHETIC MINISTRIES

Prophecy is not predestination or election. It doesn't seal the future of the individual or the church just because it has been spoken. Both individual and corporate prophetic words, or prophetic truths, are given to encourage and inspire the Gate Church toward the vision God has given. As a Gate-Church leader who is seeking to hear and implement prophetic truths, I must take responsibility for seeking out and proving the voice of God, as well as assimilating the message from God into the local church.

New truths are usually quickened old truths. They should begin with Scripture, then be inspired through prophetic preaching or prophetic words. The church today is hearing certain prophetic words that will eventually become prophetic truths and then prophetic teachings. As a pastor, I must be open but not gullible. Being open to hear God speak is not abandoning all my pastoral responsibilities of research, testing, proving, asking the right questions, moving slowly ahead, or assimilating the parts into the whole without losing the health of the whole.

COMMON ERRORS

Some common errors regarding prophecy and prophetic cutting-edge trends do exist. For example, there is the common error of deferring our responsibility and depending too heavily on the prophetic. In this case, we lean too heavily on the sovereignty of God, assuming that if God wants us to move into this prophetic word, or prophetic truth, it will happen. In other words, we don't have to do anything except let God be God. This kind of spiritual fatalism will contribute to the breakdown of a healthy Gate Church. There's danger in believing that "what will happen, will happen. God has spoken and all the demons of hell together can do nothing about it. No one can change it because God has spoken."

The reality is that all fulfillment of prophecy and truth is accompanied with the partnership of obedient, willing, praying, fasting and strategizing people. A Gate-Church leader realizes that prophetic utterances from one or several prophets are only part of the full revelation of God's will and way. A church that totally depends on prophetic words for direction, change and vision is a church that is headed for trouble. To exalt the prophetic above God's other means of speaking can put the church in peril. The Lord does not expect us to violate godly counsel, common sense, leadership skills, budget examinations, timing and taking the correct steps for fulfilling vision. The prophetic word, or prophetic cutting-edge new truths, are only a part of what the church needs to experience.

If you have properly proven a prophetic word, or truth, and have discerned that it is truly a God-given word, then you must take steps to implement the fulfillment of the word. If God promises supernatural rain but He asks you to dig the ditches, there won't be any rain until you prepare. Jesus asked for the waterpots to be filled with water before the miracle of the wine. Prophetic words and prophetic present truths usually demand that leadership take responsibility, prepare the people, teach the Word, move in faith and go forward.

Another common error is harmful comparisons. Each local church has its own personal-

> "If God promises supernatural rain but He asks you to dig the ditches, there won't be any rain until you prepare. Jesus asked for the waterpots to be filled with water before the miracle of the wine. Prophetic words and prophetic present truths usually demand that leadership take responsibility, prepare the people, teach the Word, move in faith and go forward."

ity and its own destiny to fulfill. All churches have a certain biblical mandate to accomplish; they are to preach the gospel, pray continually, worship God, make disciples and so on. How a church accomplishes these mandates, however, is varied and has something to do with the leadership team, geographical location, resources available, age of the church and the spiritual season of the church. If you are a leader, do not compare your prophetic promises to the promises for any other church. This will lead to confusion, discouragement, criticism and a misinterpreting of your church's destiny.

PROPHETIC CHURCHES FOR TODAY'S WORLD

The Gate-Church leader's biblical responsibility for prophetic words, truths and trends needs to be spelled out. God does speak, and we are endeavoring to listen carefully and wisely. My responsibility is to judge, prove, test, discern and then to move ahead with prophetic words, or truth. As a Gate-Church leader, I should receive words from the Holy Spirit with meekness and humility and with an attitude of respect and expectation for the fulfillment of those words (see 1 Thess. 2:13).

As the prophetic word is received, I must understand the test principle. God will test every word that I embrace, testing my faith and my capacity to carry that word (see Ps. 105:19; John 10:10). Prophetic words and truths are always handled with faith and patience (see Heb. 4:2; 6:12) and with a warrior's spirit (see 1 Tim. 1:18). The ministry of the prophet in today's church is needed. The voice of God from the top of the ladder is necessary for Gate Churches. Let us open our hearts to release the prophets in the Body of Christ. They have much to offer:

- ✝ Prophets inspire faith and courage (see Ezra 5:1,2).
- ✝ Prophets reveal the root cause to problems (see Judg. 6:8).
- ✝ Prophets clarify destiny and vision (see 2 Sam. 7:1-11).
- ✝ Prophets reveal and rebuke hidden acts of disobedience (see 2 Sam. 12:1-7).
- ✝ Prophets preach with prophetic power and insight (see Neh. 6:7).
- ✝ Prophets foretell future events to prepare God's people (see Acts 11:27-30).

Characteristics of Prophets ministry (over)

✝ Prophets equip the church for ministry (see Eph. 4:11,12).

✝ Prophets minister in and through local churches (see Acts 13:1-3).

✝ Prophets minister personal words to aid spiritual warfare (see 1 Tim. 1:18).

Gate Churches are prophetic churches that move into prophetic preaching, prophetic intercession, prophetic words and prophetic worship. Prophetic churches function constantly and accurately in the realm of the word of knowledge, the word of wisdom, discernment of spirits, revelation, visions and dreams. Let us seek to establish a ladder of intercession that creates an atmosphere for prophetic ministry. Let us not quench the Spirit; let us instead hear clearly what the Spirit is saying to the church that Christ is building—the Gate Church.

And behold, the LORD stood above it and said:
"I am the LORD God of Abraham your father and the God of Isaac;
the land on which you lie I will give to you and your descendants.
Also your descendants shall be as the dust of the earth;
you shall spread abroad to the west and the east,
to the north and the south; and in you and in your seed
all the families of the earth shall be blessed." Genesis 28:13,14

The Gate Church Grows in Quantity and Quality

Jacob was strengthened in the faith and supported by liberal promises because he greatly needed the assurance of divine grace. After identifying Himself as Yahweh, the God of Abraham and Isaac—thereby tying the present revelation with those preceding Jacob—Yahweh, the merciful covenant God, confirmed to Jacob the blessings of Abraham that Isaac had bestowed upon him before Jacob's departure from his home.

The first element of the promise was the possession of the land; the second element of the blessing specifically confirmed on Jacob was that of numerous descendants "like the dust of the earth" (see Gen. 13:16; 22:17). The promise was for a "spreading out." The Hebrew verb *parats* means "to break through" in the sense of bursting all restraining bonds. This word reinforces and adds to the thought of letting the expansion extend to all points of the compass, promising "a breaking out of all restraining bonds to reach even to the four corners of the earth."

SATURATING THE UNREACHED AREAS
WITHIN REACH

A healthy Gate Church is one that grows in quantitative and qualitative growth simultaneously and in good balance. The promise to Jacob is a seed promise to all Gate Churches: "Your descendants shall be as the dust of the earth. You shall spread abroad to the west and the east, to the north and the south" (Gen. 28:14). This is megagrowth, growth that spreads and enlarges from every angle. The Gate-Church calling is to grow and to reach its geographical region with the gospel of Christ.

The size of a church in relation to its city or ministry area is a significant factor. God desires that our local churches saturate our areas with the preaching of the gospel. Saturation is preaching the gospel to every available person at every available time by every available means. Acts 5:28 says, "Did we not strictly command you not to teach in this name? And look, you have filled Jerusalem with your doctrine, and intend to bring this Man's blood on us!" Clearly, the Early Church's saturation method was to present the gospel daily in the Temple and in every house; they never stopped teaching and preaching Jesus Christ (see Acts 5:12; 20:20-21).

A Gate Church has a vision for continued growth and saturation of the entire region with the gospel, making disciples of all people. The leader wrestles with any and all pressures upon the church that cause plateauing. If the church declines numerically—loses its desire to reproduce and becomes a passive consumer of information—it will slowly die. If evangelism becomes more a topic of discussion than a matter of lifestyle, the church will die. If preoccupation with nurture or internal growth replaces expansion growth, the congregation will begin to decline. These are red-alert signs.

The Gate-Church leader believes the promise of multiplication, expansion, growth and breaking out. The challenge for the Gate Church is to understand how much the culture, the people and our cities have changed. Growing a church today is not the same as it was ten, twenty or fifty years ago. The family is smaller, more mobile and harder to assimilate into the life of the church. More effort, energy and finances are required to reach the new multitude of changing families. The church has to intentionally strategize growth or growth won't happen.

The "quantity" challenge is real and ever before the Gate-Church leader who has a burden and vision for impacting his or her region. There is no real satisfaction for non-growth-producing pastors. Seeing a church decline or plateau is painful, for both the leader and the Lord. God loves the world—all races and all people—and He wants men, women and children to be saved and added to the church. God is not pleased with churches that never or seldom see people come to Christ. The church is called to preach the gospel to everyone, all the time, everywhere.

Saturation. Nothing less than saturation will penetrate our changing cities. I want to put a positive note in for large congregations. Large churches are part of our history and will remain part of our heritage. The largest congregations on record are being built now, today. As I write this book, history is being formed around the mind-boggling growth of large churches. According to John Vaughan's report on megachurches, a new congregation breaks the two thousand worship attendance barrier nearly every two weeks.[1] Chuck Swindoll, in his book *Rise and Shine*, speaks forthrightly about the large church:

> The big church has taken a bum rap. In this generation especially, size alone makes large places of worship suspect. I find that a rather curious fact since it doesn't seem to be true in other areas of life. In the domestic realm big families are not viewed suspiciously. On the contrary, it is usually the large happy family that is the envy of the neighborhood. Big is not considered bad in the commercial world. Larger stores and shopping malls are the most popular places to shop.[2]

Swindoll also offers a very insightful contrast between a neighborhood church concept and a metropolitan church concept.[3]

PHILOSOPHIES IN CONTRAST

Neighborhood Church Concept	Metropolitan Church Concept
Acts 1:15	Acts 2:41,47; 4:2; 6:1-4
‡ Smaller church of 10-300	‡ 300-100,000
‡ It is one big family where everyone knows everyone and it's easy to know everyone.	‡ One big, big extended family where you know your group and lots of faces.
‡ Pastor is pastor to everyone. He does almost everything as there are no other staff and the people want him to be available and lovable.	‡ Impossible to have one pastor relate to thousands of people. A structure to minister to this large family is complex and yet simple, pastoral ministry team.

Neighborhood Church Concept	Metropolitan Church Concept
☩ People are drawn from immediate neighborhood areas.	☩ People drawn from a vast radius of many areas. Many resources, broad influence, regional.
☩ There is a tendency toward being inbred, a one-man operation, strong centralized loyalty to "our church," don't want to change, hard to let new people in.	☩ Less inbred. Vast organization of ministries and leaders with some specialists. Team of leadership. "Open church," decentralized.

It doesn't matter whether we are a neighborhood church or a metropolitan church, we should have vision and faith for our church to break out and grow by intentionally saturating our areas with the gospel. The first church of the first century grew rapidly, influencing cities and turning the whole world upside down (see Acts 2:42-47; 4:1-10; 7:17; 12:24; 19:20). The original mandate from God was to "be fruitful and multiply; fill the earth" (see Gen. 1:26-28; 8:17; 9:1; 35:11; Heb. 6:14).

As we strategize for quantitative growth, we also need a vision for qualitative growth. The quality of spiritual life within the growing church must be kept at a high level in order to sustain healthy growth. As the church increases numerically, the tension that accompanies the search for meaningful fellowship and satisfying relationships becomes very important. Converts, transplants and new people coming into the church must all quickly find relationships and a sense of belonging. Most church-growth experts say that if a new person does not experience connectedness within five to seven weeks, that individual will not stay in the church.

THE POWER OF NETMAKING FOR CHURCH GROWTH AND CHURCH HEALTH

The quality of our church growth will be made more possible as we network all believers together. Using the image of the net, Jesus teaches spiritual principles that the disciples would use in extending the kingdom of God. To accomplish Kingdom purpose, we must understand the power of the net. To build quality Gate Churches, we must weave the people of God into a net—one that doesn't break. In Luke 5:1-10, we read how Jesus used the net:

So it was, as the multitude pressed about Him to hear the word of

God, that He stood by the Lake of Gennesaret, and saw two boats standing by the lake; but the fishermen had gone from them and were washing their nets. Then He got into one of the boats, which was Simon's, and asked him to put out a little from the land. And He sat down and taught the multitudes from the boat. When He had stopped speaking, He said to Simon, "Launch out into the deep and let down your nets for a catch." But Simon answered and said to Him, "Master, we have toiled all night and caught nothing; nevertheless at Your word I will let down the net." And when they had done this, they caught a great number of fish, and their net was breaking. So they signaled to their partners in the other boat to come and help them. And they came and filled both the boats, so that they began to sink. When Simon Peter saw it, he fell down at Jesus' knees, saying, "Depart from me, for I am a sinful man, O Lord!" For he and all who were with him were astonished at the catch of fish which they had taken; and so also were James and John, the sons of Zebedee, who were partners with Simon. And Jesus said to Simon, "Do not be afraid. From now on you will catch men."

In this passage from Luke 5, the disciples "launched into the deep," "let down their nets" and "caught a great number of fish." But the result was that "their nets were breaking." What a vivid illustration of growing churches that have faith to launch out into the deep, fill their boats with fish but end up losing much of the catch because their nets were not strong enough to handle the catch! Sinking boats and broken nets!

The Gate Church must grow with quality and sturdy nets, with strong relationships nurtured and established in the church. The word net means "a fabric made by interlocking threads, by knotting and twisting them at the points where they cross each other." The strength of the net depends on the number of twists and knots made in it. The net must be pulled and stretched into a place of strength. It is representative of how we build the relational aspect of our church. Scripture encourages a net mentality. For example, Ephesians 4:16 says, "From whom the whole body, joined and knit together by

> *"Most church-growth experts say that if a new person does not experience connectedness within five to seven weeks, that individual will not stay in the church."*

63

what every joint supplies, according to the effective working by which every part does its share, causes growth of the body for the edifying of itself in love." Verses such as 1 Corinthians 1:10; 12:26; Colossians 2:2 and Ephesians 2:21,22 all convey the same message: We need each other!

BUILDING STRONG RELATIONAL NETS

Strong relational nets provide safety, fellowship, encouragement, increased joy, faith, new friendships, teamwork, other viewpoints, unity, added resources, accountability, immediate pastoral care, interconnectedness; they are not easily broken. The Gate-Church pastor begins to weave the net by embracing the biblical reasoning for strong relationships (see Eccles. 4:9-12; Col. 2:2; Gal. 6:2: 1 John 4:7) and facing the obstacles in our culture that hinder relationships.

Unhealthy individualism lies at the very core of our American culture. We believe in the dignity, indeed the very sacredness, of the individual. Anything that threatens to violate our right to think for ourselves, judge for ourselves, make our own decisions, and live our lives as we see fit is not only believed to be morally wrong, but it is also considered to be sacrilegious. As much as we want community, we shy away from it whenever that community infringes on our autonomy. Most people are so afraid of rejection that they avoid intimacy; busy, stressful and fractured lifestyles also sabotage our need for community. The challenge to build with quality relationships is indeed the stretching and the pulling of our nets.

There is a cultural search for authentic relationship, and it is the church's responsibility to provide society with a model that is worthy of being committed to. People, philosophies and politicians are in search of the ideal harmonious society, but such a utopia has never been realized. Sin always twists the reality of healthy interpersonal relationships, leaving people hungering for the realization of relational dreams. The Gate Church that has a vision to grow quantitatively must move from a crowd to a congregation—from a cafeteria atmosphere to a family atmosphere.

Our society has become a community of nomads, rootless people who are moving and changing continually for job reasons, health reasons or just an itch for adventure and change. With so many factors working against quality relationships, we must work much harder to provide the much needed relational aspect of life for all people within the church.

THREE ASPECTS OF BIBLICAL RELATIONSHIPS

The Gate Church builds upon three aspects of biblical relationships: fellowship, Kingdom partnerships and covenant relationships.

FELLOWSHIP

The word *koinonia* is translated fellowship, sharing, partnership, contribution, association and participation. *Koinonia* is a significant Gate-Church concept found throughout the New Testament, which expresses shared participation in Christ and the bond that Christ knits between believers. It depicts a harmony between believers that is brought about by each believer's union with Christ and the Holy Spirit (see Acts 2:42; Rom. 15:26; 1 Cor. 1:9; 2 Cor. 8:4; 9:13).

KINGDOM PARTNERSHIP

The Gate Church lays a foundation of *koinonia*, and then allows for and encourages Kingdom partnership. Kingdom partnerships happen when the Holy Spirit draws teams of people together to accomplish Kingdom purposes (see Romans 16:3). When joined as partners in the work of the ministry, common commitment extends the kingdom of God. Kingdom partners are not drawn together around personalities or hobbies, but around purpose. Their closeness weaves into a tighter bond as they partner to accomplish the same thing—a two-sided relationship of giving and receiving.

The word "partner" expresses a legal relationship, a joint ownership that moves from an independent interest to join an interest that desires the greater cause and the greater vision of working together for the sake of helping others. The New Testament uses a number of words to denote Kingdom partnership: "fellow worker," "fellow laborer," "kinsman," "workers," "companion," "helper," "beloved," "servant," "servants of the church," "fellow workers in Christ." We see Kingdom partnership in the relationships of Paul and Barnabas, Paul and Silas, Paul and Priscilla and Aquilla, Paul and Timothy, Paul and Philemon, Jonathan and David (see 2 Cor. 8:23; Heb. 10:33; 1 Pet. 1:4; 5:1).

> "When joined as partners in the work of the ministry, common commitment extends the kingdom of God."

COVENANT RELATIONSHIP

The third aspect of networking the people of God into

authentic, meaningful relationships is covenant relationship. Covenant relationship may grow out of Kingdom partnership and certainly must be a significant part of Kingdom partnership, but it can have enough of a difference to be treated separately. Covenant relationships happen when God joins people together in a committed relationship that grows into a deep, godly, intimate friendship that lasts for life, in spite of relational trials, hurts, misunderstandings and geographical distances. Jesus describes this kind of relationship in John 15:12-15: "This is My commandment, that you love one another as I have loved you. Greater love has no one than this, than to lay down one's life for his friends. You are My friends if you do whatever I command you. No longer do I call you servants, for a servant does not know what his master is doing; but I have called you friends, for all things that I heard from My Father I have made known to you."

BUILDING A CHURCH WITH RELATIONSHIP NETS

Everyone has a relational pyramid that involves three kinds of relationships: acquaintances who have contact only occasionally, core friends who are known by name and who are around regularly, and intimate friends who are covenantally woven together and deeply involved in our lives. Intimate friends are those we share our most sensitive issues with; they are worthy of our deepest commitment. Not everyone attains this third category of relationship; however, for the church to be healthy, every believer should have covenant friends.

A church built upon acquaintances is shallow and unfulfilling; the people form only a superficial connection. This lack of relational depth is unhealthy and detrimental to quality growth in the church. God wants the Gate Church to know and understand *agape* kind of love. *Agape* is a covenant word that describes the ties that bind people together in a committed relationship. The Gate Church builds upon the *agape* spirit of love and uses that spirit to strengthen the net. It is the spirit of *agape* that ties people together. *Agape* love is not feeling or impulse based; it is a love of the will—a love that is constant, looking beyond the object, beyond a person's faults.

Every believer must learn to build relationships that last. We don't need more "friends of the road," or transitory relationships, in which the road runs out, life changes, and they move on. What we need are "friends of the heart," relationships that last a lifetime. As we see in the following verses, the Lord put great emphasis on this kind of friendship:

✝ John 13:34: "A new commandment I give to you, that you love one another; as I have loved you, that you also love one another."

✝ 1 Thessalonians 3:12: And may the Lord make you increase and abound in love to one another and to all, just as we do to you.

Not all people—both churched and unchurched—experience significant relationships, although most want to. The sad fact of life is that certain people in our society live on the streets, sleeping under bridges. They are homeless, living in cars with signs that say "Will work for food." These are our visible homeless. The relationally homeless are not so visible. Many single people suffer with this condition, but so do the married, the old and the young, male and female. Many people are relationally living on the street. They are unable to find significant relationship connections with other people. The Gate Church works hard and works wisely to remedy this deep and obvious societal need. The church that grows quantitatively must grow qualitatively through relationships.

Max Lucado defines relationship as "the delicate fusion of two human beings. The intricate weaving of two lives; two sets of moods, mentalities, and temperaments. Two intermingling hearts, both seeking solace and security. A relationship. It has more power than any nuclear bomb and more potential than any promising seed. Nothing will drive a man to greater courage than a relationship. Nothing will fire the heart of a patriot or purge the cynicism of a rebel like a relationship. What matters most in life is not what ladders we climb or what ownings we accumulate. What matters most is a relationship."[4]

Norm Wright speaks about the mutualability factor:

So what is a relationship? We use the term, but really, what is it? Simply put, it's the mutual sharing of life between two people. For a relationship to exist there has to be 'mutualability.' Each person has to make some contribution for the relationship to exist. Both need to participate in some way or it won't work.[5]

The Gate Church builds a healthy relational atmosphere by establishing a clear understanding of the three different expressions of covenant relationship: (1) our covenant relationship with God, (2) our covenant relationship with the church, and (3) our covenant relationship with people God places in our lives.

The goal of the Gate Church is to help people build new relationships, restore old relationships, renew some neglected relationships and commit to cultivating authentic Christian community. The Gate Church seeks to create an atmosphere of biblical *koinonia* where love, acceptance and reaching out to others flows naturally. Relationships in the congregation are the anchor to the vision and future accomplishments of the church.

The Gate Church builds covenant expressions of relationship as the core value of the church. The word "covenant" defines the agreement between two parties who are committed to guaranteeing that their relationship will be preserved based on the integrity of their word and their actions. God's principle of relationship is covenant.

OUR RELATIONSHIP WITH GOD—THE FOUNDATION FOR ALL RELATIONSHIPS

Our relationship with God operates on the principle of covenant. First John 4:20 explains that we cannot say we love God whom we cannot see if we cannot love the people of God that we can see. The heart that sacrificially reaches out in love with loyalty and patience is a heart that has been cleansed and brought into newness through reconciliation with God (see Rom. 3:23-25). In Jeremiah 31:33, God says, "I will put My law in their minds, and write it on their hearts; and I will be their God, and they shall be My people." When we enter into a covenant relationship with God through repentance, accepting His mercy and forgiveness, we are born again. Second Corinthians 5:17 defines the born-again experience by saying, "Therefore, if anyone is in Christ, he is a new creation; old things have passed away; behold, all things have become new." The Amplified Bible adds, "Behold the fresh and the new has come." The New English Bible says, "When anyone is united in Christ, there is a new world or a new act of creation."

A connection to God makes connecting to people a true possibility. We are covenant people—first with God and then with God's people (see Gen. 17:11; Exod. 2:24; 2 Chron. 6:14; 15:12; 34:31,32; Ezra 10:3; Isa. 42:9; 43:18; Acts 2:42-47).

A distorted concept of God, however, will hinder our relationship with Him and others. Norman Wright describes four distorted concepts of God:

1. **The Referee God:** Some people see God as a referee who tallies points for good performance on a huge scoreboard in the sky. These people are consumed by religious rules and the fear that they will step out of line and suffer a penalty. They may get away

with a few fouls or errors when God isn't looking, but most of the time these poor people are motivated by guilt and obsessed with avoiding God's wrath.

2. **The Grandfather God:** Many people use their interpretation of God to keep them from growing up—to avoid responsibility. And by viewing God as a warm grandfatherly figure, they remain a child. They want to be told, "There's nothing to worry about; I'll take care of everything for you."

3. **The Scientist God:** A "superior reasoning power," is how Einstein conceptualized God. "A superior mind," is how he said it on another occasion. For some, God is a withdrawn and distant thinker, too busy running the galaxies to get involved in our petty problems. God is sitting in His laboratory, conducting experiments with His door closed and a "Do Not Disturb" sign on it.

4. **The Bodyguard God:** Some people think of God much the same way a sailor thinks of a lifeboat. He knows it is there, but he hopes he'll never have to use it. These people live life without giving much conscious attention to God, but they expect Him to be there when they need Him. When we view God this way, we believe He should serve as a kind of bodyguard to protect us from pain and suffering. "If I'm living a good life," so the reasoning goes, "then God should look after me and keep me out of harm's way."[6]

The Gate Church helps to create a true picture of God so that people can have an intimate relationship with Him and with His people.

OUR RELATIONSHIP WITH THE LOCAL CHURCH—A PLACE TO GROW IN RELATIONSHIPS

The second important covenant relationship is the one we have with our local church. Some people make a spiritual decision to accept Christ but never resist the lie of "the prince of the power of the air" (Eph. 2:2) who influences a "no relationship" commitment to the local church. A local church is a congregation, or assembly of people, that joins together for prayer, worship, communion, teaching, discipline and nurture.

Christ is committed to building His church, worldwide and locally (see Matt. 16:16-18; 18:16-19). After being born again, a person needs to be added to the church (see Acts 2:47). Church membership is a tangible commitment. To develop meaningful and lasting relationships, one must be committed to and involved in his or her local church—not just attend as a spectator, but become a participator.

Americans are influenced by the spirits and attitudes of a backslidden nation. The spirit of selfishness prevails; it's an attitude of serving and living for oneself. The spirit of independence is the desire to be one's own master without any accountability to anyone, answering only to oneself. The spirit of solitariness is a desire to isolate one's actions and energies from the community of God. The problem of isolation—of individuals relocating frequently, detaching themselves out of restlessness—creates a rootlessness that works in opposition to developing relationships. Our nation's mobility has brought a sense of detachment from our neighborhoods, cities, churches and extended families. We are detached from everyone outside our own private worlds.

The same restlessness can be seen in the American church as people change frequently, moving from one church to another without biblical reasons or the Holy Spirit's leading. The Gate Church understands the pressures that work against tying the net together and—through prayer, teaching and wisely structured small groups that are available for all—fights against this problem. By weaving people together within the congregation, a Gate Church builds quantitatively and qualitatively.

Scripture provides several attitudes of convent relationship that need to be encouraged with regard to the church. These attitudes include:

‡ **Faithfulness to the house of God:** (See 1 Cor. 5:4; 11:17,18,20,33; 14:23,26.) Faithfulness in attending church is faithfulness to God and His family; it's a family-loyalty issue. Families that love each other spend time together. The house of the Lord is the place where we as believers will "dwell forever" (Ps. 23:6); it's important that we begin spending time together now. Hebrews 10:25 encourages us not to forsake "the assembling of ourselves together, as is the manner of some, but exhorting one another, and so much the more as you see the Day approaching." Meeting in the Father's house not only honors the

> "The problem of isolation—of individuals relocating frequently, detaching themselves out of restlessness—creates a rootlessness that works in opposition to developing relationships."

Father but it also builds the individual members of the family.

‡ **Loving and appreciating the house of God:** Our attitude toward the church should be, "Lord, I have loved the habitation of Your house, and the place where Your glory dwells" (Ps. 26:8). We must treat the church the way Christ treats the church. He sacrificially gave Himself for the church. Christ's wife is the church. He protects her; He loves her; He doesn't tolerate anyone speaking evil of His wife. He speaks well of her at all times—even with her spots, wrinkles and problems. He loves His church the same way a man loves His own flesh and bone (see Acts 20:28; Eph. 5:25-27). Christ attends every church meeting and dwells in the midst of the worshiping community (see Matt. 18:16-20; Heb. 1:1-9).

‡ **Participation in the house of God:** We are the television generation. Our society is so accustomed to watching an event on television without any active participation that we have developed a spectator mentality. First Corinthians 14:26 says, "How is it then, brethren? Whenever you come together, each of you has a psalm, has a teaching, has a tongue, has a revelation, has an interpretation. Let all things be done for edification." We are to be participants in God's house. Dropping the spectator mentality and becoming an active participant in corporate gatherings is truly the challenge for all members in local congregations. Many believers have bought into the American attitude of consumerism. Numerous Christians are "double dipping." Instead of becoming part of one Christian community, they attend two or more churches in a quest to have their personal needs met. They remain spectators or consumers in each church. We need to help believers see that this is not the path God desires. He desires that we be involved in one fellowship where we can give as well as receive (see 1 Cor. 12; Eph. 4:15,16).

OUR RELATIONSHIP WITH COVENANT FRIENDS—DEEPENING OUR RELATIONSHIPS

The third aspect of relational covenant is seen in our personal God-given friendships. These relationships take time, commitment and godly character; they don't just happen. Hopefully, no one really believes that people can just fall into covenant relationships with no plans, no emotions, no sacrifice, no time invested—as if the friendship just happens accidentally, easily, without any real work. True covenant relationships begin with a specific decision and continue as certain principles of integrity are respected and continually activated (see 1 John 3:16). God is adamant about covenant relationships.

In 2 Chronicles 23:1, Jehoida made a covenant commitment to a specific group of leaders he was working with: "In the seventh year Jehoida strengthened himself, and made a covenant with the captains of hundreds: Azariah the son of Jeroham, Ishmael the son of Jehohanan, Azariah the son of Obed, Maaseiah the son of Adaiah, and Elishaphat the son of Zichri."

In Amos 1:9, Jehovah judges the city of Tyre because of four sins. The fourth transgression Jehovah says will cause their judgment to not be turned away: "Thus says the Lord, 'For three transgressions of Tyre, and for four, I will not turn away its punishment, because they delivered up the whole captivity to Edom, and did not remember the covenant of brotherhood.'"

Ruth 1:14-18 records one of the most remembered and vivid pictures of covenant relationship between two people: "Then they lifted up their voices and wept again; and Orpah kissed her mother-in-law, but Ruth clung to her. And she said, 'Look, your sister-in-law has gone back to her people and to her gods; return after your sister-in-law.' But Ruth said: 'Entreat me not to leave you, or to turn back from following after you; for wherever you go, I will go; and wherever you lodge, I will lodge; your people shall be my people, and your God, my God. Where you die, I will die, and there will I be buried. The Lord do so to me, and more also, if anything but death parts you and me.' When she saw that she was determined to go with her, she stopped speaking to her."

Like Ruth and Naomi, David and Jonathan are a model of covenant relationship in the Old Testament. They grow into a deep friendship that journeys through the mountains and valleys of relationship problems and blessings. Their life experiences offer a wealth of knowledge and insight for building covenant relationship with those God puts into our lives. Every believer in the Gate Church should understand and glean from the four clear principles exemplified in David and Jonathan's relationship.

1. COVENANT RELATIONSHIP BEGINS WITH A SPIRITUAL ACT OF BEING KNIT TOGETHER

First Samuel 18:1 says that "the soul of Jonathan was knit to the soul of

David, and Jonathan loved him as his own soul." David and Jonathan were nearly the same age. Prince Jonathan had taken little interest in David as a minstrel; however, David's heroism, modesty, manly bearing, piety and high endowments kindled in Jonathan the flame of not only admiration but also affection. The word "knit" is literally "chained together." In nearly every language, friendship is considered to be the union of souls bound together by the band of love. Jonathan loved David as his own soul. The most intimate friendship subsisted with them, and they loved each other fervently with pure hearts. They had a relationship that could not be affected by changes or chances—each was worthy of the other.

Covenant relationships produce a sameness—as though one soul were in two bodies. When love grows with this kind of intensity, it is founded upon mutual values and dreams. This depth of love can bear any test because the tie is stronger than mere blood relations, making a person willing to forego all earthly advantages for the good of the relationship. Such was the love Jonathan had for David, a love that was deep and abiding—whether his friend was an outlaw and fugitive or the favorite of the court. Jonathan's love took no account of the fact that David was destined to occupy the place that he had once hoped to fill and was fully competent to fill. Although he never sat upon a throne, Jonathan's conduct gives full proof to his kingly nature.

The Hebrew word "knit together" is *qashar*, meaning "to tie, physically gird, confine, compact or mentally to love, to bind together, to become stronger because of the ties." In its simplest form, *qashar* can mean a simple joining. As used in 1 Samuel 18:1 *qashar* means a binding or tying together of two things or parties and indicates a conscious decision to do something. Basically, this root denotes binding securely and putting something together. It is used as the binding together of human beings and human relationships. People can be bound together inseparably in love and pure relationships (see Gen. 44:28; 1 Sam. 18:1-5).

The knitting together of David and Jonathan's heart was not a random act. Jonathan had been watching David and made a conscious decision to join himself, or bind himself, to David; Jonathan saw in David the same heart and passion for the Lord as he had. To be knit together with another, the strands of God-centered belief need to be tied in place (see Ps. 1:1; 2 Cor. 6:4). There must be a mutual personal commitment to the relationship that includes a mutual respect that builds the other person and does not tear down (see 1 Sam. 18:3; Ruth 1:14-18).

People can be knit together in wrong relationships, depleting instead of replenishing. A depleting relationship drains you emotionally and spiritually. It taps your energy resources and is continual hard work. A replenishing relationship energizes you, and revitalizes your spirit, soul and mind. It adds to your life; it does not diminish it.

2. COVENANT RELATIONSHIP BEGINS AND GROWS BY MAKING AND KEEPING COVENANT

"Jonathan and David made a covenant, because he loved him as his own soul" (1 Sam. 18:3). The purpose of a covenant is to guarantee that the relationship will remain healthy and will last. The covenant itself is actually a series of words that are spoken to define the nature of the relationship and the principles of commitment to it. A covenant can be a sworn oath that seals the relationship between two people. A spoken covenant reiterates the agreed upon terms between the two people involved. When covenant is the foundation for relationships, the possibility of maintaining permanence and stability is greatly enhanced. God-centered relationships should feature a unity of vision, values and passions.

An official covenant-making service is not always part of a covenant relationship, but there should be a time when a knitting together has happened and a spiritual bonding has been verbally expressed in words of commitment, loyalty, purpose, sacrifice and love.

3. COVENANT RELATIONSHIP BEGINS WITH A "GENEROUS SOUL" ATTITUDE

"Jonathan took off the robe that was on him and gave it to David, with his armor, even to his sword and his bow and his belt." (1 Sam. 18:4). A "generous soul" attitude admires the covenant friend's qualities without being jealous when personal achievements are eclipsed. Jonathan was not jealous of David, even though his own military achievements were eclipsed by David. The generous soul gives not only what is valuable and suitable to the relationship but also asks what is honorable. A "generous soul" attitude causes both people to pour out affirmation, encouragement and words of greatness; it quickly promotes the other person over self.

David was refreshed by the pleasant waters of Jonathan. Even when David was in the desert, isolated and discouraged, Jonathan's words were able to water David's soul. Some of the deepest relationships are forged in sorrow and through great trials of affliction. Empathy means to treat people as equals. It involves more listening than talking. It is feeling what the other person is feeling and going through that person's problems with him or her. A generous soul gives respect by recognizing and acknowledging the other person's worth or values. All relationships grow when the "generous soul" attitude is present.

4. COVENANT RELATIONSHIP GROWS AND STAYS HEALTHY AS WE PROTECT THE RELATIONSHIP

First Samuel 19:1-7 tells us that "Saul spoke to Jonathan his son and to all his servants, that they should kill David; but Jonathan, Saul's son, delighted greatly in David. So Jonathan told David, saying, 'My father Saul seeks to kill you. Therefore please be on your guard until morning, and stay in a secret place and hide. And I will go out and stand beside my father in the field where you are, and I will speak with my father about you. Then what I observe, I will tell you.' Thus Jonathan spoke well of David to Saul his father, and said to him, 'Let not the king sin against his servant, against David, because he has not sinned against you, and because his works have been very good toward you. For he took his life in his hands and killed the Philistine, and the Lord brought about a great deliverance for all Israel. You saw it and rejoiced. Why then will you sin against innocent blood, to kill David without a cause?' So Saul heeded the voice of Jonathan, and Saul swore, 'As the Lord lives, he shall not be killed.' Then Jonathan called David, and Jonathan told him all these things. So Jonathan brought David to Saul, and he was in his presence as in times past."

Every relationship will have its times of testing, stretching, problems and disruption. Outside pressures can be expected; however, we must handle these pressures wisely and successfully if we are to maintain true covenant relationships. We need to consistently protect the relationship by being faithful at all times with our words, attitudes and actions. Proverbs 17:17 says that "a friend loves at all times, and a brother is born for adversity." Adversity proves true relationships. The cloudy day dissolves the crowd that delights in sunshine. Mistakes and failures will prove your true friendships (see Ps. 55:12; Prov. 14:20; 18:24; 19:4; 27:10).

The relationship must be protected with honesty, compassion and sensitivity. Proverbs 17:10 explains that "Rebuke is more effective for a wise man than a hundred blows on a fool." Proverbs 27:6 confirms, "Faithful are the wounds of a friend, but the kisses of an enemy are deceitful." (See also Prov. 27:17; 29:5;

Eph. 4:13.) We protect our covenant relationship through loyalty at all times (see Prov. 11:13; 16:28; 17:9). We build a Gate Church quantitatively and qualitatively by nurturing this level of relationship in both the leadership team and the congregation. We must teach people that this principle-driven concept of relational commitment takes time, forgiveness and integrity.

Covenant relationship must be seen in the congregation's relationship with God, with spouses and other family members, with friends, with business partners and with those in ministry both inside and outside of the church. One brother in the church I pastor came to me after I spoke on covenant relationships and gave me the following description of what this level of relationship means to him:

I will step into your world and stay there.

I will be your covenant friend through thick and thin.

God's not going to let go, and I'm not going to let go.

I know you have a lot of potential and a lot of problems.

I also know you're a God-person.

I'm stepping into your life during a crisis.

I know I have reason not to feel good about you.

I will plead your cause to my own hurt.

Wherever you go, I will go.

God grant us the wisdom, authority and spiritual power to build a Gate Church that offers both quantity and quality. Give us the heart and passion to knit together every person into the net—and then, with that net, do the work of ministry in this generation.

NOTES

1. John Vaughan, "Megachurches and American Cities," *Church Growth Today*, p. 28.

2. Charles Swindoll, *Rise and Shine* (Portland, Oreg.: Multnomah Press, 1989), p. 97.

3. Ibid.

4. H. Norman Wright, *Relationships That Work* (Ventura, Calif.: Regal Books, 1998), p. 11.

5. Ibid., p. 12.

6. Ibid., p. 169-170.

"And through you and in your seed all the families of the earth shall be blessed." Genesis 28:14

The Gate Church Blesses and Builds Families

Jacob had encountered the God of his father and grandfather. God had revealed himself to Jacob in a dream, a dream so real that Jacob received it as a divine visitation and responded with a deep commitment in the form of a vow. Jacob had been touched and something in him had changed. The Lord met Jacob in his need and granted him the support of His grace by giving him promises. These words were given by Yahweh to strengthen Jacob for a lifetime and give him a prophetic vision for his future. Jacob was without family, home, provision or protection. He was alone and grieving over his past. The voice of the Lord broke through for Jacob, and breaks through for us, in the darkest hours, the lonely times, when the future looks bleak and our souls are in need of a heavy deposit of divine grace and hope.

THE PROMISE

The Lord began by promising Jacob possession of the land where he lay sleeping. The promise didn't fit Jacob's present circumstance. He was an exile, homeless. He wondered, How could it ever happen? The Lord also promised that through Jacob, all the families of the world would be blessed. Jacob's blessing would touch the families of the world. The blessing that God promised to

Jacob could only be totally fulfilled through a spiritual seed with spiritual influence great enough to impact all the families of the world. The promise was that in Jacob and "in his seed," all families would be blessed.

Galatians 3:16 clarifies the "seed" as a spiritual seed fulfillment: "Now to Abraham and his Seed were the promises made. He does not say, 'And to seeds,' as of many, but as of one, 'And to your Seed,' who is Christ." Verse 29 goes on to explain that, "if you are Christ's, then you are Abraham's seed, and heirs according to the promise." Galatians 4:28 continues with, "Now we, brethren, as Isaac was, are children of promise" (see also Gen. 17:7; 22:18; Rom. 8:17).

God had made it very clear to Isaac and Rebekah that the promise would be continued, not through the line of Esau, but through the line of Jacob (see Gen. 25:33; 27:27-29). All the promised blessings given to Jacob would find ultimate fulfillment in Christ and the church. It was not through Isaac or Jacob that all the earth would be blessed but through the ultimate seed of Christ, the Blesser of all nations, all peoples, all families of the earth (see Gen. 3:15; John 8:56; Heb. 11:13,17-19). God's promise to Abraham, Isaac and Jacob in its richest spiritual meaning was to be fulfilled in connection with one—and not more than one—definite person, Christ, the true Seed. Everyone who is in Christ is in His seed and this seed has the power to fulfill the promise. The church is the seed of Christ and the fulfiller of this promise: "And all the families of the earth shall be blessed."

THE GATE CHURCH STRATEGIZES TO BUILD FAMILIES

The Gate Church is a family-blessing and family-building church by strategic design. It is biblically responsible for developing a family-blessing and family-building atmosphere through teaching, preaching, counseling, mentoring, small groups, classrooms, sermons and modeling what Scripture teaches about family. The Gate Church must not only concentrate on saving the lost outside the church, but it should also focus on preserving the fruit from the biological reproduction that has been placed by God in the church. If we save the world and lose our own children, we will relinquish leadership to a generation

> "If we save the world and lose our own children, we will relinquish leadership to a generation without the strength of a Christian heritage."

without the strength of a Christian heritage.

The Gate Church equips families to be spiritually healthy, which is no easy task in our day and age. Because the family is so important, the church should be a place of training, counseling and ongoing strength. Often, however, family doesn't appear to be as crucial to the church as it is to the public. Thank God for Dr. James Dobson, founder of Focus on the Family, and the many other para-church organizations that have rallied to the challenge of ministering to the family in this generation. One has to wonder whether the church has felt over-whelmed by the net or simply been preoccupied with other issues.

Where has the church been during the past fifty years concerning the family? Our nation has adopted a "family is in" attitude with family ranking high on most American's lists of priorities—yet the family is falling apart! In his book *Family Ministry*, Charles S. Sell addresses the church's failure to meet the need in this one ministry, family. In the early 1970s, H. Norman Wright surveyed Christian education and youth directors and discovered that relatively little was being done by the church for families. Two thirds of those who responded reported that within the previous two years, their churches had offered no fam-ily-related programs whatsoever—not even a sermon preached on a family theme. Wright goes on to say, "Today the national association of evangelicals has uncovered the same lack of family ministry. In a recent study, few pastors indicated having taken significant steps to help people whose families were in trouble, even though they also said that family disintegration is a relatively common problem in their congregations. Why this shortage of family min-istry?"[1]

Lyle Schaller wrote at the beginning of the 90s, "Perhaps the most significant implication is the attractiveness to church shoppers of the church that can deliver on the promise that their distinctive role is to strengthen the family. Fulfilling that promise has become one of the guaranteed parts to numerical growth today. The other is high quality, memorable, motivational and persua-sive biblical preaching."[2]

THE WORLD OF CHANGING VALUES

We live in a world of changing systems and values. There has never been a greater need to investigate what the Bible has to say about family, marriage, values, parenting and relationships, and the church is responsible for equipping believers in these areas. The Gate Church takes this part of its ministry seriously and uses strategic planning to do so. The Gate Church must build a ministry that ministers to all aspects of society: the single desiring biblical guidelines for relationship, the young pre-married couple needing preparation for marriage, and young marrieds wanting to learn the art of successful relationships. The Gate Church should provide marriage-enrichment courses, retreats, seminars, parenting curriculum for all ages, divorce and other recovery groups, help for special-child needs, assistance for restoring prodigal children, men's ministries and women's ministries. Clearly, this assignment is no small undertaking, especially when combined with all the other tasks of biblical church building, such as worship and music, evangelism, missions, city/community outreaches, youth ministry, senior saints, budgets, staff, preaching, counseling and all others. The challenge is real and complicated for the Gate-Church leader who truly seeks to tackle the family-ministry need.

The promise we have is that in Christ's seed and through Christ's seed all the families of the earth will be blessed. We have the promise as well as the provision through the Word and the Spirit to fulfill this promise. Our families need and deserve a better approach than a yearly shot in the arm or an annual weekend seminar. The Gate Church will develop the family ministry as part of its weekly ministry program, just as it does worship, prayer, preaching and giving of finances.

FAMILY BUILDING TAKES PRIORITY AND HIGH VISIBILITY

To gain priority and visibility, the leader—or minister, senior pastor, bishop, overseer, whatsoever the title—is supposed to guide the church into its God-given vision. If the leader does not see family ministry as a priority and is not willing to teach, preach, structure, budget, plan and implement, the vision for family will struggle to find its place of priority. I might go as far as to say that it's virtually impossible for family to become the priority unless the pastor-shepherd leads the flock into this specialized area of ministry.

The pastor or leader who does embrace family ministry as part of every church's responsibility must obey the command to bless and build the family. When the family ministry is finally brought into the hub of the vision, it should then be defined in a mission statement, a ministry philosophy with plans and goals. Leaders of Trinity Baptist Church in Syracuse New York wrote their family mission statement as follows:

Our desire is to respond to the needs and interests of families within our community with the relevance of Christianity. We wish to foster an atmosphere that embraces the virtues of a loving family of acceptance, nurture and forgiveness. In doing so, we will provide a place where singles, couples, parents and children can enjoy a strong sense of belonging. Our task is to build godly families through discipleship, that we might effectively bear the Gospel throughout every area of life and serve as beacons of light in a dark world."[3]

FAMILY BUILDING TAKES CLEAR EDUCATIONAL GOALS

The Gate-Church leader shows the church how to establish a family-sensitive and family-building atmosphere; the leader also equips the family through long range family curriculum that is highly visible to the whole church. The goal is to educate and re-educate all persons about God's design for family life—training them in essential family-living skills, creating a resource pool that covers all issues of family life, ministering to families with special needs and concerns, and equipping members with biblical knowledge to strengthen the marriage covenant. The church must be prepared to minister to dysfunctional singles and dysfunctional families; it must be ready to minister to new converts with old and new problems. The Gate Church does not ignore dysfunctional people or families with needs—it helps them to handle their problems, to change and to become strong so that they can serve God, the church and the community in a responsible manner.

The devil hates the family and hates the Gate Church that seeks to strengthen the family because...

✝ The family is a place to establish identity and security.

✝ The family is a place to teach and transmit values.

✝ The family is a place to make and store lifetime memories.

✝ The family is a place to develop hidden talents and potentials.

✝ The family is a place to learn how to love and forgive.

✝ The family is a place to grow in a safe environment.

✝ The family is a place to learn honesty and transparency.

✝ The family is a place to fail without criticism or condemnation.

✝ The family is a hiding place during the storms of life.

✝ The family is a place to experience the kingdom of God in action.

✝ The family is a place to translate Scripture into living realities.

America is a war zone and most people don't even recognize it. Satan is viciously fighting for the soul of our nation. The chief battleground is the home, where family unity and future generations are at stake. All the artillery of hell has been aimed at our homes. Every shell in that artillery is a lie, and those lies assault us in the form of negative influences that seek to erode the family structure: television misuse, negative styles of music, easy access to tobacco, alcohol, drugs, various ungodly public communications, pornography and, most recently, easy access to the Internet with a whole new world of temptations to ensnare young and old alike. More than ever, the family must have a family-building Gate Church that will be like Noah of old who built an ark of safety for his family.

THE GATE CHURCH BUILDS AN ARK OF SAFETY

The Bible says that "as it was in the day of Noah, so it will be also in the days of the Son of Man" (Luke 17:26; Gen. 6:5). The world was destroyed because of its wickedness, but Noah and his eight family members were saved from the flood. The Gate-Church leader builds the ark of safety for the family. The atmosphere in which we are now living and seeking to raise our families in is indeed as corrupt as it was in the days of Noah (see Matt. 24:36-39; Heb. 11:7; 1 Pet. 3:20; 2 Pet. 2:5,6).

Another corrupt time where only three family members were saved was in the days of Lot in Sodom and Gomorrah (see Gen. 19:16,29; 2 Pet. 2:6-9). Second Peter 2:7-14 describes the days of Lot, Sodom and Gomorrah, a description that is very similar to our present day:

✝ Desire dominated by lust

✝ Daring of shameless deeds

✝ Dedicated to obstinacy

✝ Deluding self and deluding others

✝ Degenerated morals without embarrassment

✝ Dedicated to greed

✝ Destroying the souls of their children

OUR PROMISE OF PRESERVATION

With God's help, we can build an ark of safety in these troublesome, perverted times. We should claim the following promises of preservation:

✝ Job 10:12: You have granted me life and favor, and Your care has preserved my spirit.

✝ Psalm 12:7: You shall keep them, O Lord, You shall preserve them from this generation forever.

✝ Psalm 31:23: Oh, love the Lord, all you His saints! For the Lord preserves the faithful, and fully repays the proud person.

✝ Psalm 97:10: You who love the Lord, hate evil! He preserves the souls of His saints; He delivers them out of the hand of the wicked.

✝ Ephesians 6:13: Therefore take up the whole armor of God, that you may be able to withstand in the evil day, and having done all, to stand.

The Gate Church must heed the signs of our times and arise with faith for our families just as Noah did: "By faith Noah, being divinely warned of things not yet seen, moved with godly fear, prepared an ark for the saving of his household, by which he condemned the world and became heir of the righteousness which is according to faith" (Heb. 11:7). Noah had a responsive heart to God's forewarning about the destructive flood that was to come, even though it was 120 years away. Noah built the ark according to the divine pattern. He did what God told him to do, right down to the inch (see Gen. 6:15,22). When the ark was finished, Noah and his household "entered in" and were safely protected. We must build the church according to God's pattern; the flood of evil is already here!

According to Isaiah 59:19, "When the enemy comes in like a flood, the Spirit of the Lord will lift up a standard against him." The flood will consist of waters that seek to overflow the family, and it will eventually sweep the family away unless Gate Churches with family-building ministries are in place to secure it (see Jer. 47:2; Dan. 11:22). We must build wisely "like a man building a house, who dug deep and laid the foundation on the rock. And when the flood arose, the stream beat vehemently against the house and could not shake it, for it was founded upon the rock" (Luke 6:48). The flood will rise and beat against the family, but we can be assured of victory if we will build upon the Rock (see Ps. 1:1-3; Josh. 1:8; Matt. 7:24; Rev. 12:15,16).

FOUR ABSOLUTES FOR BUILDING FAMILIES

The decline and failure of the family is not some story about a faraway nation. It is a reality in our nation NOW! We must aid all family leaders, marriage partners and those who are preparing for marriage. We do this when we:

1. Lay the biblical foundation for belief in the Bible as the book of absolutes, not suggestions;

2. Lay the biblical foundation that the family is the cornerstone of society;

3. Lay the biblical foundation that Christ, His Word and His Spirit, when obeyed, will solve any and all complicated and simple family problems;

4. Lay the biblical foundation for right thinking about marriage, parenting and family by resisting public opinion, refusing weak theology and exposing questionable family practices in unstable, wavering, lukewarm Christians.

In the middle of a constantly changing culture, we have a God who is relevant, current and timely because He is the Author of timeless, changeless truths. In the middle of a world that has changed all the price tags, we have a God who loves us enough to give us undistorted standards to live by. If we are to be a family-blessing and a family-building Gate Church, we must pay attention to God's blueprint for marriage and family.

STRENGTHENING AND SAVING MARRIAGES

The Gate Church strengthens the marriages of the church with a definite faith in God's purpose for marriage. Obviously, we must be a healing refuge for those who have experienced a failed marriage, helping them to forgive, to find new life and to experience God's abundant mercy. At the same time, however, we must teach those who are presently married to strengthen their relationships, resisting the easy divorce route. God's kind of marriage requires a total commitment that is established through covenant. Marriage is a covenant between God, man and woman, which means that both the man and the woman lay down their lives for the other so that each lives out a new life through the other.

Marriage is a covenant of love (see Prov. 2:17; Mal. 2:14), a commitment of permanence through perseverance (see Heb. 13:5), a bond of committed love that is not easily broken. The demands and trials of life will work to perfect and strengthen the love between those whose marriage is based on commitment (see Gen. 2:24; Matt. 19:5; Mark 10:7,8; Eph. 5:3). Marriage is a total commitment and a total sharing of the total person with another person for the total of one's life until death.

The Gate Church is acutely aware of the destructive forces that are successfully destroying multitudes of marriages. People whose marriages are in trouble will be kept from destruction if the Gate Church seriously believes that the family ministry must be kept as priority and with high visibility. A group of divorced couples were asked to share the effects of their broken marital commitments. Their remarks were:

- ✝ It is never over for anyone completely.
- ✝ It devastates families.
- ✝ It makes people wonder if being a Christian makes any difference.
- ✝ It produces so much pain to the people involved.
- ✝ It does anything but demonstrate God's glory.
- ✝ It breaks up families for generations to come.
- ✝ Children's loyalties are torn between two people they love.

The pain of broken marital bonds must be revealed so that we will be compelled to warn those tempted to break their marriage vows. The high cost of broken commitments in marriages today serves to show us why God has such a high regard for the marriage commitment. God loves us and does not want His people to be fractured and broken through the wreckage left in the wake of divorce (see Gen. 2:24,25; Mal. 2:13,14; Eph. 5:25-27; 1 Pet. 3:7).

Many marriages carry a heavy load of unrealistic expectations. One source for many conflicts is unmet expectations: husbands and wives often do not get what they expected to receive, and they receive what they did not expect to get. Marriage vows are not usually broken because of one incident; they erode over a period of time. Here are some comments made by those whose marriages have failed: "We just grew apart." "He stifled my intellectual growth." "She didn't meet my sexual needs." "I lost my respect for him." "He was more interested in his hobbies than in me." "She was always moody or depressed." "All we ever did was argue." "I'm not sure I loved him in the first place." "I got married to get out of the house, away from my parents." "I was too young to know what I wanted."

As the Family and Marriage Ministry of the church develops into a high visibility ministry, marriages are instructed to face these patterns of failure in marriage with biblical principles that will strengthen and secure the marriage covenant. Strong marriages and families are built through constant work and a great deal of God's mercy and love (see Prov. 2:17; 14:23; 24:30-34).

The church is faced with a culture that is in opposition to God's Word; it is not a family-building culture. Our culture encourages no absolutes, gives open freedom to homosexuality, accepts public adultery, offers easy and frequent divorce. It encourages sexual freedoms, has little or no respect for God and refuses to accept the Bible as absolute truth. Our culture embraces all religions under the guise of religious tolerance. It promotes convenient abortion of the unborn for lifestyle purposes and encourages gay rights. The Gate Church must prepare the family to survive these perilous times. It takes strategy!

PARENTING IN TODAY'S WORLD

The goal for the Gate Church is to equip every parent to raise champion children. The family must be seen as a tightly knit unit with parents and children who form a household of harmony and beauty. This is a place where the atmosphere is positive and full of faith—where parents believe that their children were designed for accomplishment, engineered for success and endowed with the seeds of greatness. Godly parenting is the starting point for producing long-lasting health, happiness and a biblical, positive self-image. Negative experiences with heavy doses of criticism, ridicule, sarcasm or continual put downs help to destroy children.

Parents must start early. Books, magazines and parental educational material all echo the message that the time to start is now: "The first four years shape all of life." "Behavior is set by five." "Train citizens in the cradle." "Don't wait for the school bell." "Combat crime in infancy." The church must purpose to keep the children and lower the rate of prodigals by equipping people to be great parents. The Bible speaks of parents who lost their children (see Gen. 49:3-7; 1 Sam. 1:6-10; 2:1-25; 4:1-18; 8:1-5; 2 Sam. 15-19), and parents are still losing their children today. Parents should avoid the following proven ways to drive children away from home and the church:

✝ Expressing approval only when the child is good

‡ Threatening the child

‡ Ridiculing the child

‡ Screaming at the child

‡ Being too busy to listen

‡ Giving the child the silent treatment

‡ Having a continually critical attitude

‡ Using the child's name negatively

‡ Expressing disappointment or disgust for the child's actions

‡ Breaking the love routine by acting inconsistent in loving the child

‡ Neglecting or ignoring the child

‡ Abusing the child physically or psychologically

‡ Finding fault continually

‡ Refusing to listen to the child

‡ Being a poor parental example

‡ Expressing conditional love

‡ Expecting the child to do things you didn't or don't do

‡ Neglecting to be involved in the child's life

‡ Failing to build family togetherness, pride and loyalty

‡ Seeking from the child what you should be getting from your spouse

‡ Allowing negative peer influence

‡ Being too permissive

‡ Being overly demanding intellectually, spiritually, physically or emotionally

‡ Having double standards, one for the parent and one for the child

‡ Moving or changing standards

‡ Pressuring the child to be a carbon copy of yourself or someone else

‡ Expressing disrespect or disappointment

‡ Exercising unbiblical parenting principles

Now that we have looked at what not to do, let's consider some of the things that we can do. The following guide gives twelve tested pointers for raising kids God's way.

PARENTS' DAILY DOZEN FOR CHAMPION CHILDREN

1. Help each child to feel loved, appreciated and wanted. Never use negative words to correct them.

2. Provide the child with moral and religious values that are clearly transmitted in the home by becoming and associating with godly role models.

3. Cultivate open and honest communication with the child daily: listen to him or her and discuss his or her daily events.

4. Teach your child traditional values such as honesty, integrity, love, loyalty, faith, truth, dependability and humility.

5. Cultivate a spiritual hunger in the child by reading biographies of godly and successful people.

6. Develop a positive atmosphere in the home. Encourage positive language by using it yourself and not allowing negative words.

7. Be consistent in loving discipline. Yes, even spank a young child for misbehavior.

8. Give your child responsibility at an early age. Establish reasonable, age-appropriate responsibilities and expect the child to fulfill those responsibilities.

9. Always know your child's friends, where your child is and who he or she is with when away from home. Remember that friends can either help or ruin your child. Don't let your child have the final say on who his or her friends will be.

10. Make sure your child's life has a sense of purpose and meaning coupled with the ability to make wise decisions and solve problems.

11. Teach respect to your child. Respect him or her and teach the child to respect others—not to talk when others are talking, to say "excuse me" and "thank you," etc.

12. Teach your child to worship and pray at an early age. Help him or her to learn how good God is, how big God is and how much Mom and Dad love God!

The Gate Church takes a proactive strategy in ministering to the families within the congregation. This means that the church should consider a "family life" pastor as a future staff position. It should also implement a well-structured marriage and family curriculum, small groups for marrieds, support groups, seminars, classes, and make sure that resources are made available. Let's take seriously our biblical mandate to be the church that Christ is building so that "through you and your seed all the families of the earth shall be blessed." With this as our goal, the family is destined to survive the floods of adversity that war against it.

BECOME A TERRIBLE TILLY

The winter storms that rage against the Oregon coast can be devastating. The waves and tide have undermined cliffs and homes, causing neighborhoods to be destroyed. In the midst of these onslaughts is a lighthouse called Terrible Tilly that stands on an acre of rock, one mile off shore in the Columbia River channel. The storms have not moved her. The waves have not undermined her foundation. She stands unmoved through the storms to guide ships through a dangerous channel during fog and adverse conditions. We are to be like Terrible Tilly, a guiding light for all families. The Gate Church is built upon the Rock and assists all families to build their homes upon the Rock of Christ and His unchanging principles.

NOTES

1. Charles S. Sells, *Family Ministry* (Grand Rapids: Zondervan Publishing, 1995), p. 13.
2. Kenneth Gasgel and James Wilhoit, *Christian Educator's Handbook on Family Life Education* (Grand Rapids: Baker Books, 1996), p. 9.
3. Charles S. Sells, *Family Ministry*, p. 358.

*"Behold, I am with you and will keep you wherever you go,
and will bring you back to this land; for I will not leave you until
I have done what I have spoken to you." Genesis 28:15*

The Gate-Church Door
of Divine Opportunity

The Gate-Church leader can identify with Jacob every step of the way as he encounters God and the continual unveiling of God's vision for his life and work. What begins as a dream will, through persevering faith, become a reality. Jacob's dream was pieced together with symbols, prophetic promises and future hopes. As with Jacob, God's dream becomes our dream: A dream for a place where the atmosphere is charged with God's supernatural living presence—clean, spiritually alive, energetic, life changing. A place where the ladder of intercession can be established to connect the resources of heaven with earth. A place where the voice of God is heard and new present truths are believed and assimilated. A place where people are born again daily, added to the church and then multiplied—"like the dust of the earth...spread abroad to the west, the east, the north and the south."(see Gen. 28:14). A place where the family is blessed and built by a positive atmosphere and powerful teaching.

Jacob, the Gate-Church leader, received fresh and life-changing promises. God had invaded his world and changed him forever. The Lord God Jehovah gave Jacob the promise that His divine presence was to be both a source of encouragement and, at times, a source of protection. Jacob would be on the move. His journey would offer many doors of opportunity as well as potential dangers, snares and possible harm. God promised Jacob that He would fulfill all that He had spoken to him. He reassured Jacob, "I am with you...I will keep you...I will bring you back...I will not leave you...I will do everything I have spoken."

OPEN DOORS

In God's shaping and making of a Gate-Church leader, God's promises become foundational for the journey. We, like Jacob, have a dream, a call and a vision for the Gate Church that we are to build in our cities or regions. At times and during various seasons, however, God will burst upon the scene to change the way we view things. He sets before us doors of opportunity. These doors may be hidden behind crises, obstacles, disappointments or a host of other difficulties, but they are doors opened by God. Jacob had a difficult time discerning those doors because he did not desire to go through them.

I see a connection between the doors of opportunity promised to Jacob and the letter written to the church of Philadelphia in Revelation 3:7-13. This letter offers the Gate-Church leader a promise, a provision and a prophetic future. It echoes with the same promises given to Jacob in Genesis 28:14-16. Jacob was a lonely sojourner on an untried journey pursuing an uncertain fate. What could have been more comforting or assuring than God's promises of protection, a blessed future, success in his mission, a place with opened heavens, anointed stones and pillars, the voice of God and a gate of heaven! And yet, only God Almighty could bring to pass all these things; only God could open a door that no man could shut and shut a door that no man could open. God would shut doors in Jacob's life; He would also open new doors that would become doors of destiny, doors of opportunity.

We have the same promise given to Jacob: "I will be with you. I will keep you. I will not leave you. I will do everything I have spoken." Our promise is recorded by God in the letter to the Philadelphia church in Revelation 3:7,8:

> He who has the key of David, He who opens and no one shuts, and shuts and no one opens. I know your works. See, I have set before you an open door, and no one can shut it; for you have a little strength.

This letter contains five key factors that prepare Gate Churches for the future. As we frame in these factors, let us broaden our framework by considering the importance of Christ's commendations, warnings and challenges to the seven churches.

CHRIST AND HIS CHURCH

Our present-day churches must come under the scrutiny of Christ, the Head of the church. If you have ever moved to a new city and set out to find a new church home, you know how difficult it is to examine and evaluate a church and its ministries. Imposing buildings may house a dying or dead congregation, while modest structures can belong to healthy and alive congregations. The church we think to be rich might be poor in God's sight, while the poor church is actually rich. Only the Head of the church, Christ, can accurately inspect each church and know its true condition. He sees the internal, not just the externals. Churches are made up of people whose individual spiritual lives determine the spiritual health of the church as a whole.

The first three chapters of Revelation reveal the connection between Christ and His church. The most famous first-century letters are addressed to seven city churches in Asia and bear the names of those cities. These letters are written from Christ, the Head of the church, to the seven churches. Christ stands in the midst of the seven golden lampstands with the seven stars or angels of the seven churches in His hands. The stars are held in His right hand, symbolizing His favor and protection over them. He has a message for each star, the angel of the church, which is to be given to the whole church (see Rev. 1:20).

This vision is the natural introduction for all that follows, indeed it defines the main purpose of the whole book—it shows Christ sustaining, directing and indwelling His churches. The seven angels or seven messengers (*angelos* can mean either angel or messenger) refers to the recognized heads and representatives of the seven churches. The messenger or *angelos* of each church had the letter addressed to him and he was spoken to in words of rebuke and exhortation; he was seen as one who could sin and repent, who could be persecuted and die, who could fall into heresies and be perfected through suffering. The following list provides a brief description of the seven lampstands or churches.

> "He sets before us doors of opportunity. These doors may be hidden behind crises, obstacles, disappointments or a host of other difficulties, but they are doors opened by God."

THE SEVEN LAMPSTANDS, THE SEVEN CHURCHES

Church	Greek Meaning	Seen As
1. Ephesus (2:1-7)	Desirable	The careless church
2. Smyrna (2:8-11)	Myrrh	The crowned church
3. Pergamos (2:12-17)	Marriage	The compromising church
4. Thyatira (2:18-29)	Continual sacrifice	The corrupted church
5. Sardis (3:1-6)	Remnant	The feeble church
6. Philadelphia (3:7-13)	Brotherly love	The faithful church
7. Laodicea (3:14-22)	People's rights	The foolish church

The letter for each church begins with a revelation of Christ and a commendation, usually followed by a warning and a challenge. Christ knew exactly what was going on in the lives of each church's congregation. He knew their successes and their failures, their victories, their problems and their difficulties. He commended their virtues more than He warned of their faults. He knew what each one needed. Today's churches face the same conditions, the same challenges as did these first-century churches.

THE PHILADELPHIA CHURCH

Now let's zero in on the letter to the church of Philadelphia. This letter is important for Gate Churches because it is written to a gate city with a gateway promise. Philadelphia was a very young city located some twenty-eight miles southeast of Sardis. It had been founded by Attalus II Philadelphus and was called "Little Athens" because so many temples were located in the city.

PHILADELPHIA WAS A GATEWAY CITY

Philadelphia had a remarkable characteristic: This city was on the edge of a great plain called the *katakekaumene*, which means "burned land." It was a great volcanic plain bearing the marks of lava flow and the ashes of volcanoes. Philadelphia was situated in a strategic place on the main route of the imperial post from Rome to the East and was called the Gateway to the East.

PHILADELPHIA WAS A GLOOMY CITY

Despite its hope-filled name—a city of brotherly love—Philadelphia was a bleak and oppressive city, and its people were shadowed and dispirited. In A.D. 17 a massive earthquake destroyed Philadelphia. It wasn't this one earthquake, however, that brought such hopelessness to the city—it was the daily after-shocks that continued for years. These aftershocks weren't just once-in-a-while tremors, but daily events. Every time the people began to rebuild, another tremor would destroy what they had started. Every time Philadelphians returned to their homes, another tremor would chase them back to the coun-tryside. Every time one of these tremors occurred, the people were reminded of the previous destruction and the potential danger that was under their feet. Every tremor reminded them of the past disaster and opened the door to fear and hopelessness. Minor shocks became panic shocks as life was interrupted continually. Gaping cracks appeared in the walls of homes and some parts of the city remained in ruins. People concluded the city had no future and began to move away. This was a city that had no future.[1]

The city and its leadership were in desperate need of a fresh, clear word from the Lord. They had lost their gateway spirit and vision; they had given up their gateway faith. They had developed a "dead-end" attitude: "We're finished here. This is a city with no future."

Have you found yourself in one of those "no future" cities with a "no gate-way here" mentality? Are you thinking: *Build a Gate Church here?* It is possible, but it isn't probable. No church has ever prospered in our county, region or city. How can I have the faith to believe for building a Gate Church in this city when every tremor reminds me that no spiritual breakthroughs have occurred here? Where are the healings? Where are the souls being saved? Where is the passion for prayer, for worship and for the Word? Where are the gates of heaven open over this city? Let me encourage you, fellow sojourner: God has a gateway for you. He has a gateway for your ministry, for your church and for your city! Build upon God's promise to you: "I will be with you. I will keep you. I will not leave you. I will do everything I have spoken" (see Gen. 28:14,15). God has not left you or your city. The promise to every pastor or leader is a "Philadelphia church" promise; it is a Gate-Church promise for gateway cities. Let's read it again:

‡ Rev. 3:7,8: And to the angel of the church in Philadelphia write, "These things says He who is holy, He who is true, He who has the key of David, He who opens and no one shuts, and shuts and no one opens. I know your works. See, I have set before you an open door, and no one can shut it; for you have a little strength, have kept My word, and have not denied My name."

A Gate Church has a God-given vision that originates from above, from the voice at the top of the ladder, from a vision with prophetic perspective that sees from God's point of view. We must grasp our Gate-Church prophetic promises.

A Gate Church is a church that is lifted above the disasters, the gloom, the hopelessness into the realm of God's voice. The prophetic strength of the Philadelphia church is seen historically. From A.D. 100—160, the church prospered under the ministries of a prophetess named Ammia, who was recognized as ranking with Agabus and the four daughters of Philip in her possession of the gift of prophecy. God's calling for the Gate Church in every gate city is to believe these promises. These words from Christ to His church are relevant for you and me today, words that we can believe in and build upon:

‡ Rev. 3:7-13: And to the angel of the church in Philadelphia write, "These things says He who is holy, He who is true, He who has the key of David, He who opens and no one shuts, and shuts and no one opens. I know your works. See, I have set before you an open door, and no one can shut it; for you have a little strength, have kept My word, and have not denied My name. Indeed I will make those of the synagogue of Satan, who say they are Jews and are not, but lie—indeed I will make them come and worship before your feet, and to know that I have loved you. Because you have kept My command to persevere, I also will keep you from the hour of trial which shall come upon the whole world, to test those who dwell on the earth. Behold, I am coming quickly! Hold fast what you have, that no one may take your crown. He who overcomes, I will make him a pillar in the temple of My God, and he shall go out no more. And I will write on him the name of My God and the name of the city of My God, the New Jerusalem, which comes down out of heaven from My God. And I will write on him My new name. He who has an ear, let him hear what the Spirit says to the churches."

IF GOD SAYS IT, I BELIEVE IT!

The Gate Church and its leader esteems highly both the written Word and the spoken words of God (see vv. 6,7). The Holy Spirit is still speaking today to all who have "ears to hear" what He is saying. What the Holy Spirit speaks is right, livable, buildable and doable—in spite of what others might say or think. Faith is merely affirming what God has said in His Word by His Spirit.

As a Gate-Church pastor, I will not submit to the atmosphere of my city—nor will I submit to the gloom and negativity of my surrounding culture. I will not allow the media, newspapers, politicians, economists, educators, scientists, psychologists or religious leaders to have more influence over my thinking than the Spirit of God has. I will not allow the words of men, spirits or angels to captivate my mind. I will be a Holy Spirit-governed person (see Rev. 2:7,11,17,29; 3:6,13,22). I will believe a reliable source: "These things saith He that is holy and true." These are the words I choose to put my faith in. These are the words of truth, the words from the "Reliable One," the real words for life and ministry.

KINGDOM KEYS

The "key of David" mentioned in Revelation 3:7 represents the authority of his royal office. Jesus is the genuine Messianic King who makes David's throne eternal (see Acts 2:30,32,36; 3:14,15). Isaiah 22:22 says, "The key of the house of David I will lay on his shoulder; so he shall open, and no one shall shut; and he shall shut, and no one shall open." Jesus already has that authority and was and is already manifesting His royal authority and power by using the key to open doors that no one can shut (see Matt. 28:18).

The reference to the key of David in Revelation 3:7 alludes to Isaiah 22:22 and the incident of transferring the post of secretary of state in Judah from the unfaithful Shebna to the faithful Eliakim. The key signifies the power of the keys that were normally held by the king himself, unless delegated to another. Christ, the Head of the church—your church, my church, all churches—holds the keys to everything. He has all power and authority, and today—right now—He has delegated the keys to us His people, His church.

Matthew 16:19 says, "And I will give you the keys of the kingdom of heaven, and whatever you bind on earth will be bound in heaven, and whatever you loose on earth will be loosed in heaven." As a Gate-Church leader, I must receive faith to use the keys Christ has put into my hands. The word "key" means "opener." I need to open those locks that God will grant me authority to open, using the keys He has designated.

THE KEY OF DAVIDIC WORSHIP, A NEW RELEASE OF PRAISE AND WORSHIP

The "key of David" in Revelation 3:7 also refers to praise and worship. David was a man after God's heart, a worshiper from the beginning, who built the Tabernacle of David that was known for its 24-hour, seven-day-a-week worship (see Amos 9:11-15; Acts 9:15,16). All Gate Churches need to find the key that releases a new level of worship (see Ps. 149:1-9; Acts 16:25,26).

THE KEY OF KNOWLEDGE, A NEW LEVEL OF TEACHING AND LEARNING

The key or "opener" of spiritual knowledge brings the understanding that causes the church to enter into truth. Luke 11:52 says, "Woe to you lawyers! For you have taken away the key of knowledge. You did not enter in yourselves, and those who were entering in you hindered." (See also Matt. 23:1-35; Jer. 3:15.) This key opens people's understanding, causing them to grasp something that has been difficult in the past for them to understand. In Jesus' day, the Pharisees resisted the key Christ had—a key of Holy Spirit power and anointing. Matthew 7:29 says, "For He taught them as one having authority, and not as the scribes." When the key of knowledge is removed from the Gate Church, the people become stubborn and self-willed (see Exod. 33:3; Deut. 9:27; Ps. 32:9; Prov. 29:1; Matt. 11:29; Acts 7:51), the vineyard is destroyed (see Prov. 24:30-34) and moral weakness abounds (see Prov. 6:32).

THE KEYS OF DEATH AND HELL, A POWER FOR PREACHING THE GOSPEL

When this key is used, death and hell must loose their grip upon the souls of people who believe the gospel message. The gospel is the Isaiah 61:1-3 description of Christ's message as quoted in Luke 4:18. When the gospel key is used, it unlocks the power "to open their eyes, in order to turn them from darkness to light, and from the power of Satan to God, that they may receive forgiveness of sins and an inheritance among those who are sanctified by faith in [Christ]" (see Acts 26:18). The gospel preached properly is a message of victory and the good news is proclaimed with power (see Ps. 68:11; Isa. 40:10; 52:7; Luke 4:43; John 3:8).

For the apostle Paul, the heart of the good news is the story of Jesus and His suffering, death and resurrection. The gospel does not merely bear witness to salvation history—it is itself salvation history. It breaks into the lives of people, refashioning and creating new people, new churches and ultimately penetrating the whole city with its power (see Ps. 102:20; John 8:32-36; 11:44; Rom. 3:21-26). When the key for power-preaching the gospel is used, salvation is in Christ alone (see Col. 1:3,22; 2:14; Gal. 2:28; 6:14), people are delivered from the domain of darkness (see Luke 11:34-36; Col. 1:13; 2 Pet. 1:19), people are transplanted into new life (see Ps. 1:1-3; Col. 1:13), people are set free from spiritual slavery (see Rom. 3:24; 2 Cor. 5:21; Col. 1:14) and they receive full forgiveness for all sins and iniquities (see Ps. 103:12; Rom. 4:7; Eph. 1:7).

CLAIM YOUR DOORS OF OPPORTUNITY

Revelation 3:8 says that God knows "your works. See, I have set before you an open door, and no one can shut it; for you have a little strength, have kept My word, and have not denied My name."

This is an awesome promise to the Gate-Church leader and the Gate-Church congregation. Would you right now begin to absorb the spiritual significance within this promise for you and for your future? In essence the Lord is saying, "Take notice! I have placed before you a door which has been opened—mark it. I have set before you an opportunity. This door having been opened, and thus remaining open, no man, no power, no spirit, no angel can shut because I have opened it for you." The Lord has set before you an open door, and it shall remain open until you are able to enter in. You will enter in sooner than you think; and when your moment of opportunity comes, your strength will not be wasted in an effort to make the conditions favorable. "You shall enter in at once because I have opened the door for you."

We usually move through the doors of divine opportunity when we hurt enough to step forward, or get so fed up with where we are that we are compelled to move through them. It may even be that we have learned enough in the school of faith to risk stepping over the threshold of opportunity (see Hos. 2:15; Acts 16:6-9; 2 Cor. 2:12).

The Lord promises to open doors that no one is able to shut. The word "no one" suggests that someone may be trying to shut the doors and to stop, or to interfere with, what the Lord is holding open for you. Adversaries may be many (see 1 Cor. 16:9). They may try to close the doors of divine opportunity, but they will not succeed! When your work and your motivation are acceptable to the Lord, you can expect to receive His help—and no earthly power can stand against the Lord God Almighty!

Put the fear of the future behind you. The future will not be like the past. Don't be satisfied with your

> "They may try to close the doors of divine opportunity, but they will not succeed! When your work and your motivation are acceptable to the Lord, you can expect to receive His help—and no earthly power can stand against the Lord God Almighty!"

present status or with your past successes. The greatest doors of divine opportunity for your life and church have yet to be opened. You must combat the spirit of intimidation that limits your vision for the future. Your church may be small in size, but it does not need to be small in the influence it has within your community. The Gate Church may have "little strength" in the natural realm, but human weakness is God's open door to show His mighty hand. Our limitations are the basis for divine possibilities (see 2 Cor. 12:10; 2 Tim. 1:7).

FROM WEAKNESS TO GLORY

Consider the limitations placed on Winston Churchill's life the next time you are tempted to doubt your future. He was a man, full of ambition and great dreams, yet he faced many obstacles, crises and disappointments. Winston's father, Lord Randolph Churchill, could see no great future for his son. Sent to a private school, Winston failed most of his classes year after year. Lord Randolph Churchill wanted his son to go to into the infantry cadetship. Winston, however, failed the test three times, and each time had to face his father's disappointment. Lord Randolph had to tell his good friend, the Duke of Cambridge, that his son was too stupid to become an infantry officer. A week after failing the entry test for Sandhurst Officer's School, Winston received the following letter from his father.

> Never have I received a really good report of your conduct in your work from any master or tutor you had from time to time to do with. Always behind hand, never advancing in your class, incessant complaints of total want of application, and this character, which was constant in your report, has shown the natural results clearly in your last army examination. Thus you have failed to get into the sixtieth rifles, one of the finest regiments in the army. Do not think I am going to take the trouble of writing to you long letters after every failure you commit and undergo. I no longer attach the slightest weight to anything you may say about your own acquirements and exploits. If you cannot prevent yourself from leading the idle, useless, unprofitable life you have had during your school days and later months, you will become a mere social waste, one of the hundreds of public school failures and you will degenerate into a shabby, unhappy and futile existence. If that is so, you will have to bear all the blame for such

misfortunes yourself. Your mother sends her love.

Lord Randolph Churchill [2]

A later letter also described his father's view of Winston:

> I have told you often and you would never believe me that he has
> little claim to cleverness, knowledge or any capacity for settled
> work. He has great talent for show-off, exaggeration and make-
> believe. [3]

Winston Churchill's father could not hold a mirror up to the future. He only saw the present—which was anything but encouraging! Winston's school records were a catalog of misconduct and scholastic failure. He was always in trouble, always disobedient and always making and breaking promises. Winston's life seemingly held no sense of promise. But within his future, God had placed many hidden doors of opportunity that would change his character, his course and ultimately the destiny of England, his country. No one could see the latent potential in Winston Churchill. But Winston had unbelievable drive and great vision. He knew that he was called to something great and unique; He knew that God would help him fulfill his dream.

What about your dream? Will you trust that God has already opened the doors of divine opportunity for you? Will you dare to face your fears about tomorrow? Why not rise to the famous challenge that Sir Winston Spencer Churchill presented at Harrow School: "Never give in! Never give in! Never, never, never, never—in nothing great or small, large or petty—never give in except to convictions of honor and good sense!"

NOTES

1. Frank E. Gaebelein, *Expositor's Bible Commentary* (Grand Rapids: Zondervan Publishing), p. 451.
2. William Manchester, *The Last Lion: Winston Spencer Churchill* (Boston: Little Brown and Company, 1983), Vol. I, pp. 182-183.
3. Ibid.

Then Jacob awoke from his sleep and said,
"Surely the LORD is in this place, and I did not know it."
And he was afraid and said, "How awesome is this place!
This is none other than the house of God,
and this is the gate of heaven!" Genesis 28:16,17

The Gate Church
Has Awesome Worship

God's wake-up calls are different in each one of our lives—and so are our responses to them. These two featured verses from Genesis 28:16,17 record Jacob's awakening to his dream, the effect of that dream and the words he spoke while the dream was still fresh in his memory. Jacob probably felt severed from God's presence because of his shameful past. He remembered that Yahweh had manifested His gracious presence in his father's house; but now, alone, on the run, Jacob could hardly have felt any manifestation of God. The presence of Yahweh was not unknown to Jacob, but he was surprised that God in His condescending mercy would desire to come near to him right where he was, far from the security of his father's house and far from places consecrated to worship.

Yahweh was birthing in Jacob an insatiable hunger and unquenchable thirst for the living presence of God. He wanted to impart to Jacob a sacred awe toward Himself that would seal Jacob's lifelong pursuit of God's genuine manifested presence. He intended to reveal Himself to Jacob in such a way that even the place where Jacob slept would be a "dreadful" place because of the nearness of God.

THE FEAR OF GOD

The nearness of God makes an alarming impression upon unholy people: the consciousness of sin grows, and the fear of God becomes a reality. Initially, Jacob was "afraid and said, 'How awesome is this place'" (Gen. 28:17). The house of God should be an awe-inspiring place, a gate opening into a personal revelation of God's powerful, manifested presence. The awareness of His power and splendor should always lead to a sense of His awesomeness, but that doesn't always happen.

The Hebrew word *nora* translated "awe-inspiring" is the passive participle of *yare*, "to be afraid." The translation could render, "He was awed, saying, 'How awesome!'" *Yare* is used to describe something awesome or terrifying. It may describe awesome places (see Gen. 28:17), an awesome God (see Exod. 15:11), an awesome name (see Deut. 25:18), awesome deeds (see Exod. 34:10) and the awesome day of the Lord (see Joel 2:31).

Yare may also refer to the God-fearer, the person who has encountered God in such a way that he or she becomes a devout follower of God. The God-fearer will implement his or her newly found awe for God in practical righteousness, being careful to avoid evil, to honor God and to walk differently before God (see Job 1:1; Ps. 128:1). The God-fearer's change of heart is evidenced by a response to God's voice, or God's message. Scripture promises many things to the God-fearer: blessings (see Ps. 112:1), goodness from God (see Ps. 31:19), provision for meeting needs (see Ps. 34:9), protection (see Ps. 3:18,19), overshadowing mercy (see Ps. 103:11) and fulfilled desires (see Ps. 145:19).

In Psalm 22, the phrase "those who fear God" parallels "sons of Jacob" and "sons of Israel" on the one hand (see v. 23) and the "great congregation" on the other hand (see v. 25). The parallel suggests that this Hebrew phrase is used to refer to the worshiping congregation that is gathered for worship. As the Gate-Church congregation gathers around a revelation of God's awesomeness, two things are released: powerful worship of God as awesome and a corresponding manifestation of God's presence.

THE GATE CHURCH CELEBRATES THE AWESOME GOD

We worship an awesome God...

✝ Deuteronomy 7:21: You shall not be terrified of them; for the LORD your God, the great and awesome God, is among you.

✝ Deuteronomy 10:17: For the LORD your God is God of gods and Lord of lords, the great God, mighty and awesome, who shows no partiality nor takes a bribe.

Who does awesome deeds...

✝ 1 Chronicles 17:21: And who is like Your people Israel, the one nation on the earth whom God went to redeem for Himself as a people—to make for Yourself a name by great and awesome deeds, by driving out nations from before Your people whom You redeemed from Egypt?

By His awesome power...

✝ Nehemiah 9:32: Now therefore, our God, the great, the mighty, and awesome God, who keeps covenant and mercy: Do not let all the trouble seem small before You that has come upon us, our kings and our princes, our priests and our prophets, our fathers and on all Your people, from the days of the kings of Assyria until this day.

Therefore, we sing and proclaim God as awesome Lord over all...

✝ Psalm 47:2: For the LORD Most High is awesome; He is a great King over all the earth.

✝ Psalm 66:3: Say to God, "How awesome are Your works! Through the greatness of Your power Your enemies shall submit themselves to You."

✝ Psalm 66:5: Come and see the works of God; He is awesome in His doing toward the sons of men.

(See also Ps. 68:35; 99:3; 111:9; 145:6; Isa. 28:21; Dan. 9:4.)

The Gate-Church leader understands the importance of establishing a worshiping congregation, one that encounters the awe-inspiring presence of God. In his book *Churchquake*, Dr. C. Peter Wagner gives the eight most significant changes from traditional worship to apostolic worship: [1]

- From classical to contextual
- From performance to participation
- From hymns to songs
- From pipe organ to percussion
- From cerebral to celebration
- From awe of God to intimacy with God
- From liturgy to liberty
- From meditation to mission

A GATE CHURCH IS A
"PRESENCE OF GOD" CHURCH

A church functions at its best when it is on fire for the Lord and when His presence is the focus of corporate church life. The Hebrew word "presence," *paniym*, is used seventy-six times in the Old Testament. It is derived from the root word *panah*, meaning "to turn" or "to turn the face toward." This word denotes the blessing and favor of God turned toward those who worship Him. The presence of God is a presence that fills up, pervades, permeates and overspreads all who come under it. The omnipresence of God simply means that God is everywhere all the time; His presence fills all and covers all (see Ps. 139:6-8; Jer. 23:24). God is all present, unlimited by space or time; He is everywhere present at all times. The manifest presence of God is experienced when God chooses to reveal Himself sovereignly (see Gen. 3:8; 4:16; Lev. 22:3; 2 Chron. 5:11-14). The felt, revealed, personalized presence of God is the presence that is available to God's people as they follow a pattern of worship that allows the "gate of heaven" to be opened (see 2 Chron. 5:14; Ps. 16:11; 22:3; 31:20; 51:11; 95:2; Acts 3:19).

Moses' famous response after God offered an angel to go with him is our passion for God's presence verbalized:

- Exod. 33:14,15: And He said, "My Presence will go with you, and I will give you rest." Then he said to Him, "If Your Presence does not go with us, do not bring us up from here."

Moses knew the value of God's presence: the manifold blessings, the strength and the provision.

THE GATE CHURCH PRODUCES "PRESENCE PEOPLE"

What are "presence people"? They are...

A PEOPLE WHO HUNGER AND THIRST FOR GOD'S PRESENCE

Divine desires, which are prompted by the Holy Spirit, become greatly enhanced in the atmosphere of true worship. Only the presence of God can satisfy the craving of a soul that has been truly aroused by the working of the Holy Spirit (see Ps. 27:1-6; 42:1-4; 63:1-6). People who have experienced God's presence and tasted true worship will hunger and thirst after it. They know that "in [His] presence is fullness of joy" (Ps. 16:11).

A PEOPLE WHO DESIRE TO HIDE AND ABIDE IN THE SECRET PLACE

The Gate Church creates an atmosphere in worship that can only be described as "the secret place"—a scriptural term identifying the Most Holy Place in the Tabernacle of Moses. It was the place where the ark of the covenant abided. The ark was made of acacia wood overlaid with gold, inside and outside. On top was a mercy seat of pure gold that was shadowed by the wings of two gold cherubims that faced each other (see Exod. 25:18-20). To enter into the Most Holy Place, the high priests would encounter the ark of the covenant where the voice of God could be heard and His *shekinah* glory manifested (see Exod. 29:42; 30:6,36; Num. 7:89). This is where the psalmist received his revelation of dwelling under the shadow of the wings of God, the secret place, the place where God's presence and voice is found (see Ps. 27:5; 63:7; 91:1,4; Isa. 37:16; Matt. 6:4,5).

A PEOPLE WHO TASTE THE AWE-INSPIRING PRESENCE OF GOD

"Tasting the presence of God" is not speaking of the natural five senses; it is referring to the spiritual senses that need to be opened to the spiritual realm. When a person is born again, his or her spirit is made alive and that person's soul—mind, will and emotions—is quickened by the new spirit within (see Rom. 8:15; Gal. 4:4-6). New desires begin to emerge because the Holy Spirit's life has been implanted into that person's spirit and He now has the ability to influence that person's soul (see John 14:21; 1 Pet. 2:1,2; 1 John 3:14; 5:15,16). The person develops a new hunger for spiritual things; and as he or she matures, spiritual taste buds begin to change. Hebrews 5:14 says, "But solid food belongs to those who are of full age, that is, those who by reason of use have their senses exercised to discern both good and evil." Hebrews 6:4 tells us that "it is impossible for those who were once enlightened, and have tasted the heavenly gift, and have become partakers of the Holy Spirit." And Psalm 34:8 says, "Oh, taste and see that the LORD is good; Blessed is the man who trusts in Him!"

These scriptures and more teach that people can taste. Let's look at Hebrews 6:5: "And have tasted the good word of God and the powers of the age to come." Can people taste the presence of God in your worship services? Can people taste the "good word," "the powers of the age to come" when they enter into your church? Can people sense that the gate is open and heaven has touched down upon earth in the very place where they are standing? We must create a worship atmosphere where spiritual taste buds are made alive so that people crave to eat at the table of the Lord—where people leave saying that they "have tasted that the Lord is gracious" (1 Pet. 2:3; see also Ps. 34:8; Luke 14:24).

A PEOPLE WHO PREPARE THEMSELVES FOR ENTERING INTO GOD'S PRESENCE

Preparation for entering the worship part of our Gate-Church service is very important and absolutely necessary. Hebrews 10:19 talks about "having boldness to enter the Holiest by the blood of Jesus." The Holiest refers to the Most Holy Place in the Tabernacle of Moses where the ark of the covenant abided and the presence of God was manifested. We, as the priests of the Lord (see 1 Pet. 2:5-9), come into His holiest by having cleansed and washed our souls and spirits in Jesus' blood (see Heb. 10:20-22; 1 John 5:1-6). The worship service should always begin with a preparation time, a time of prayer in which to "wash up" before going in. God promises to meet with us, speak to us, cleanse us, direct us (see Exod. 29:42-46). We should prepare for the awe-inspiring presence that we are about to encounter. Why prepare?

- People may come to the worship service unprepared to hear from God and unprepared to minister to both God and others.
- People may have busy minds, busy lives and be in need of time to empty themselves of those things that hinder true worship.
- People may come with defeated spirits, spiritual bondages, satanic harassment and need time to prepare.

110

People may come with the dust of the world upon the mind, will or emotions of their souls and need time to seek God, to ask for cleansing, apply Scripture and prepare for worship (see Gen. 35:2,3).

A PEOPLE WHO BY FAITH RECEIVE FROM GOD'S PRESENCE

We worship God because He is worthy of our worship. We would and should worship Him whether He gives us anything or not. Whether He does anything for us or not, we still worship God. Our first approach toward worship is to give our best unto God. We come as givers first. And yet, our giving to God as the priority does not negate the fact that we also activate our faith to receive what He has promised to give us, especially that which grows out of our worship time. True spiritual worship ought to contribute something powerful and lasting to the believer's spirit, soul and body. Sincere worship delights the heart of God, refreshes the soul of humans and releases the presence and power of God in the lives of His people. As we worship, God promises the release of joy (see Ps. 16:11), strength (see 1 Chron. 16:27), power (see Isa. 40:29), liberty (see 2 Cor. 3:17), transformation (see 2 Cor. 3:18), refreshing (see Acts 3:19) and boldness (see Acts 4:13).

THE GATE CHURCH WORSHIPS BEFORE THE THRONE OF GOD

Religion binds. Every person is bound somewhere, somehow—to a throne, to a government, to an authority, to something that is supreme, to something for which he or she offers sacrifice, burns incense or bends his or her knees. Worship at the throne of God involves attitudes (awe, reverence, respect) and actions (bowing, praising, serving). It is both subjective and objective activity. Worship is not an unexpressed feeling, nor is it an empty formality. True worship involves the mind, the emotions and the will. It is based upon clear biblical passages. True worship must reach deep within and be motivated by love. It must lead to obedient actions that glorify God. True worship is the total adoring response of humans to the eternal God who is self-revealed in time.

> We must create a worship atmosphere where spiritual taste buds are made alive so that people crave to eat at the table of the Lord—where people leave saying that they "have tasted that the Lord is gracious."

We are not speaking about cheap entertainment, not an "escaping from life's reality by some out-of-control hype." Worship is not a selfish experience. True worship leads to personal enrichment and enablement, the kind of spiritual strength that helps the believer carry the burdens and fight the battles of life. The Gate Church focuses on the throne of God, which speaks of God's authority as the King on the throne (see 2 Chron. 18:18; Esther 5:1-2; Ps. 9:7). God's throne is higher than man's throne. His throne is in heaven (see Ps. 11:4) and lasts forever and ever (see Ps. 45:6-8; 89:29,36). During worship, we need to see the Lord "sitting on His throne high and lifted up"; it is a throne of mercy and truth (see Isa. 22:23; 66:1; Matt. 19:28; Acts 7:49; 12:21; Heb. 1:8). We need to encourage God's people to come before His throne and worship openheartedly and fervently. The throne we worship before is:

‡ The set throne (see Rev. 4:2)

‡ The occupied throne (see Rev. 4:3; 5:7)

‡ The covenantal throne (see Rev. 4:3)

‡ The throne surrounded by overcomers (see Rev. 4:4)

‡ The throne where the voice of God is heard (see Rev. 4:5)

‡ The energizing throne (see Rev. 4:5)

‡ The transforming throne (see Rev. 4:6)

‡ The throne of continuous praise (see Rev. 4:6-11)

(See also Rev. 5:7,11,13; 6:16; 7:9,10; 8:3; 14:3-5; 19:4,5; 22:1,3.)

THE GATE CHURCH WORSHIPS THE BIBLE WAY

We simply must read, study and apply the Scripture. We are not to be driven by our personalities, our traditions, our likes or our dislikes. We are to be driven by God and obedience to His Word. Let's look at what Scripture says about praise, worship and entering into God's awe-inspiring presence. The seven Hebrew words used for our English word "praise" should give us some idea of what God expects. They are:

1. *Halal*: To laud, to boast excitedly, celebrate with rejoicing 1.

2. *Yadah*: To stretch out the hands, confess, publicly acknowledge

3. *Barak*: To kneel, bless, remember joyfully, adore

4. *Tehillah*: Laud, praises sung extravagantly, celebration

5. *Zamar*: To involve instrumental music in accompanying the voice

6. *Todah*: Thanksgiving with hands extended, a sacrifice of praise

7. *Shabach*: To shout, command, boast, exclaim praise with a loud voice, proclaim victory of the enemy, give forth a war cry

These seven Hebrew words describe worship that sounds anything but boring, stale, routine, uninspiring, dull or lifeless. Instead, they describe worship that is alive, exciting, energetic, life changing, wonderful, majestic, powerful. The Gate Church opens the gate of heaven with its biblically based pattern of worship. In his exhaustively researched book on worship, Ernest Gentile states, "A balanced worship program will be monitored by a sound theological foundation, an accurate biblical structure, a meaningful historical substance and a living pneumatic presence." [2]

The Gate Church builds a solid foundation for continual worship that is experienced without hindrances by respecting and applying the enormous number of clearly defined Bible passages on how to worship (see Ps. 47:7; 111:1). Gate-Church worship cannot be limited by tradition or determined by style.

We are experiencing a second reformation that is affecting our worship. Jack Hayford says, "I want to underscore the reformation in worship that is in progress. It has already begun and its fruit has been tested and proven worthy in a sufficient number of situations to show we are not simply dealing with a fad." [3] Jack makes a wise and important statement regarding tradition, "Worship is being redefined in terms of its form and focus. It isn't valid traditions that must be scorned or discarded, but that newness must refill them with meaning." [4] The meaning part of worship is pivotal to establishing a biblical heart toward worship. We can object to styles we do not personally like or even think are biblically wrong. It is easy to reject something we are not comfortable with.

C. Peter Wagner quotes Gary McIntosh of Talbot seminary concerning people who resist new trends in worship.

> There are several reasons for opposing it. One, it's too new. Two, it's often worldly, even blasphemous. The new Christian music is not as pleasant as the more established style. Because there are so many new songs, you can't learn

"The meaning part of worship is pivotal to establishing a biblical heart toward worship."

them all. It puts too much emphasis on instrumental music rather than godly lyrics. This new music creates disturbances, making people act indecently and disorderly. The preceding generation got along without it. It's a money-making scene and some of these new music upstarts are lewd and loose. [5]

Some of you are probably thinking, *Yes, that's exactly how I feel about all the new choruses and CDs. There are so many new worship songs. Where are the old hymns?* The previous quote though was attacking Isaac Watts, now regarded as the father of American hymnody, in 1723! Isaac Watts' hymns were regarded as worldly and blasphemous with too much emphasis on instrumental music!

The fact is that God uses music and styles that are rooted in our generation's culture and time. Rick Warren, pastor of the world-famous Saddleback Church in California, comments on worship:

> There is no correct style of worship. Jesus only gave two requirements for legitimate worship. "God is Spirit and His worshipers must worship in spirit and truth (John 4:24)." I don't think God is offended or even bothered by different styles of worship as long as it is done in spirit and in truth. In fact, I'm certain that God enjoys the variety. Remember, it was His idea to make us all different. The style of worship that you feel comfortable with says far more about your cultural background than it does about your theology. Debates over worship style are almost always sociological and personality debates couched in theological terms." [6]

In order for a Gate Church to flow in unity of vision and philosophy, the vision, principles, philosophy and procedures for worship must be clearly articulated. Our church is committed to a biblical practice of worship as part of our core theology and ecclesiology. We follow a definite set of principles and values, and we do not assume that everyone understands our vision, philosophy and principles of worship. Our church-membership class outlines the basics of worship, and our services reflect those basic principles.

A few years ago I created an entry-level class called Worship Ministry 101, which is a first step toward serving in our Worship Ministry department. This class is required for anyone seeking to be involved in leading worship, the choir, bands, orchestras or assisting with worship in any way; it was designed to guarantee unity concerning worship. When a person has completed Worship

Ministry 101, he or she is cleared to go into the Worship Ministry department, which we call the School of David. For those of you who are wondering, let me briefly state the main portion of Worship Ministry 101.

Because I believe the worship ministry must begin with the overseeing pastor, this class has roots in my own vision, principles and philosophy. I do reflect what the larger leadership team believes, and I think it is necessary for singers and musicians to hear from their senior pastor.

The following is my commitment to build a worshiping church:

- ‡ I am committed to sustaining a fervent spirit of worship in our congregation through the biblical expressions of worship as taught in Scripture (see 1 Pet. 2:5-9).

- ‡ I am committed to maintaining proper spiritual preparation for worship through opening-service prayer for all worshipers, especially those who lead in worship (see Gen. 35:2,3; Exod. 30:18-21; 40:12-16; Heb. 10:22).

- ‡ I am committed to furthering a spirit of excellence in our music (mentioned 839 times in the Bible) and worship ministry-excellence in attitudes, dress, modesty, etcetera.

- ‡ I am committed to the river of God as being the power and the purpose for our worship. I am not interested in techniques, methods or creativity that does not enhance the river of God. All songs and worship should be in the river of God, in the flow of the Holy Spirit. We are a people of His presence (see Acts 3:19).

- ‡ I am committed to teaching that the Tabernacle of David is a pattern for New Testament worship (the order of singers and musicians).

- ‡ I am committed to pursuing the prophetic word and prophetic song released in the presence of true worship.

- ‡ I am committed to the theology of creativity and spontaneity as it is rooted in God's Word, allowing for new, contemporary, cutting-edge expressions in both music and song. God is alive—living, changing and growing through us—so our worship must be new, growing, changing and open to what God is desiring to do and say in our worship.

✝ I am committed to worship and praise through instruments (see Ps. 150). We shall endeavor to nurture more skilled musicians, more stringed instruments and more prophetic spirit upon the instruments.

✝ I am committed to nurturing a dynamic, unified, committed, spirited, anointed, flexible, prophetic, cutting-edge, edifying, stronghold-breaking, devil-chasing, worshiping church (see 1 Chron. 15:16; 2 Chron. 20:21; Neh. 7:1).

Worship Ministry 101 allows those seeking ministry in the worship department to understand my heart and vision; it introduces them to the School of David.

Seven biblical basics form the foundation for our worship ministry (see 1 Chron. 25:1-7; Jer. 30:21). They include:

1. A spirit of dedication (see 1 Chron. 25:1; Josh. 14:8,9,14; Rom. 12:1; 2 Tim. 4:6; 1 Thess. 5:23)

2. Prophetic anointing (see 1 Chron. 25:1)

3. Skill and discipline (see 1 Chron. 25:1)

4. A servant's heart (see 1 Chron. 25:2)

5. A teachable and submissive spirit (see 1 Chron. 25:2,3,6)

6. A commitment to the House of the Lord (see 1 Chron. 25:6)

7. Instruction in the Song of the Lord (see 1 Chron. 25:7)

The following acronym for David reflects the groups that serve under the umbrella of our Worship Ministry department, or School of David:

D = Davidic worship
A = Arts
V = Voice
I = Instruments
D = Drama

Meetings for the School of David begin with corporate teaching, intercessory prayer and worship. The various segments of the school are then dismissed to join their own groups for practice and preparation for the upcoming weekend services: orchestra, choir, rhythm section, worship leader, drama team, special music, etc. This unified approach allows us to continually teach and impart our worship vision, principles and philosophy. As the senior pastor of our church, I make it a priority to speak to the School of David on the first Thursday of each month; I also meet with all the heads of each segment (orchestra, rhythm band, choir, worship leaders) before that meeting for dinner and discussion. Because I understand the importance of worship, I willingly give my time to this ministry.

A healthy worship ministry is vital to sustaining an open gate to heaven and enjoying the power of God's presence. Worship is key to establishing an atmosphere where people can seek God for who He is and not what He can give. Worship helps to purify our motives for wanting an audience with the Lord. It is through worship that the hidden agendas in our hearts are exposed so that we can enter His presence seeking Him and Him alone.

A PURE MOTIVE

We were created to know God because we are fully known by Him. The following story by Max Lucado shows that when our motives have been purified, our hearts will be satisfied in relationship.

> John Blanchard stood up from the bench, straightened his army uniform and studied the crowd of people making their way through Grand Central Station. He looked for the girl whose heart he knew, but whose face he didn't, the girl with the rose.
>
> His interest in her had begun thirteen months before in a Florida library. Taking a book off the shelf, he found himself intrigued— not with the book, but with the notes penciled in the margin. The soft handwriting reflected a thoughtful soul and insightful mind. In the front of the book, he discovered the previous owner's name, Miss Hollis Maynell.
>
> With time and effort, he located her address. She lived in New York City. He wrote her a letter introducing himself and inviting her to correspond. The next day he was shipped overseas for service in World War II. During the next year and one month, the two grew to know each other through the mail. Each letter was a seed falling on a fertile heart. A romance was budding.
>
> Blanchard requested a photograph, but she refused. She felt that if he really cared, it wouldn't matter what she looked like.
>
> When the day finally came for him to return from Europe, they

scheduled their first meeting—7:00 P.M. at Grand Central in New York. "You'll recognize me," she wrote, "by the red rose I'll be wearing on my lapel."

So at 7:00 he was in the station looking for a girl whose heart he loved, but whose face he'd never seen.

I'll let Mr. Blanchard tell you what happened.

"A young woman was coming toward me, her figure long and slim. Her blonde hair lay back in curls from her delicate ears; her eyes were as blue as flowers. Her lips and chin had a gentle firmness, and in her pale green suit, she was like springtime come alive. I started toward her, entirely forgetting to notice that she was not wearing a rose. As I moved, a small provocative smile turned her lips. 'Going my way, sailor?' she murmured.

"Almost uncontrollably I made one step closer to her, and then I saw Hollis Maynell.

"She was standing almost directly behind the girl. A woman well past 40, she had graying hair tucked under a worn hat. She was more than plump, her thick-ankled feet thrust into low-heeled shoes. The girl in the green suit was quickly walking away. I felt as though I was split in two. So keen was my desire to follow her, and yet so deep was my longing for the woman whose spirit had truly companioned and upheld mine.

"And there she stood. Her pale, plump face was gentle and sensible, her gray eyes had a warm and kindly twinkle. I did not hesitate. My fingers gripped the small worn blue leather copy of the book that was to identify me to her. This would not be love, but it would be something precious, something perhaps even better than love, a friendship for which I had been and must ever be grateful.

"I squared my shoulders and saluted and held out the book to the woman even though while I spoke I felt choked by the bitterness of my disappointment. 'I'm Lieutenant John Blanchard, and you must be Miss Maynell. I am so glad you could meet me; may I take you to dinner?'

"The woman's face broadened into a tolerant smile. 'I don't know what this is about, son,' she answered, 'but the young lady in the green suit who just went by, she begged me to wear this rose on my coat. And she said if you were to ask me out to dinner, I should go and tell you that she is waiting for you in the big restaurant across the street. She said it was some kind of test!'" [7]

Gate-Church believers will pass the test. They will see God's face because they have learned to pursue His heart in worship.

NOTES

1. C. Peter Wagner, *Churchquake* (Ventura, Calif.: Regal Books, 1999), p. 158.

2. Ernest Gentile, *Worship God* (Portland, Oreg.: City Bible Publishing, 1994), p. 39.

3. Jack Hayford. *Worship His Majesty* (Waco, Tx.: Word Books, 1987), p. 21.

4. Ibid., p. 22.

5. C. Peter Wagner, *Churchquake*, p. 161.

6. Rick Warren, *The Purpose-Driven Church* (Grand Rapids: Zondervan, 1995), p. 240.

7. Compiled by Alice Gray, *Stories for the Heart* (Sisters, Oreg.: Multnomah Books, 1996), pp. 117-118.

CHAPTER NINE

"Then Jacob rose early in the morning, and took the stone
that he had put at his head, set it up as a pillar,
and poured oil on top of it." Genesis 28:18

The Gate Church Builds
with Stones and Pillars

Jacob had been sovereignly captured through unique circumstances on the journey to his Uncle Laban's house. He had left home with nothing but vivid, recurring memories of fractured relationships and shameful deeds. It was Jacob's mother, Rebekah, who sought to frustrate Isaac's plan to give the first-born blessing to Esau. She was the one who had strategized to secure the blessing for her favorite son, Jacob. But Jacob was not innocent; he had conspired with his mother. While Esau was out hunting, Rebekah and Jacob had pulled off their subtle, deceitful plot to steal the blessing...and their plan worked. Isaac blessed Jacob and would not revoke the blessing, even after discovering that it had been given to Jacob rather than his firstborn, Esau.

Jacob was sent to Padan-aram to his mother's relatives with instructions to seek a wife. As he traveled from Beersheba, where he had lived so many years with his parents, to Haran, his destination, Jacob camped at the side of the road overnight. Genesis 28:10 says that "he lighted upon a certain place," indicating the apparently accidental yet divinely appointed choice of this God-place. After making a pillow with the stones, Jacob fell asleep and had a dream in which he saw a ladder resting upon earth with the top reaching to heaven. The angels of

121

God were ascending and descending the ladder while Jehovah Himself stood at the top. This ladder was positioned there upon the earth, at the very place where Jacob was lying in solitude, poor, helpless and forsaken by people.

This accidental place became a sovereign place, which was an awesome place. Jacob proclaimed this place of visitation to be the "house of God and the gate of heaven," a place where the awesome revealed presence of God dwelt and a way was opened to heaven.

Jacob represents many of God's chosen leaders, young and old alike, educated and uneducated, denominational and nondenominational, charismatic and non-charismatic. We are hungry for God to reveal Himself and to turn our accidental places into sovereign, God-visited places. Our passion is to set up a ladder that connects all the resources of heaven to earth so that a great house will be built, a Bethel, which in Hebrew means "house of God."

Yeah Baby!

The Gate-Church leader envisions a church with a gate open into the supernatural activity of God where His voice, His presence, His power and His provision are experienced. Like Jacob, we need to "awake" from our sleep and receive new vision through a new awareness of God. We all need to be shaken from our slumber so that we can awaken to a new day in God.

A stone Becomes a pillar.

BUILDING A HOUSE WHERE GOD CAN DWELL

Jacob has discovered that the gate of heaven is the house into which God moves. And what materials are needed? Stones and pillars. "And Jacob took the stone...and set it up as a pillar" (Gen. 28:18). Every house of God that seeks to become a Gate Church must build with stones and pillars. Proverbs 24:3,4 says that "through wisdom is a house built and by understanding it is established. By knowledge the rooms are filled with all precious and pleasant riches." We need the wisdom of God to build great houses, churches. Jesus said, "I will build My church" (Matt. 16:18). We are to partner with Him as wise master builders to build a great house that is able to withstand the attacks of our culture and of the devil (see Matt. 7:24-27). Scripture refers to the church as the temple, or the house of God (see Heb. 3:1-6; 1 Tim. 3:15), which is to be built according to the pattern God gives.

The Temple of Solomon is one of the great prophetic pictures of the church that Christ would build (see footnote 1). Solomon, a man of wisdom, determined to build a great house where God would live (see 2 Chron. 2:1,9; 6:2; Ps.

127:1; 1 Cor. 3:10). Solomon's Temple is a foreshadowing of the great house we are to build; it yields many great prophetic truths that describe the Gate Church.[1]

BUILDING WITH STONES

Solomon's house was built with the same two materials that Jacob used to build his prophetic memorial: stones and pillars. A great house that is destined to be a Gate Church will build with stones (see Hag. 2:9; 2 Tim. 2:20; Heb. 3:1-4; Rev. 21:19).

Let's look at some Scriptures that have to do with stones (italics added):

‡ 1 Kings 5:17,18: And the king commanded them to quarry large *stones*, costly *stones*, and hewn *stones*, to lay the foundation of the temple. So Solomon's builders, Hiram's builders, and the Gebalites quarried them; and they prepared timber and *stones* to build the temple.

‡ 1 Kings 6:7: And the temple, when it was being built, was built with *stone* finished at the quarry, so that no hammer or chisel or any iron tool was heard in the temple while it was being built.

‡ 1 Peter 2:5: You also, as living *stones*, are being built up a spiritual house, a holy priesthood, to offer up spiritual sacrifices acceptable to God through Jesus Christ.

The stones are symbolic of what I call the stone people; people who build great churches have a stone-type nature. The living stones used to build a spiritual house are people who are stable, know where they fit, and function there faithfully. They follow spiritual principles and submit to godly authority. They are not necessarily those with highly visible gifts; however, they do supply a quiet, enduring strength and stability with a visible joy and contentment. They are easy to work with in almost any situation. "Loyalty," "transparency," "faithfulness," "consistency," "dependability," these are the words that come to mind when you think of stone people.

> *"The living stones used to build a spiritual house are people who are stable, know where they fit, and function there faithfully."*

Our church has a focused process that we endeavor to use for nurturing all people so that they can become stone people. We have discovered that few people come to the house of God as stones or pillars. Most come in as weak, unstable, fragile people with major character flaws, lacking principles and spiritual disciplines. The Gate-Church leader must design a process whereby these "reed"-type people can transition into stone people. A reed in the Old Testament was used to weave baskets. It was a long, hollow bamboo-type plant that was easily blown about by the wind. You would not use bamboo reeds to build a strong house; they would not be strong pillars.

People must be taught to see themselves as they really are so they will be motivated and willing to change (see Rom. 12:3).

The challenge is: What do you do when you find out that you are not a stone, you are not a pillar, but you are a reed? Do you avoid facing yourself? Do you cover up your flaws with more activities? Do you retreat into a world of fantasies and daydreams? We teach that people must face the facts with faith. Face your failures with the hope of change; face your future with determination. "I will become a stone person by the grace of God!" Settle it! You can change!

Second Corinthians 3:18 explains that "we all, with unveiled face, beholding as in a mirror the glory of the Lord, are being transformed into the same image from glory to glory, just as by the Spirit of the Lord." We are people who are in the process of being changed (see John 1:42; 1 Pet. 2:5). Change, however, takes time (see Eccles. 3:11). It requires pressure, personal challenges and positive choices (see 2 Pet. 1:1-10). Change takes willingness and responsiveness (see Rom. 9:20-22); it is accompanied by the Holy Spirit's work in our lives (see 2 Cor. 3:18).

Reed people are basically unstable, easily moved by circumstances and emotions. They are known to be moody and cannot be trusted with responsibility. They have not discerned the difference between rights and responsibilities. Reed people may look good, having personality charms. They may have charisma and know how to talk the talk. They may even have a desire to do right, but they do not transfer that desire into action.

Have you ever been surprised by thinking you were building with a couple of stones but instead found yourself building with bamboo people who were easily bent and destroyed by pressure? I have.

I was totally shocked. I had no warning, no idea, that Tom was so spiritually and domestically unstable. Our meeting was to be a casual get together over coffee with small talk and fellowship. Then I was hit with the brick: "Our marriage is in trouble; we're also filing bankruptcy. We're not happy with the church, and we're leaving."

I was stunned and confused. I wondered: *Is this the same couple that I was so excited about incorporating into leadership in the church? They've been through the church-membership class and through leadership training. How could I have missed such a deep character flaw? Why haven't they ever confided in me? Why haven't they been honest in sharing their problems? How could I have been so duped? I thought they were pillars, but they aren't even stones.*

Throughout my thirty years of ministry, this same scenario has happened several times. I don't dwell on the negative; however, because more often than not, I have been pleasantly surprised. Pete was the perfect example of an unstable, non-buildable kind of person. From a failed marriage, he entered a wasteful single lifestyle that was destroying himself financially—gambling, parties, expensive trips, wasting his time, energy and resources. He was a reed. Then it happened. After being badgered by his parents, Pete finally visited our church one Easter Sunday morning. That day, he turned his life over to God and was genuinely transformed. He completed the church-membership class and joined our church family as a full-fledged member. He also committed himself to the small-group ministry and began to put his life in order. His money, his time, his friendships, his family, his morals, everything was brought into alignment. Eventually Pete became a cell leader and started to help pastor other people. From a reed, he became a stone and is on his way to becoming a strong pillar.

In order to build a Gate Church, we must have an abundance of pillar people who are strong, immovable and always in their place. A Gate Church will never open up the resources of heaven by depending on reed people.

In the book *The Anatomy of a Great Executive*, John Markham lists both the signs of immaturity and the signs of a person with his head on straight. These signs can easily be seen as the comparison with the reed person to the stone person.

SIGNS OF IMMATURITY

1. Has poor judgment.

2. Feels a sense of entitlement, that he should be looked after and his feelings should be respected. When in trouble, he expects everyone to drop what they're doing and come to his rescue, becoming upset if people don't. Needs everyone's attention all the time.

3. Sees himself as an innocent victim. Is quick to blame others for the things that go wrong in his life.

4. Does not learn from past mistakes, but repeats the same ones over and over again his whole life.

5. Is incredibly selfish. Is absolutely self-absorbed and shows little concern for the interests or feelings of anyone else. Is only interested in his own feelings. Expects other people to make the effort to get along with him, but does not make the effort to get along with others. Has the attitude: "What's in it for me? Will I be rewarded, recognized, promoted? If not, I'm not interested."

6. Has a bad case of irresponsibility. Has the attitude: "None of this is my responsibility. I didn't make the mess and I won't clean it up." Has one hundred excuses why he doesn't need to lift a hand to solve a problem, to get involved or to do something that doesn't really affect himself.

7. Has a disregard for consequences. Has the attitude: "The devil made me do it." Does not curb his impulses because he cannot see very far ahead.

8. Has a pleasure madness. His philosophy of life is "Let's play!" His maturity lies in learning to forego immediate pleasure to meet the demands of reality. Lacks self-discipline.

9. Demands to make his feelings known all the time. Throws temper tantrums. Manipulates people with tears, anger or quietness, or by withdrawing.

SIGNS OF A PERSON WITH HIS HEAD ON STRAIGHT

1. Accepts responsibility for his own behavior. Learns from failure. Does not repeat past errors.

2. Is pleased to receive constructive criticism and is sincerely glad to have the opportunity to improve.

3. Doesn't expect special treatment.

4. Meets emergencies with poise.

5. Is not impatient with reasonable delays. Realizes that the world runs to its own pace. Expects to have to make reasonable compromises.

6. Wins without gloating. Endures defeat and disappointment with equanimity. Tries to learn from every loss.

7. Harbors no jealousy. Is sincerely pleased for others when they enjoy success or good fortune.

8. Is considerate of the opinions and feelings of others. Is a careful listener. Doesn't become defensive, closed-minded or unduly argumentative when discussing opinions.

9. Plans for the future, rather than trusting the inspiration of the moment.[1]

Stone people are placed people. Through right decisions and right responses to Scripture, they become faithful and vital parts of the house of the Lord. Our process for developing stone people involves (1) joining and completing our membership class, (2) becoming a vital part of a small group called cells; and (3) developing and deploying their gifts through equipping by being involved with our School of Equipping.

I have a written member's profile so that every person coming into our church knows the kind of person we are developing.

MEMBER PROFILE

The goal of our ministry is to help every member become a person who is born again, water baptized and filled with the Spirit—who is faithful to the corporate church gatherings, cell ministry and School of Equipping—who joyfully gives his or her tithe, enjoys prayer and worship, has a heart for winning our city to Christ, a vision for world missions, a commitment to uphold family values and a love for God that is expressed with all of his or her heart, soul, mind and strength.

We also have a lay-pastor profile and an elder profile.

LAY-PASTOR PROFILE

A City Bible Church lay pastor is one who has the pastoral gift—one who is trained and released to do the work of pastoring although is possibly still employed in full-time secular work and not necessarily ordained as an elder. The lay pastor may be involved in areas such as pastoral counseling, altar work, teaching, public ministry, teaching of membership classes and departmental leadership, but the lay pastor has no governmental decision-making responsibility or legal stewardship over the church and is not ordained.

ELDER PROFILE

A City Bible Church elder should be actively involved in the fulfilling of the vision statement by his or her function as a leader. As an overseer of a major segment of the vision, the elder also has governmental responsibility and legal stewardship in the functioning of the church. The elder should also be involved in and accountable for discipling new leaders and hands-on mentoring while being an example of enthusiasm, passion for prayer, worship, evangelism and hospitality. Elders who are district pastors should attend all Sunday services, coming early and staying late. As an expression of their hearts for the corporate gathering, all other elders should desire to be involved in all services and be in attendance whenever possible at all major or special meetings hosted by the church.

PLACEMENT OF STONES

When a person chooses our church, we immediately begin to prepare him or her to be a stone person. The stone is then placed into the house not only as a strength to the whole house but also as a strength to all the other stones. Placement of the stones is very important.

1. Placement means that I develop the conviction that God has placed me in the local church of His choosing, for His pleasure and purpose and for my good (see 1 Cor. 12:18).

2. Placement means that I put down spiritual roots by committing myself to the God-given place He has chosen for me (see 2 Sam. 7:10; Ps. 1:3; 92:12-14; Isa. 61:1-3).

3. Placement means that I determine to respond to God's planting. I will allow time for my roots to bear fruit (see Prov. 12:12).

4. Placement means that I oppose everything that would cause me to leave the place of my planting (see Eccles. 10:4).

5. Placement means that I commit myself, my money, my talents and my energy to serve unselfishly and sacrificially (see Rom. 12:3-7).

6. Placement means that I will not neglect the corporate gathering of God's people (see Heb. 10:25).

MOVING FROM STONES TO PILLARS

When we read that Jacob "took the stone... set it up as a pillar, and poured oil on top of it" (Gen. 28:18), we are reminded that it is the stone people who build the church, but it is the pillar people who expand the church. Pillars allow the natural house or temple to expand, the same is true with people pillars in the house of God. It is the pillar people who help to build great churches. The church's spiritual vitality is directly dependent on the people who compose it. A Gate Church with strong people who take pillar-type responsibility will be a strong, healthy church. Efficiency is increased—not only by what is accomplished but also by what is relinquished. Pillar people both accept and delegate responsibility. They know how to build. Even as you are reading this, you're probably thinking of those whom you would consider to be pillar people. You know who your pillar people are!

The word "pillar" means "to support, hold up, carry or bear weight, to lift up or relieve pressure successfully." Every great church will have many pillar people carrying the burden and relieving the pressure. A pillar person is free of moodiness, faithfully providing strength and support, without the need for recognition or reward. This kind of person finishes all tasks, does not procrastinate or make excuses for spiritual laziness and stands alone if necessary. A pillar person is a mature Christian for whom holiness is more attractive than happiness. He or she is dissatisfied with the milk of the Word only and craves solid food. The pillar person has a growing discernment that helps to discriminate between truth and error, good and evil. He or she prefers serving others to being served by others and giving rather than receiving. This person is dynamic—not static—and accepts spiritual discipline.

CHOOSING PILLARS

As we Gate Church leaders, or pastors, choose those who could become pillar people, we are choosing people to function in various levels of leadership. God has specific ideas about what constitutes a leader, and He has given us a specific list of attributes to look for (see 1 Tim. 3:1-7; Titus 1:5-9; 1 Pet. 5:1-3). Let's be careful when we select people for any level of leadership function. We must get beyond the superficial and choose instead individuals who have biblical qualifications for

> "A pillar person is a mature Christian for whom holiness is more attractive than happiness.... He or she prefers serving others to being served by others and giving rather than receiving."

the task at hand. Character is the priority, not just charisma or personality.

Let's be realistic. No one is perfect, except God. We are all sinners, saved by grace, and we live in a fallen world with people who have been affected by sin. No one can live up to every aspect of God's checklist 100 percent of the time. Grace and mercy are needed along with standards and qualifications. The most qualified are not always the most obvious; they are not necessarily the most vocal or the ones up in front radiating with charisma. They may be stones hidden from sight because of all the things piled on top of them.

A pillar person is a mature believer who has developed enough of Christ's nature to be able to serve and support the church in a faithful manner, contributing to the health of the church, its stability and its future (see Gal. 2:9).

The apostle Paul tells us in Colossians 1:28 that his desire is to present every man perfect. The word "perfect" in the Greek is *teleios* and signifies an end, a goal, a limit, a full development of one's powers, attainment of a certain goal or standard. To be complete and full-grown implies ripeness in character and experience. *Teleios* is used to denote full development of adulthood as compared with the immaturity of childhood. God wants many of the stone people to develop into pillar people.

One of the tools I have used for developing pillar people is the *Timothy Training Program*, a leadership training program (available through City Bible Publishing). I invite individually selected men and women to meet together for teaching, discussion and relational, hands-on discipling using the material in the *Timothy Training Program*. These individuals are stone people, potential leaders, with whom I work to train and impart vision to become pillar people, strong leaders to serve the church.

The making of a pillar involves the development of the total person: spirit, soul and body. Developing a pillar person means helping to renew that person's mind, will and emotions as well as providing a proper biblical foundation with heavy doses of non-negotiable principles. This process will take both mentoring and classroom instruction. Pillars do not just self-create; they are made through wisdom and hard work. Notice the effort mentioned in the following verses (italics added):

‡ 2 Chronicles 3:15: Also He *made* in front of the temple two pillars.

‡ 2 Chronicles 3:17: Then He *set up* the pillars before the temple.

‡ 1 Kings 7:22: So the *work* of the pillars was finished.

These Scriptures are taken from the making of the two pillars named Jachin and Boaz which were in Solomon's Temple. First Kings 7:15-22 gives a detailed account of how these pillars were made—cast in a bronze mold—and how they were decorated—lattice network, wreaths of chainwork, seven chains, pomegranates and lilies. These pillars received an investment of intricate and detailed work. What a picture of how God makes us into pillars for His house, working within us the beauty of His nature, adorning us with His power and authority, fashioning us after His own pillar nature! Throughout the Old Testament Scriptures, God demonstrates Himself by appearing in a "pillar of fire" or a "pillar of cloud," which was indicative of His nature as a pillar God (see Exod. 13:21,22; 33:9,10; Num. 12:5; 14:14; Deut. 31:15; Neh. 9:12,19; Ps. 99:7; Rev. 3:12).

CHARACTERISTICS OF PILLAR PEOPLE

The church's pillars are crafted by the Holy Spirit and through the hands of wise-hearted leadership. Using six key passages on pillars, let's consider some clear, biblical characteristics of pillar people.

PILLAR PEOPLE MUST BE ANOINTED WITH THE OIL OF THE HOLY SPIRIT

> ✝ Genesis 28:18: [Jacob] set it up as a pillar, and poured oil on top of it.

> ✝ Genesis 31:13: I am the God of Bethel, where you anointed the pillar.

The oil is symbolic of the Holy Spirit and is to be received by every person desiring to be a strong pillar in the house of God. The holy anointing oil was used in the Tabernacle of Moses (see Exod. 30:25,31; 35:8,14) to anoint all the pieces of furniture and all the ministering priests (see Exod. 40:9-13). Anointing oil was used to consecrate new kings and new prophets (see 1 Sam. 10:1; 16:1,13; Ps. 89:20) and promised to believers who are the Lord's sheep (see Ps. 23:5; 45:7).

The stone person who has established a firm foundation will be saved by the Spirit, filled with the Spirit, led by the Spirit and covered by the Spirit. Pillar people must have an abundance of what the stone people have and more, anointed by the oil of the Holy Spirit. The pillar person needs to be filled with the Holy Spirit in such an obvious manner that the oil is seen upon his or her life. To be Spirit-filled is to have the Holy Spirit, the oil of heaven, poured from God's throne into our being, overflowing and running over! People are the pillars of the temple (see 1 Cor. 3:16; 6:19; Eph. 2:21) that God is building today, and we are in need of a double portion of fresh Holy Spirit oil (see Ps. 92:10). The house of the Lord should be filled with the sweet fragrance of the oil poured out upon the pillars (see Heb. 1:9; John 11:2; 12:3).

The New Testament, or new covenant, anointing is not a physical anointing as with oil being poured upon the body, but rather a spiritual empowering, or outpouring, of the Holy Spirit upon the blood-washed believer. By this outpouring, God Himself consecrates each believer to Himself and equips each believer with the Holy Spirit. The anointing is a divine enablement for the one singled out and chosen for a particular task. The anointing oil is always symbolic of the power and influence of the Holy Spirit in a person's life, penetrating and saturating (as oil does) what a person is, says and does.

PILLAR PEOPLE ARE TO BE SUPPORTIVE IN ALL WAYS

✠ Exodus 17:11,12: And so it was, when Moses held up his hand, that Israel prevailed; and when he let down his hand, Amalek prevailed. But Moses' hands became heavy; so they took a stone and put it under him, and he sat on it. And Aaron and Hur supported his hands, one on one side, and the other on the other side; and his hands were steady until the going down of the sun.

The word "pillar" means to support or hold up, carry the load, bear the weight, relieve the pressure. These two verses from Exodus tell us that Moses' hands became "very heavy" and that he needed support. Aaron and Hur "supported his hands," one on the right side and one on the left side. They demonstrated the attitude and action of supporting the leadership that God has put over and in your life. Aaron and Hur understood and responded correctly to biblically delegated authority.

Don't criticize people because their hands are heavy and they have let up a little or because they show signs of humanness. Support them. Move to their side and offer spiritual and emotional support. Pillar people who support well are those who know their placement and are able to give their strength in a team effort, supporting with their gifts, attitudes, actions, words and influence to build and to add to, not to tear down or subtract.

Pillar people know their limitations and understand delegated authority. Aaron and Hur supported Moses' rod in a time of crisis. They did not run to get their own rods to take Moses' place. Pillars must uphold the load and give security to the building. They must be strong enough to sustain the weight that is to rest evenly upon all the pillars. If one pillar falters, it causes all the other pillars to have increased pressure and weight. Pillar people should not need propping up and persuading or continual support to secure their pillar function. Pillar people should independently and tenaciously give continual strength.

Pillar people must be aware of the hidden flaws that might one day be the cause of the destruction of the whole house. The discovery of a serious flaw in the moral character of a leading pillar in a church has sometimes brought immediate weakening and sometimes even widespread destruction. Pillar substance must be suitable and staunch material. Just any substance will not do for pillars. Wood, hay and stubble are not suitable materials for building pillars because they are unsturdy and liable to catch fire. Pillars are made of the spiritual virtues encouraged in Galatians 5, Philippians 4 and 2 Peter. These are all character virtues that should be growing strong in a person's life. Pillar people must provide support during good reports and evil reports, in dry times and revival times, in growth times and no-growth times; they should be supportive in every season of the church's life.

PILLAR PEOPLE ARE TO UPHOLD THE STANDARDS

‡ Exodus 38:9-20: Then he made the court on the south side; the hangings of the court were of fine woven linen, one hundred cubits long. There were twenty pillars for them, with twenty bronze sockets. The hooks of the pillars and their bands were silver. On the north side the hangings were one hundred cubits long, with twenty pillars and their twenty bronze sockets. The hooks of the pillars and their bands were silver. On the north side the hangings were one hundred cubits long, with twenty pillars and their twenty bronze sockets. The hooks of the pillars and their bands were of silver. And on the west side there were hangings of fifty cubits, with ten pillars and their ten sockets. The hooks of the pillars and their bands were of silver. For the east side the hangings were fifty cubits. The hangings of one side of the gate were fifteen cubits long, with their three pillars and their three sockets, and the same for the other side of the court gate; on this side and that were hangings of fifteen cubits, with their three pillars and their three sockets. All the hangings of the court

all around were of woven fine linen. The sockets for the pillars were bronze, the hooks of the pillars and their bands were silver, and the overlay of their capitals was silver; and all the pillars of the court had bands of silver. The screen for the gate of the court was woven of blue and purple, and scarlet yarn, and fine linen thread. The length was twenty cubits, and the height along its width was five cubits, corresponding to the hangings of the court. And there were four pillars with their four sockets of bronze; their hooks were of silver, and the overlay of their capitals and their bands was of silver. All the pegs of the tabernacle, and of the court all around, were bronze.

The Tabernacle of Moses was called the church in the wilderness (see Acts 7:38); it displays God's intentions for pillars in His house. The Tabernacle of Moses had a total of ninety-six pillars, each with a brass foundation, a silver cap and anointed with oil. The outer court pillars were the structure for hanging the white linen that separated the Tabernacle proper from the congregation. Fine, twined linen is one of the most prominent materials used in the Tabernacle. Between four thousand and five thousand square feet of it were used in the construction of the Tabernacle and in the clothing of the priests.

The white linen throughout Scripture represents the righteousness of God, holiness and purity (see Ps. 132:9,16; Isa. 61:10; Phil. 3:9). Revelation 19:8 states, "And to her it was granted to be arrayed in fine linen, clean and bright, for the fine linen is the righteous acts of the saints." Then in Revelation 19:14, we read: "And the armies in heaven, clothed in fine linen, white and clean, followed Him on white horses."

The pillars of the Tabernacle were the only source of structure to uphold the linen, pillars with feet of brass and caps of silver. Pillar people are to uphold the righteous standards of God's Word in their personal lives and in their personal ministries (see Isa. 62:10).

The Bride of Christ will be adorned in fine, gleaming white linen garments, the fruits of her righteous conduct put on display (see Rev. 19:6-8).

PILLAR PEOPLE ARE SELF-CONTROLLED

The pillar person who upholds the godly, righteous standards of God's Word, the standards directly stated in Scripture for leadership, must be a person who has added temperance, or self-control, to his or her character (see 2 Pet. 1:6). It was said of Alexander the Great, "He conquered the world; himself he could not conquer." What we fail to control will soon control us: anger, lust, envy, pride. Any habit or work of the flesh left outside of the lordship of Christ will potentially ruin us in the future (see 1 Cor. 9:25-27). The word temperance in the Greek is *enkratia* which is used four times in the New Testament: control your passion (see Acts 24:25); self-restraint (see Gal. 5:23); keeping oneself in hand (see 2 Pet. 1:6 and Titus 1:8).

Pillar persons must have power over themselves in all areas of the mind, will and emotions. We would say these people have a "grip" on themselves, can govern their own behavior, are not excessive in anything and are inwardly strong. These men and women have the power to do what is right, even when they don't feel like it. The Scriptures demand that pillar people be sober-minded (see Titus 2:2), temperate (see 1 Tim. 3:11) and abstain from all weaknesses of the flesh (see 1 Thess. 4:3; 5:22; 1 Pet. 2:11).

Our society has developed a philosophy of self-indulgence that has resulted in every form of addiction. Because of our affluence and excessive leisure time, we have learned to pamper our appetites for pleasures. A pillar person will discipline himself or herself to uphold the white linen of right living, holy conduct, righteous thinking, purity of heart. Pillar people are necessary in order to build a house with standards. Self-control does not come by human willpower alone but by the power of the Holy Spirit (see Gal. 5:23-25; 2 Cor. 12:9). Self-control comes by ruling our own souls, mind, will and emotions (see Prov. 16:32).

When considering a person to set in place as a pillar, ask the following questions. Personal Life: Do this person's internals square with his or her externals? Does this person's private world with God match up with his or her public performance in God's service? Domestically: Would this person's family vote for him or her? Would this person's spouse and children agree that he or she would make a significant contribution? Publicly: Would the community be surprised or confirming? Conduct: Does this person's conduct reflect a life lived according to clear biblical principles, or is this person ruled by emotions or cultural acceptability? Have his or her standards grown out of principle?

> *"A pillar person will discipline himself or herself to uphold the white linen of right living, holy conduct, righteous thinking, purity of heart."*

PILLAR PEOPLE ENDURE PRESSURE AND CRISIS SUCCESSFULLY

‡ 2 Chronicles 3:15-17: Also he made in front of the temple two pillars thirty-five cubits high, and the capital that was on the top of each of them was five cubits. He made wreaths of chainwork, as in the inner sanctuary, and put them on top of the pillars; and he made one hundred pomegranates, and put them on the wreaths of chainwork. Then he set up the pillars before the temple, one on the right hand and the other on the left; he called the name of the one on the right hand Jachin, and the name of the one on the left Boaz.

These two pillars in Solomon's Temple were named Jachin, which means "he shall establish," and Boaz, meaning "in it is strength." These two pillars are prophetic pictures of what all pillar people should be—immovable and established. Taking responsibility means coming under pressure. Pressure can press a person out of shape and possibly out of control. There is no better proof that a person is qualified to function as a pillar than through his or her ability to persevere, hold his or her ground, remain steadfast.

The word for persevere in the Greek is *hupomone. Hupo* means to remain or stay and *mone* means to stay under, remain in your place. *Hupomone* is to remain in your place in spite of opposition, pressure or direct attack. None of these things move a pillar person. *Hupomone* is a military word used to describe a soldier on the frontlines who is to "hold the line," to face the enemy with no thought of retreating or surrendering; it is a battle word. Perseverance is the ability to continue in the faith and resist all pressures of the world, the flesh or the devil. Perseverance is to be steadfast in purpose, not swerving aside; it is to continue on course in spite of difficulties and obstacles, refusing to consider giving up as an option!

The pillar person makes a commitment to a vision and stays with the commitment in times of pressure and trials. The pillar person will unite with those of like mind and strengthen the others in order to reach the vision, setting aside privileges that weaken the persevering attitude.

King David was a pillar person with a commitment to pursue and not give up (see 1 Sam. 30:4-10). Shammah was a model pillar person who would not give up any ground to the enemy (see 2 Sam. 23:11,12). The apostle Paul continued on in spite of setbacks, discouragement and pressure (see 2 Tim. 4:7). Hebrews 12 warns of nine threats to all pillar people who choose to endure and hold their ground. The following are some threats to our perseverance:

‡ The threat of hidden insignificant sins (see Heb. 12:1)

‡ The threat of undefined goals and purposes (see Heb. 12:1)

‡ The threat of deadly distractions (see Heb. 12:2; Phil. 3:12-14)

‡ The threat of losing motivation (see Heb. 12:2; 6:11,12)

‡ The threat of becoming weary (see Heb. 12:3; Gal. 6:9)

‡ The threat of wrong focus (see Heb. 12:4; Rom. 8:18)

‡ The threat of reacting against God-sent correction (see Heb. 12:5-11)

‡ The threat of discouragement that destroys (see Heb. 12:12,13; Isa. 35:3)

‡ The threat of bitterness that weakens (see Heb. 12:14-17; Deut. 29:18)

PILLAR PEOPLE MUST HAVE GODLY WISDOM

Proverbs 9:1 reads, "Wisdom has built her house, she has hewn out her seven pillars." All pillar people need a heavy dose of the wisdom of God to function successfully for long periods of time. Our natural man and mind will continually weaken the work of God. We must see things from God's perspective and do all things by the wisdom of God. Spiritual ends can be achieved only by spiritual people who employ spiritual methods that are saturated in the wisdom of God. The word "wisdom" means "sound judgment, discernment, seeing life from God's point of view." Wisdom is the ability to use the facts and the knowledge of God's Word to correctly discern how to build one's life in God's house. Pillar people with wisdom will represent the stability of God's Word in God's house (see Isa. 33:6).

There is a kind of person who is undoubtedly clever with an acute brain and skillful tongue, but one whose effect upon any committee, group or team in the church will bring trouble. He or she may have wisdom in the natural sense, but lacks godly wisdom. As we see in the book of James, there are two kinds of wisdom—one from above which is godly wisdom and one from below which is evil wisdom:

‡ EVIL WISDOM

‡ James 3:14,15: But if you have bitter envy and self-seeking in your hearts, do not boast and lie against the truth. This wisdom does not descend from above, but is earthly, sensual, demonic.

✦ Earthly wisdom: Its standards and sources are earthly. It measures success in wrong, worldly terms, and its aims are worldly aims.

✦ Sensual wisdom: Its source is fleshly, destroying the moral fiber. It is sensual, and its results are always destructive.

✦ Devilish wisdom. Its source is evil, and it produces the kind of situation that the devil delights in.

✦ Confusing wisdom. It results in disorder, and it is rooted in arrogance and bitterness. Instead of bringing people together, it drives them apart. Instead of producing peace, it produces strife.

✦ GODLY WISDOM

✦ James 3:17,18: But the wisdom that is from above is first pure, then peaceable, gentle, willing to yield, full of mercy and good fruits, without partiality and without hypocrisy. Now the fruit of righteousness is sown in peace by those who make peace.

✦ Pure (*hagnos*): It is cleansed of all ulterior motives and of self so that it has become pure enough to see God.

✦ Peaceable (*eirenikos*): It produces right relationships between man and man and between God and man. True wisdom produces right relationships.

✦ Gentle (*epieikes*): It knows how to apply the letter of the law, uses principles and standards with great gentleness. When the law could be fatal, gentleness is used. Godly wisdom knows how to make allowances and when not to stand upon personal rights; it knows how to temper justice with mercy and always remembers that there are greater things in the world than rules and regulations. "Sweet reasonableness" is the ability to extend to others the kindly consideration we would wish to receive.

✦ Easy to be entreated (*eupeithes*): It is easy to persuade, not in the sense of being pliable and weak, but not being stubborn (unwilling to listen to reason and to appeal); it is not rigid but willing to listen, knowing wisely when to yield.

✦ Full of mercy (*eleos*): It shows pity for the man who is suffering unjustly or suffering because it is his or her own fault—not judgmental or condemning.

‡ Without partiality (*adiakritos*): It is undivided, not wavering or vacillating; it knows its own mind; chooses its course and abides by that decision.

‡ Without hypocrisy (*anupokritos*): It is honest; it never pretends to be what it is not; it never acts or plays a part to gain its own end.

PILLAR PEOPLE MUST BE OVERCOMERS

‡ Revelation 3:12: He who overcomes, I will make him a pillar in the temple of My God, and he shall go out no more. And I will write on him the name of My God and the name of the city of My God, the New Jerusalem, which comes down out of heaven from My God. And I will write on him My new name.

Pillar people are not weakened by the devil or the flesh. When self-life has run its course, we find ourselves in a spiritual desert. Fleshly actions will hurriedly lead to spiritual dryness. But when the flesh life is overcome, the well of new life begins to flow. When a pillar person who has determined to overcome all weaknesses of the flesh fails, that person humbles himself or herself immediately through repentance and cleansing. Failures promote a life of brokenness that leads to a teachable spirit, a servant's attitude and a willingness to be obscure.

Pillar people, who have gone through the process of brokenness, dying to the flesh, do not push for the limelight, the front row of attention, titles or privileges. Pillars overcome the dark ambitions of the heart; they embrace the servant's attitude of working without pay and without thanks, without being honored by men. Pillars can be built into the house of God without worrying about who they are pleasing.

Pillars overcome. They are able to prevail, to gain total and complete victory in the struggle of unbroken fleshly habits. Pillar people have overcome the wicked one (see 1 John 2:13-14), the spirit of antichrist (see 1 John 4:3-4), the world (see 1 John 5:5) and fleshly bondages (see 2 Pet. 2:19,20).

Every Gate-Church builder will take time to make stones and pillars that will guarantee a great house. Just as Jacob poured oil on the stones and set them up to be pillars, we Gate-Church pastors must pour oil on our potential stones and set them up to be great pillars in the house of God.

NOTES

1. The following descibes the Temple:

– A house where His name is recorded (see 2 Chron. 2:1)

– A house where His Kingdom is established (see 2 Chron. 1:1)

– A house where sweet incense is offered (see 2 Chron. 2:4)

– A house where sacrifices are offered up (see 2 Chron. 2:4; 7:12)

– A house built according to divine pattern (see 2 Chron. 3:3)

– A house built with strong, godly foundations (see 2 Chron. 3:1; 1 Kings 5:17)

– A house built with beautiful, costly stones (see 2 Chron. 3:6; 1 Kings 5:17,18; 6:7)

– A house built with prepared pillars (see 2 Chron. 3:15)

– A house with a brazen altar for redemption (see 2 Chron. 4:1-3)

– A house with brazen lavers for washing (see 2 Chron. 4:6)

– A house with golden candlesticks for oil (see 2 Chron. 4:7)

– A house with a table of shewbread (see 2 Chron. 4:8)

– A house with singers and instruments (see 2 Chron. 5:12)

– A house with praise and thanksgiving (see 2 Chron. 5:13)

– A house finished in the month of harvest (see 2 Chron. 5:3; 7:11)

– A house of holiness and sanctification (see 2 Chron. 7:16)

– A house with the eyes and the heart of God (see 2 Chron. 7:16)

– A house with the presence of the Lord (see 1 Kings 8:10)

– A house with the voice of God (see 1 Kings 9:3)

– A house with happy servants (see 2 Chron. 9:7)

– A house that was finished and God came (see 1 Kings 8:10,11)

2. John Wareham, *The Anatomy of a Great Executive* (Scranton, PA: Harper Collins, 1991), n.p.

*"And he called the name of that place Bethel;
but the name of that city had been Luz previously."*

Genesis 28:19

The Gate Church Is a
Word-Driven Church

God's visitation changed Jacob's whole life, past, present and future; it also changed his vision and his purpose for living. This out-of-the-way place, this accidental stopping point, became a place marked by God's presence. God found this spot to be the most important center on earth at that moment for this elect individual. God's name, power and presence were supernaturally attached to that place.

Before then, the city had simply been named after a hazelnut tree—the city of Luz, the Hazelnut City! In other words, Nowheresville, a place of no significance! But when God attached His name, His power and His grace to that place, it was called Beth-El, the House of God. God has called you and me to build a place of visitation, a Gate Church, a Bethel, a house for God.

The word "Bethel" is used sixty-nine times in the Bible and takes on a prominent prophetic and symbolic meaning throughout Scripture. The modern Tell Beit is on the watershed route twelve miles north of Jerusalem. Abram camped to the east of Bethel when he built an altar to Yahweh (see Gen. 12:8). For Jacob, Bethel was the starting point in his realization of God who was for him, "the God of Bethel" (see Gen. 31:13; 35:7). He named this place of vision Bethel, meaning "the house, or dwelling place, of God." Bethel later became a place of the prophets (see 1 Kings 13:10,11; 2 Kings 2:2,3) and a place where people came to seek God, to hear God's Word and gain fresh perspective for their lives. In the New Testament, our Bethel is the church, the house of God.

THE GATE CHURCH, A WORD AND SPIRIT CHURCH

If we are to build a Bethel, we must build with God's Word and His Spirit. Both are essential and need to be highly visible. Both evangelical and charismatic traditions bring a rich legacy to the church. In his book *The Word and Power Church*, Doug Bannister gives his perspective on evangelicals and charismatics.

> The evangelical legacy includes expository preaching, an emphasis on the authority and sufficiency of Scripture, a realistic affirmation that the kingdom of God is not fully here, a belief that spiritual growth is a process and a belief that the Word must be studied in community.

> The charismatic legacy includes an emphasis on prayer, a hopeful affirmation that the Kingdom is here in part, a belief that God speaks today, an emphasis on participatory worship and a belief that the Spirit must be experienced in community. [1]

We should not think in terms of either/or. Instead, we must think in terms of both. The church often swings from one extreme to the other, rarely finding the balanced middle. We are called to embrace both the Spirit and the Word. All churches have this responsibility. Gate Churches build with the pillar of God's Word (see 2 Tim. 3:16) and the power of God's Spirit. As a Spirit-hungry leader, I am totally committed to building a Word-driven church where the people develop an appetite for both the Word and the Spirit.

The Gate Church creates an atmosphere where the Word of God is alive, powerful, highly respected and sought after so that lives can be changed by its truth. Many people today are infected with uncertainty about everything. They seem to be confused, unsure of what is right and wrong, unsure of their beliefs, unsure about how to make wise decisions or how to raise their children or help their marriages. The Word provides the answers.

Differing views of the Bible, however, may discourage the average person from reading or studying the Bible, believing that it is hard to understand. Amos 8:11 warns, "'Behold, the days are coming,' says the Lord God, 'That I will send a famine on the land, not a famine of bread, nor a thirst for water, but of hearing the words of the Lord.'" Amos predicts a time when the Word will be lost and when people will be vexed with uncertainty and perplexity. The Gate Church realizes this famine and seeks to remedy it by building a Word church.

John Wesley once wrote, "I am a creature of a day, passing through life as an arrow through the air. I am a spirit, coming from God, and returning to God; just hovering over the great gulf; a few months hence I am no more seen; I drop into an unchangeable eternity! I want to know one thing—the way to heaven...God himself has condescended to teach the way. He hath written it down in a book. O give me that Book! At any price, give me the book of God!" 2

Part of the Anglican Confession reads, "The Scripture of God is the heavenly meat of our souls. It is a light lantern to our feet. It is a sure, steadfast and everlasting instrument of salvation. It comforteth, maketh glad, cheereth and cherisheth our conscience. The words of Holy Scripture be called, words of everlasting life, for they be God's instrument, ordained for the same purpose. They have power to turn, through God's promise and being received in a faithful heart, they have ever a heavenly spiritual working in them."

THE POWERFUL WORD OF GOD

The Gate-Church leader believes the Word of God to be heavenly food for our weary souls. A supernatural work happens when people expose their lives to the anointed Word of God. Hebrews 4:12 indicates that the Word is living, powerful and is effective now, today for whomever and whenever. Let's look at this verse in the light of three different translations:

‡ New King James: For the word of God is living and powerful, and sharper than any two-edged sword, piercing even to the division of soul and spirit, and of joints and marrow, and is a discerner of the thoughts and intents of the heart.

‡ Amplified: For the Word that God speaks is alive and full of power [making it active, operative, energizing, and effective]; it is sharper than any two-edged sword, penetrating to the dividing line of the breath of life (soul) and the [immortal] spirit, and of joints and marrow [of the deepest parts of our nature], exposing and sifting and analyzing and judging the very thoughts and purposes of the heart.

‡ The Message: God means what he says. What he says goes. His powerful Word is sharp as a surgeon's scalpel, cutting through everything, whether doubt or defense, laying us open to listen and obey. Nothing and no one is impervious to God's Word. We can't get away from it—no matter what.

The written Word of God is not to be taken lightly. The reader who will not listen faces God Himself. The Word demands a response; God does not tolerate indifference (see John 10:35-36; Luke 16:17; Acts 7:38; Rom. 3:2). He has given the Word for a purpose. Second Timothy 3:16 explains that "all Scripture is given by inspiration of God and is profitable for doctrine, for reproof, for correction, for instruction in righteousness."

THE WORD IS GOD'S REVELATION

The Bible presents itself as revealed truth from God; it is God's revelation, the very pure Word of God. God has unveiled that which is absolutely true, not conjectured, not hypothesized. When the Bible speaks, God speaks. This is hard for some people to believe or grasp, but it is true. The ultimate Author of Scripture is God Himself. The Scriptures as a body were written by the inspiration of the Holy Ghost and are thus the Word of the Living God, His infallible wisdom. The authority of Scripture is the authority of Jesus Christ; the two are indivisible. To attempt to distinguish the two is like asking which blade of a pair of scissors is more important or which leg of a pair of pants is more necessary. We know Christ through the Bible, and we understand the Bible through the knowledge of Christ. The two cannot be separated.

God's Word is living, active, full of power and energetic! (See 1 Pet. 1:23.) Martin Luther is credited with the saying, "The Bible is alive; it speaks to me. It has feet; it runs after me. It has hands; it lays hold on me."

THE WORD REFLECTS GOD'S CHARACTER

The Word of God reflects the true character of God Himself, the source of all life. This kind of Word life is full of energy to achieve its declared end. A revelation that is living has a constant application to the minds of its recipients. It is living, altogether like God in its power. It is an outflow of His life and therefore indistinct with the same divine, imperishable, powerful life, either to kindle similar life in us or to react against all opposition.

God does not separate Himself from His Word. He does not disown it as if it were a foreign thing to Him. His it remains when it comes into our ears, into our hearts, into our mouths and into our total lives. He knows it well as His own Word, as the expression of His own life. Therefore, it is never dead matter, insensible to what is done with it, for it is a bond of union with the Living God (see John 1:12; 1 Cor. 1:18; Phil. 3:21; Col. 1:29). A thing may be alive but dormant. The nature of true life, however, is that it springs into activity and challenges on every front those who fall short of its standards. The Word of God is full of living energy to carry out the will of God by either blessing or cursing as the case may be. What folly to treat the Word of God as though it is subject to our minds, our views, our opinions! It is electric and spites him who tampers with it. It is electric to light him who bows beneath it!

THE WORD IS RAZOR SHARP

The Word of God is sharp as a two-edged sword, cutting deeply. In the ancient world the double-edged sword was the sharpest weapon available in any arsenal. The Word is as sharp as a surgeon's scalpel that uncovers the most delicate nerves of the body (see Isa. 49:2; Eph. 6:17; Rev. 1:16). The Word of God pierces and penetrates, dividing asunder the soul and spirit, slicing between what the human eye cannot see (see Heb. 4:12; 1 Thess. 5:23). The Word has the power to "go through," to penetrate the innermost part of a person, either to change that individual inwardly into a new man or woman, or—in a case of self-hardening—to lay bare all his or her deadly guilt.

The Word judges even our thoughts and intentions of the heart. It can tell the difference between the desires and the intentions of the human mind, detecting the innermost thoughts, sifting, analyzing and judging the whole of our inner world (see John 12:47,48). The Word of God is the searchlight of the soul.

As the surgeon has to be able to decide in an instant what to do, so God's Word—like the surgeon's eye—sees the secret lurking doubt and unbelief of the thoughts and intents of the heart (see Ps. 139:1-3,12). The surgeon carries a bright and powerful light for every dark crevice and a sharp knife for the removal of all the infection revealed by the light. Nothing evades the scope of God's Word. What we hold as

> "Martin Luther is credited with the saying, "The Bible is alive; it speaks to me. It has feet; it runs after me. It has hands; it lays hold on me."

most secret, we will find subject to the scrutiny and judgment of His Word.

The Gate Church is a Word church, a Word-preaching and Word-teaching church (see Isa. 2:3; Mic. 4:2). Only the Word of God has the full power to change lives and redirect destiny.

THE THREEFOLD MINISTRY OF JESUS

The Gate Church makes a concerted effort to avoid short-changing people's brains and impoverishing their spirits through a lack of the Word. The Gate Church must be a teaching church, imparting instruction, instilling doctrine, explaining and expounding Scripture—teaching so that people learn. The Bible says that "Jesus went about all Galilee, *teaching* in their synagogues, *preaching* the gospel of the kingdom, and *healing* all kinds of sickness and all kinds of disease among the people" (Matt. 4:23, italics added; see also Matt. 9:35). The threefold balanced ministry of Jesus is:

1. Teaching: Systematic instruction

2. Preaching: Systematic proclamation

3. Healing: Supernatural works of the Holy Spirit

Stretching forth from the inception of the Christian faith down to this very hour, there is an unbroken succession of teachers and teaching. Wherever preaching was at its best, the sermons contained a large amount of teaching content. Jesus was frequently called a "rabbi" or teacher. Of the ninety times He was addressed in the gospels, sixty times Jesus was called "Rabbi," or Teacher. Furthermore, the thought of the speaker in at least part of the thirty remaining cases was directed toward Jesus as a teacher, using the Greek word *didaskolos* which refers to "one who teaches concerning the things of God and the duties of man" and is translated both "teacher" and "master" (see Matt. 7:28,29; 22:16; 28:19,20; Mark 6:6; 9:38; Luke 10:25; 18:18; 19:39; 20:39; John 3:2; Eph. 4:11).

THE FIRST CHURCH WAS A WORD CHURCH

The first-century churches referred to in the book of Acts were Gate Churches that focused on teaching as a primary function of the church. Because these Scriptures are so important for emphasizing teaching in our Gate Churches, I will list them here (italics added):

‡ Acts 5:42: And daily in the temple, and in every house, they did not cease *teaching* and preaching Jesus as the Christ.

‡ Acts 6:7: Then the *word of God* spread, and the number of the disciples multiplied greatly in Jerusalem, and a great many of the priests were obedient to the faith.

‡ Acts 11:26: And when he had found him, he brought him to Antioch. So it was that for a whole year they assembled with the church and *taught* a great many people. And the disciples were first called Christians in Antioch.

‡ Acts 15:35: Paul and Barnabas also remained in Antioch, *teaching* and *preaching* the *word* of the Lord, with many others also.

‡ Acts 20:20: How I kept back nothing that was helpful, but proclaimed it to you, and *taught* you publicly and from house to house.

‡ Acts 28:31: Preaching the kingdom of God and *teaching* the things which concern the Lord Jesus Christ with all confidence, no one forbidding him.

‡ Acts 13:1: Now in the church that was at Antioch there were certain prophets and *teachers*: Barnabas, Simeon who was called Niger, Lucius of Cyrene, Manaen who had been brought up with Herod the tetrarch, and Saul.

‡ 1 Corinthians 12:28: And God has appointed these in the church: first apostles, second prophets, third *teachers*, after that miracles, then gifts of healings, helps, administrations, varieties of tongues.

TEACHING IN THE NEW TESTAMENT

Clearly, the teacher was a central figure of the first-century church. In this age of many books and much radio and television, it is rather difficult to fully appreciate how successfully the apostles and their successors carried on by means of an oral ministry. Textbooks were unknown; even the record of the words and works of the Lord Jesus were not committed to writing until thirty years after the Resurrection. But the apostolic church was the burning expression of personalities who had been made new creatures in Christ Jesus and who went everywhere teaching the Good News.

The eminent church historian, Philip Schaff, gives tribute to the place and importance of the teaching ministry in the Early Church in the following words:

> It is a remarkable fact that after the days of the apostles, no great missionaries are mentioned until the Middle Ages. There were no missionary societies, no missionary institutions, and no organized efforts in the ante-Nicean age. Yet in less than 300 years after the death of the disciple John, the whole population of the Roman empire, which then represented the civilized world, was nominally Christianized.[3]

TEACHING AGAINST THE CHURCH OF THE REFORMATION—THE JESUITS

Both Protestant and Catholic historians agree that the religious schools set in motion by the Jesuits as a counter movement to the Protestant Reformation arrested its triumphant advance. When Protestantism threatened to sweep Catholicism from the face of Europe, Ignatius Loyola and Francis Xavier conceived the plan of reaching the children and rearing up a new generation of lovers and defenders of Roman doctrine. The effective tools of the Jesuits were not the inquisition chambers, but their schools. The Jesuit priests stated, "Give me a child until he is six years old and then you may have him." Those Protestant denominations, which have recognized the place and importance of teaching, have also been significantly successful.

TEACHING IN THE CHURCH OF THE TWENTIETH-CENTURY—THE SOUTHERN BAPTISTS

Prior to 1900, the Southern Baptist Convention had never emphasized the teaching ministry. One of its members said at that time, "We have organized; we have evangelized; we have preached, but we have never taught."

During the 1900s, Dr. J. B. Gambrel, the president of the Convention, declared:

> The time has come for us to further the teaching ministry. I believe the most significant of all modern movements is the work of teacher training. Upon his recommendation, the denomination adopted the slogan, "A certificate for every teacher" and began to concentrate all its resources upon the preparation of Sunday school teachers for their task. Since that time, teacher training has

been stressed on every platform and in every paper with the result that the Sunday School Board is now issuing more than a hundred thousand awards annually.[4]

TEACHING DEFINED IN THE OLD TESTAMENT

The words used in the Old Testament to describe the teaching and learning process open up more windows for understanding the powerful affect of teaching the Word properly.

‡ *Lamadh*: This word may have originally meant "to beat with a rod, to chastise" and may have originally referred to the training of beasts. By a noble evolution, the term came to describe the process of disciplining and training men in war, religion and life (see Isa. 2:4; Hos. 10:11; Mic. 4:3). As teaching is both a condition and an accompaniment of disciplining, the word often means simply "to teach or to inform" (see 2 Chron. 17:7; Ps. 71:17; Prov. 5:13). The glory of teaching was its harmony with the will of God, its source in God's authority and its purpose to secure spiritual obedience (see Deut. 4:5,14; 31:12,13).

‡ *Yarah*: This word means to throw, to cast as an arrow or lot (see Josh. 18:6; 2 Kings 19:32). It is also used of thrusting the hand forth to point out or show clearly (see Gen. 46:28; Exod. 15:25). The original idea easily converts into an educational conception since the teacher puts forth new ideas and facts as a sower casts seed into the ground. But the process of teaching was not considered external and mechanical but internal and vital (see Exod. 35:34-35; 2 Chron. 6:27).

‡ *Bin*: This word, meaning "to separate or to distinguish," is often used in a causative sense to signify "to teach." The idea of teaching was not an aggregation of facts bodily transferred like merchandise. Real learning followed genuine teaching. This word suggests a sound psychological basis for a good pedagogy. The function of teaching might be exercised with reference to the solution of difficult problems, the interpretation of God's will or the manner of a godly life (see Neh. 8:7-9; Ps. 119:34; Dan. 8:16,26).

‡ *Sakhal*: The verb from which the various nominal forms for "wisdom" are derived means "to look at, to behold, to view" and in the causative stem describes the process by which one is enabled to see for himself or herself

what had never before entered his or her physical or intellectual field of consciousness. The noun indicates a "wise person, or sage, whose mission is to instruct others in the ways of the Lord" (see Prov. 16:23; 21:11). In Daniel 12:3 we read, "Those that are wise (margin: teachers) shall shine like the brightness of the firmament."

✝ *Yadha*: This verb literally means to see and consequently to perceive, to know, to come to know and cause to know or teach. It describes the act of knowing as both progressive and completed. The causative conception signifies achievement in the sphere of instruction. It is used of the interpretation and application by Moses of the principles of the law of God (see Exod. 18:16,20), of the elucidation of life's problems by the sages (see Prov. 9:9; 22:19) and of constant providential guidance in the way of life (see Ps. 16:11).

✝ *Zahar*: This verbal root signifies "to shine, to bring to light" and when applied to the intellectual sphere indicates the function of teaching to be one of illumination. Ignorance is darkness; knowledge is light. Moses was to teach the people statutes and laws or to enlighten them on the principles and precepts of God's revelation (see Exod. 18:20). The service rendered by the teachers—priests, Levites and fathers—sent forth by Jehoshaphat, was one of illumination in the twofold sense of instruction and admonition (see 2 Chron. 19:8-10).

✝ *Ra'-ah*: The literal meaning of this verb is "to see" and the nominal form is the ancient name for prophet or authoritative teacher who was expected to have a clear vision of spiritual realities, the will of God, the need of man and the way of life (see 1 Sam. 9:9; 1 Chron. 9:22; 2 Chron. 16:7).

✝ *Nabha*: The most significant word for "prophet," *nabi,* is derived from the verb which means "to boil up or forth like a fountain" and consequently to pour forth words under the impelling power of the spirit of God. The Hebrews used the passive forms of the verb because they considered the thoughts and words of the prophets due not to personal ability but to divine influence. The utterances of the prophets were characterized by instruction, admonition, persuasion and prediction (see Deut. 18:15-22; Ezek. 33:1-20).

✝ *Ra'ah*: This word means "to feed a flock." The name "shepherd," so precious in both the Old and New Testaments, comes from a verb meaning "to feed," hence to protect and care for out of a sense of devotion, ownership and responsibility. It is employed with reference to civil rulers in their positions of trust (see 2 Sam. 5:2; Jer. 23:2), with reference to teachers of virtue and wisdom (see Prov. 10:21; Eccles. 12:11), and preeminently with reference to God as the Great Shepherd of His chosen people (see Ps. 23:1; Hos. 4:16). Ezekiel 34 presents an arraignment of the unfaithful shepherds or civil rulers. Psalm 23 reveals Yahweh as the Shepherd of true believers and John 10 shows how religious teachers are shepherds under Jesus the Good Shepherd.

TEACHING DEFINED IN THE NEW TESTAMENT

The words describing the teaching process in the New Testament are also very helpful for all Gate Churches in evaluating their teaching ministries:

✝ *Didasko*: This usual word for "teach" in the New Testament signifies either to hold a discourse with others in order to instruct them or to deliver a didactic discourse where there may not be direct personal and verbal participation. In the former sense, it describes the interlocutory method, the interplay of the ideas and words between pupils and teachers; in the latter use, it refers to the more formal monologues designed especially to give information (see Matt. 4:23; 13:36; John 6:59; 1 Cor. 4:17). A teacher is one who performs the function or fills the office of instruction. Ability and fitness for the work are required (see Rom. 2:20,21; Heb. 5:12). The title refers to Jewish teachers (see John 1:38), to John the Baptist (see Luke 3:12), to Jesus (see John 3:2; 8:4) and to Paul (see 1 Tim. 2:7; 2 Tim. 1:11), and to instructors in the Early Church (see Acts 13:1; Rom. 12:7; 1 Cor. 12:28). Teaching, like preaching, was an integral part of the work of an apostle (see Matt. 28:19; Mark 16:15; Eph. 4:1).

✝ *Manthano*: The word translated as "disciples" comes from *manthano*. The central thought of teaching is causing one to learn. Teaching and learning are not scholastic but dynamic and imply personal relationship and activity in the acquisition of knowledge (see Matt. 11:29; 28:19; Acts 14:21). There were three concentric circles of disciples in the time of our Lord: learners, pupils, superficial followers; the multitude, the body of believers who accepted Jesus as their Master; and the twelve disciples whom Jesus also called apostles.

✝ *Paratithemi*: This word means presentation. The presentative idea involved in the teaching process is intimately associated with the principle of adaptation. When it is stated that Christ put forth parables unto the people, the sacred writer employs the figure of placing alongside of or near one, hence before him in an accessible position. The food or teaching should be sound, or hygienic, and adapted to the capacity and development of the recipient (see Matt. 13:24; Mark 8:6; Acts 16:34; 1 Cor. 10:27; 2 Tim. 4:3; Heb. 5:12-14).

✝ *Diermeneuo*: This word means to interpret or elucidate. On the walk to Emmaus, Christ explained to His perplexed disciples the Old Testament Scripture in reference to Himself. The work of an interpreter is to make truth clear and to affect the edification of the hearer (see Luke 24:27; 1 Cor. 12:30; 14:5,13,27).

CREATING A HUNGER FOR THE WORD OF GOD

The Gate Church creates an atmosphere for learning the Word of God. This atmosphere is immediately impacting upon the new convert, the visitor, the seeker and the member alike. A hunger for the Word is in the air. It is everywhere, in every aspect of church life. The Word is lifted up by all the leaders, and it is used by all the leaders for all things: counseling, training, correcting, singing and preaching. The Word of God is the centerpiece, the main thing.

Years ago E. F. Hutton, a prominent investment corporation, inundated the media with its compelling advertising: "When E. F. Hutton speaks, everybody listens!" The commercial opened with a large, noisy group of people mingling and talking incessantly. Someone would then whisper, "E. F. Hutton says...," and the room would become a silent chamber. Everyone wanted to learn E. F. Hutton's secrets for investing so that they, too, could enjoy "the good life."

That is the kind of image the Gate Church should nurture toward God's Word. Every believer should be encouraged to learn God's Word, realizing that the secrets it contains will promote a flourishing and godly life. We learn about what we are interested in. What are you interested in? What do you really love? If you love golf, you will play golf, watch golf, talk golf, read golf and pray golf! Golf will occupy your heart because you have an interest in or love for it.

Anyone who stops learning is old, whether that person is twenty or eighty! Anyone who keeps learning stays young. The greatest thing in life is to keep your mind young and alive, especially with the Word of God. A learner is one who:

‡ Is interested in new ideas, new information and new experiences.

‡ Is keenly aware of how much he or she doesn't know.

‡ Believes that personal growth is the best investment of time he or she can make in the future.

One of the profound miracles of the human brain is its capacity for memory. Mental skills get rusty from disuse. Learning of any kind cleans off the rust and restores the gears to full function. When we put ourselves into and under the Word of God, the results are mind-boggling. The Gate Church is committed to being a Word-driven church, a place where Bethel is established by building pillars of truth.

We can expect the following results when we establish a Word-driven Gate Church:

‡ Divine guidance (see Ps. 119:105,133)

‡ Spiritual cleansing (see Ps. 119:9,11)

‡ Spiritual health and vitality (see Prov. 4:4,20-22)

‡ Security and safety (see Ps. 18:30; 19:8)

‡ Foundational truths (see Heb. 5:12-14; 6:1-3; 1 Pet. 1:12)

‡ Equipping for the work of the Lord (see Eph. 4:11-13)

‡ Darkness being driven out (see 1 Pet. 2:9; 1 John 1:6,7; Col. 2:6)

‡ Instruction in the principles of warfare (see Ps. 18:34; 144:1; 2 Sam. 22:35)

One of our practical applications to the challenge of helping people grow in the Word is our School of Equipping. In the Appendix at the back of this book, you will find a typical layout of our eight tracks and the different classes offered in each. As you will notice, we offer a systematic approach to learning the Word of God.

APPLYING THE WORD

One of the reasons that we provide a School of Equipping is to ensure that those who learn the Word of God also receive proper guidance in applying it. Ruth Bell Graham has reportedly told the story of how her two young daughters heard the Word and knew the Word but misunderstood its application.

> One day Ruth heard loud screams coming from the kitchen. Running to investigate the problem, she found three-year-old Bunny with tears streaming down her face; her hands were clinging to her cheeks. Five-year-old Anne piped up, "Mommy, I'm teaching Bunny the Bible. I'm slapping her on one cheek and teaching her to turn the other one so I can slap it too!"

The Gate Church teaches God's children not only how to love and to know the Word of God but also how to apply it correctly.

NOTES

1. Doug Bannister, *The Word and Power Church* (Grand Rapids: Zondervan, 1999), p. 12.

2. John Wesley, *The Preface to Sermons on Several Occasions from the Works of John Wesley 1* (Bishop, Tex. Conrad Archer, 1746), p. 104.

3. Philip Schaff, *History of the Christian Church*, Vol. II, Second Period Anit-Neican (Grand Rapids: Erdmans Publishing, 1910), n.p.

4. C. B. Eavey, *Principles of Teaching for Christian Teachers* (Grand Rapids: Zondervan, 1982), n.p.

*"And this stone which I have set as a memorial
shall become a house of God and
everything that thou wilt give me,
I shall repeatedly tithe unto thee."* [1] Genesis 28:22

The Gate Church
Is a Giving Church

In Jacob's place of visitation, which he describes as the gate of heaven, Jacob sets up a stone and anoints it with oil, calling it the house of God. His next response to the awesome presence of God is a heart commitment expressed in the form of a vow. Genesis 28:20-22 says that "Jacob made a vow, saying, 'If God will be with me, and keep me in this way that I am going, and give me bread to eat and clothing to put on, so that I come back to my father's house in peace, then the Lord shall be my God. And this stone which I have set as a pillar shall be God's house, and of all that You give me I will surely give a tenth to You.'"

The reach of Jacob's vow was unusual. It covered his possessions, his ways, his heart—his total life. Jacob was unwilling to stand in God's presence without securing a covenant with God for his future. He wanted to hear the Lord's voice all the days of his life ("Remember your oath!"). Jacob surrendered himself and his future to God; he surrendered a fixed portion of his income as a token of his fixed commitment to God. Jacob wanted the awesome presence and favor of God ("If God be with me") to continually abide with him as he journeyed into the future.

God's abiding presence in a person's life is manifested in wisdom, courage, success and satisfaction (see 1 Sam. 18:14,28; 2 Sam. 5:10; Ps. 4:6,7; 36:7-9). Thus, Jacob's plea, "and will keep me in this way that I am going" (Gen. 28:20), gave evidence of divine counsel and providential protection. Interesting is Jacob's promise to give a fixed portion of all his income, "a tenth" (v. 22), to God. He promised a tenth during all seasons of life—storms, calamities, crises, disappointments, blessings, peace and prosperity. The tenth was promised without any sense of bargaining. This was the act of a young leader who was just starting out in life. Jacob made a decision to give a fixed amount, not on impulse, but by commitment and plan, a decision made once and carried out during his lifetime.

THE VOW: GIVING BACK
WITHOUT GIVING IN

A settled habit of giving is promoted by a settled expression of giving. The Gate Church is a place of committed giving by people who have made a vow to God. The tithe giver understands that the tithe is only the beginning of giving, only the foundation for more generous acts of faith and sacrifice. As the Gate Church experiences the awesome presence of God—through dreams, visions, the anointing oil of God, a connection between heaven and earth, and the receipt of heaven's resources—then the correct response is a vow to give back a tenth of all that God has allowed to flow through our hands. Anything less than such a vow would surely be a wrong response—a clue that the heart is in need of more visitation, more restoration and more changing. If someone who faithfully attends a Gate Church (where God has opened the gate of His presence) does not make a vow that touches all of his or her material life, that person must set out to discover whether or not he or she has truly been touched by God and what keys are needed to unlock the secretly locked doors within his or her heart.

The success of the Gate Church will be found in people who understand the significance of a vow and who value the importance of commitment to that which has been vowed, even when life is filled with contradictions. The Hebrew word for vow indicates a pledge or a promise made to God. A vow was always an expression of unusual devotion or commitment and was usually voluntary. When we make a vow, we fast forward to a point of time that is not yet present, deciding what will happen in that distant time. To vow means "to spring horizontally from one place to another," quickly placing oneself in another place by springing over the intervening space and keeping one's eye on the future, or a future goal.

As we consider Jacob's vow, we find that Jacob is committing his heart to faithfully giving back to God, whether facing poverty or prosperity. Jacob prays that God will keep his character and that he be given strength not to forfeit any of his spiritual or moral integrity. The connection between the awesome power and presence of God and the giving of the tenth is vitally important to the Gate Church. Tithing is a token of consecration; it is a visible sign that we have surrendered all and have made Him Lord of all. If He is Lord of all, then we are merely stewards of all that He has given us.

ESTABLISHING GATE-CHURCH STEWARDSHIP

A steward is a guardian over the interests of another. The steward owns nothing but is careful to guard, protect and increase the prosperity of the one whom he or she serves. We are stewards of our time, strength and ability, as well as our money (see Luke 16:1-3). Stewardship is an act of worship; thus, we must recognize that God is the owner of all things, and in everything we do, we must keep in mind His objectives, His best interests and His glorification.

The stewardship lifestyle of the believer in the Gate Church has these basic elements:

- ‡ Giving: "Honor the Lord with your substance and with the first fruits of all your increase" (Prov. 3:9). Giving activates the divine law that releases the work of God in our private worlds.

- ‡ Receiving: "Your barns will be filled with plenty" (Prov. 3:10). God responds to our giving by opening up opportunities to receive divine provisions both directly and indirectly from His hand.

- ‡ Prospering: "Your vats will overflow with new wine" (Prov. 3:10). God wants us to receive abundantly and have more than enough to become liberal givers.

GIVING

Someone once said, "Give according to your income lest God make your income like your giving." Giving sets in motion divine law. Proverbs 3:9 says, "Honor the Lord with your substance and with the first fruits of all your increase." Martyred missionary Jim Elliot lived his life by the motto, "He is no fool who gives what he cannot keep in order to gain what he cannot lose."

The believer's expression of giving is found in two acts of obedience: the giving of tithes and the giving of offerings. Malachi 3:8-10 reads:

> "Will a man rob God? Yet you have robbed Me! But you say, 'In what way have we robbed You?' In tithes and offerings. You are cursed with a curse, for you have robbed Me, even this whole nation. Bring all the tithes into the storehouse, that there may be food in My house, and try Me now in this," says the LORD of hosts, "If I will not open for you the windows of heaven and pour out for you such blessing that there will not be room enough to receive it."

The tithe is the tenth part of anything. It is the first part of our income, of all that we earn, and it already belongs to the Lord. Giving the tithe is our responsibility; it is a biblical minimum in our financial commitment (see Gen. 28:21; Lev. 27:30). It does not limit our giving; tithing opens the door to a genuine life of financial stewardship.

Prices keep going up, and the rate of interest keeps changing, but God still only asks for ten percent. The believer in the Gate Church sees tithing as a biblical response to God's Word, God's presence and God's power. Tithing is not optional; it is an automatic heart response. Our old nature is stubborn, stingy, selfish, doubting, reasoning and manipulating; it is not borne out of a giving, sacrificing and believing heart. Our new nature represents a new heart, which must take dominance over our old nature if we are to obey God's Word and walk in His ways. In Ezekiel 36:26 the Lord says, "I will give you a new heart and put a new spirit within you; I will take the heart of stone out of your flesh and give you a heart of flesh." Paul tells us in 2 Corinthians 5:17 that "if anyone is in Christ, he is a new creation; old things have passed away; behold, all things have become new."

> "Giving the tithe is our responsibility; it is a biblical minimum in our financial commitment."

New life in Christ means that we make Jesus lord over our lives, Master of everything. The outward giving of possessions and finances is merely a reflection of the inner condition of the heart; giving is a spiritual barometer that allows a person's soul to know the condition of his or her spirit. We are to give ourselves to Him (see Rom. 12:1,2). We are also to give Him our money; wealth is a trust from God and must be earned and managed according to spiritual principles (see Matt. 19:16-22; Luke 12:15-20). Jesus is, or should be, lord over our finances. Our giving should not be randomly or emotionally based; it should be done by principle. God expects us to be givers, to give generously and consistently. He accepts no excuses for stinginess. Our lives are materially affected by our generosity.

One of the most overlooked teachings in the American church today is the truth that nothing we have belongs to us. According to Psalms 24:1,2, "The earth is the Lord's, and all its fullness, the world and those who dwell therein. For He has founded it upon the seas, and established it upon the waters." George Barna's research indicates that only thirty-five percent, or one third, of all Christians who attend church believe that the Bible teaches us to tithe; two-thirds believe that the Bible offers suggestions about giving but that it leaves the final choice totally up to us. We do have a choice in the amount we give in offerings, but the tithe has been established by God and recorded in His Word. Proverbs 3:9,10 says, "Honor the Lord with your possessions, and with the first fruits of all your increase; so your barns will be filled with plenty, and your vats will overflow with new wine."

Some people believe that their first responsibility is to tend to their personal needs, then to give God a slice of the leftovers. The word "first" refers to that which is before anything else in the order of time, place or consideration. The "first fruits" is the fruit, or produce, that matures first and is collected first in the season. All that we have, all that we are, all that we possess, all that we earn are equally the gifts of God. We should acknowledge God as the Giver of all good things, all the support and comfort of our natural lives; then, because we do, we give back to God our first and best (see Gen. 28:22; Deut. 8:11-20; 26:10). So why and how are we to tithe?

‡ Tithe is the first of our wages and the firstfruits of our increase (see Deut. 26:10,26).

‡ Tithe is the acknowledgment that all we have already belongs to the Lord (see Gen. 28:22; Deut. 26:10).

‡ Tithe is to be given with an attitude of worship as a rejoicing offering (see Lev. 22:17-22, 29; John 12:3-5; 2 Cor. 9:7).

✝ Tithe is to be given from our increase (see Deut. 26:12).

✝ Tithe is the sacred portion that we set aside as the Lord's; it is holy (see Deut. 26:13; Lev. 27:30).

✝ Tithe is not to be used for personal needs (see Lev. 27:30; Deut. 26:12-15).

✝ Tithe is to be given as an act of spiritual obedience (see Deut. 26:12-15).

✝ Tithe is the basis for releasing God's covenantal blessings or curses (see Deut. 26:15-19; Mal. 3:8-11; Luke 6:38).

✝ Tithe is the provision for releasing ministry in the house of the Lord (see Neh. 13:10-12; 1 Cor. 9:9; Acts 28:10).

✝ Tithe is not just Old Testament teaching (see Matt. 6:1; 23:23; 1 Cor. 16:1,2).

✝ Tithe is the biblical minimum and will not limit our giving; it will open the door to a genuine stewardship lifestyle.

✝ Tithe is the acknowledgment of ownership, that God is owner of all, and I am only a steward, or trustee, over my human estate.

Malachi 3:8,9 states, "Will a man rob God? Yet you have robbed Me! But you say, 'In what way have we robbed You?' In tithes and offerings. You are cursed with a curse, for you have robbed Me, even this whole nation."

This passage brings up the matter of the curse that can be placed upon our finances. No one likes the thought of potentially having a curse attached to his or her money, but this Scripture states clearly that it can happen. It tells us that people can rob God, thus placing a curse on their finances. Robbery means taking either by fraud or by a violent act that which belongs to another and appropriating it to one's own use. It is not only taking what is not ours but also keeping back for ourselves what belongs to someone else. Robbing God is permitting something else to have a stronger power over us than His will does. People who retain God's money in their treasures will find it a losing proposition.

A story is told about an eagle who was hunting for game to feed her young ones back in the nest. As she circled high above the ground, she looked for a rabbit, a bird, something she could catch to take back to her nest. Movement caught her eye, and she saw a priest placing a sacrifice on an altar. The eagle dove toward the altar and grabbed a piece of the meat, gloating at the easy day of hunting she had just had. Instead of spending hours circling and trying to catch live game, all she had to do was swoop down and steal fresh meat from those helpless priests. What she didn't realize was that a live coal from the altar had adhered to the sacrifice. When she dropped the stolen meat into her nest, that coal came to life and destroyed the nest where her young had once been safe. Taking a bit of meat from the sacrifice may seem like an easy solution to our problems, but it can be a source of destruction to our lives.

Like the eagle who thought it was safe to steal from the priests, the following verses assure us that our actions do not go unnoticed by God:

✝ Proverbs 26:2: Like a flitting sparrow, like a flying swallow, so a curse without cause shall not alight.

✝ Malachi 2:2: "If you will not hear, and if you will not take it to heart, to give glory to My name," says the Lord of hosts, "I will send a curse upon you, and I will curse your blessings. Yes, I have cursed them already, because you do not take it to heart."

✝ Haggai 1:6: You have sown much, and bring in little; you eat, but do not have enough; you drink, but you are not filled with drink; you clothe yourselves, but no one is warm; and he who earns wages, earns wages to put into a bag with holes.

✝ Haggai 1:9-11: "You looked for much, but indeed it came to little; and when you brought it home, I blew it away. Why?" says the Lord of hosts. "Because of My house that is in ruins, while every one of you runs to his own house. Therefore the heavens above you withhold the dew, and the earth withholds its fruit. For I called for a drought on the land and the mountains, on the grain and the new wine and the oil, on whatever the ground brings forth, on men and livestock, and on all the labor of your hands."

We are to bring the tithe into the storehouse. The Old Testament storehouses were places that God designated for bringing and distributing abundance. The storehouse also referred to His Tabernacle where His name was established. Today the storehouse refers to your local church, the place where you receive your spiritual food, nurture, fellowship and worship, the place you call your spiritual home (see Gen. 28:8; 41:56; Ps. 1:1-4; 27:1-4).

RECEIVING

We should believe and expect God's blessings upon our tithe giving. God issues an invitation to prove His promises, to test Him. He offers a guaranteed direct and abundant return on our investment. Malachi 3:10 promises, "'Bring all the tithes into the storehouse, that there may be food in My house, and try Me now in this,' says the Lord of hosts, 'If I will not open for you the windows of heaven and pour out for you such blessing that there will not be room enough to receive it'" (see Gen. 12:2; Prov. 10:6, 28:20). The Scriptures boldly claim that it is more blessed to give than to receive (see Acts 20:35). Luke 6:38 encourages us to "give, and it will be given to you: good measure, pressed down, shaken together, and running over will be put into your bosom. For with the same measure that you use, it will be measured back to you." Deut. 8:18 adds, "And you shall remember the Lord your God, for it is He who gives you power to get wealth, that He may establish His covenant which He swore to your fathers, as it is this day."

We have the right to believe that our barns will be filled with plenty and our vats will overflow with new wine (see Prov. 3:10). God wants us not only to give but also to receive abundantly so that we can have more than enough to become liberal givers. God responds to our giving by opening up opportunities to receive divine provisions, both directly and indirectly from His hand. Proverbs 11:24 assures us that "there is one who scatters, yet increases more; and there is one who withholds more than is right, but it leads to poverty." The Lord's storehouse of blessing is unlimited; the only restriction on how much you or I might receive depends on our ability to contain or use it. Proverbs 10:32 says that "the lips of the righteous know what is acceptable, but the mouth of the wicked what is perverse." God longs to open the shut windows of heaven and pour out a personalized custom-made blessing (see Deut. 28:13; 15:4,10,18; Ps. 132:15; Eccles. 2:8-11). God wants these heavenly windows to be opened and to remain opened.

The windows of heaven are not representative of a bank where we store up good deeds and gain interest, but they are openings from which all life's blessings flow. The Bible uses the word "windows" to describe the source from which God blesses. When windows are open over your house, there is joy and happiness. When windows are open over your business, there is fruitfulness and prosperity. When windows are open over your mind, there is peace and confidence. When windows are open over your body and soul, there is health and contentment. I don't believe for one minute that tithing buys God's blessings, but I do believe that it opens a door, or better, a window of release for God to bless mightily and continually.

Malachi 3:10 promises a "blessing" that there will not be room enough to receive it. The Hebrew word used for blessing in this verse means "to evolve with power for success, power to receive prosperity, longevity, to receive riches and abundant life" (see Ps. 133:3; Prov. 10:22; Ezek. 44:30). The Gate Church must be filled with believers who have faith in God's Word and in God's ways, who believe that they will receive what is promised as they practice the principle of covenant tithing.

I find that many people tithe and enjoy giving, but they do not expect to receive from God-nor do they even pray about receiving His promises. And yet Matthew 7:8 says, "For everyone who asks receives, and he who seeks finds, and to him who knocks it will be opened." Again in Mark 10:30 we read, "Who shall not receive a hundredfold now in this time—houses and brothers and sisters and mothers and children and lands, with persecutions—and in the age to come, eternal life." We are to open our hearts and our hands expecting to receive after we have sown our seed into the ground. Expecting a return is not presumptuous or selfish; it is doing business with God. Planting a bigger field means reaping a bigger harvest.

The Greek word translated "receive" in our New Testament is rich in its meaning and encourages us to do what it means (see Acts 3:5, 2:38; 1 Cor. 3:14; 1 John 3:22). This word "receive" means to take or receive with open hands, to take to oneself and hold on to, expecting results from what has been invested or sown, to partake of, to welcome or receive gladly, to make room for what is to be received.

The believer is to expect the Promiser to bring to pass what He has promised. Our part is expectation-faith—an attitude of readiness to receive. The promise is a pledge, a word of honor, a vow, an oath, a warranty, a guarantee or a covenant. It is the ground of hope, expectation and assurance in which we plant the promises God has given through His Word (see Isa. 55:10,11; 2 Cor. 1:20; Gal. 3:22; Heb. 6:18; 10:23).

When we ask, we must believe that God is able and willing to fulfill His promises. Think about that as you read the following verses:

‡ Numbers 23:19: God is not a man, that He should lie, nor a son of man, that He should repent. Has He said, and will He not do? Or

has He spoken, and will He not make it good?

✝ 1 Kings 8:56: Blessed be the Lord, who has given rest to His people Israel, according to all that He promised. There has not failed one word of all His good promise, which He promised through His servant Moses.

We are to follow in the steps of Abraham as stated in Romans 4:20: "Yet he did not waver through unbelief regarding the promise of God, but was strengthened in his faith and gave glory to God." When we have a clear word of promise like the one in Malachi 3:8-11 concerning our tithe giving and tithe receiving, we should lay hold of that word by faith without wavering. We have a sure word that we are to pursue the promise until it becomes a reality (see Ps. 78:19; 2 Kings 7:2; Luke 1:34). We are not to "stagger," or "waver," in our faith as we pursue the promise, even if it seems quite impossible.

To stagger at the promise is to consider the promise and all the difficulties that lay in the way of its fulfillment and thus dispute it. We don't fully cast it off nor do we fully embrace it, but we waver. Wavering back and forth in unbelief prevents us from laying hold of the promised blessings. Unbelief is the end result of doubt; it emanates from fear, or an inner problem with believing the truth that God can, or that God will, do what He said.

Tithing requires a step of faith and a life of faith. Anytime we take our money or material goods and give them away, faith is needed to see beyond the natural realm into the spiritual realm. Strong faith must be supported by right thinking based upon Scripture. The reasons that justify our believing in God's promises are the same reasons that justify our believing in Him most firmly. He can't lie. He is all-powerful. He is a good and generous God. Is anything too hard for the Lord? Strong faith judges God as faithful to what He has promised. If we can't trust God with our money, how can we trust Him with our lives, our children and the future? We must grow in faith, and a great place to start is in the giving of our tithes.

PROSPERING

Tithing is only one aspect of the believer's lifestyle of stewardship. The Scriptures also speak about the giving of our offerings. An offering is an undesignated, unlimited amount given as a free-will love gift unto the Lord. The Word of God encourages us to grow in the grace of giving; and although the amount of the tithe always remains a ten percent gift of our incomes, offerings are unlimited sums that we should be giving. Offerings provide the opportunity to grow in liberality, generosity, faith and sacrifice.

Because God is a giver, He loves to see His children give. Second Corinthians 9:7 says that "God loves a cheerful giver." Luke 6:38 says that when we give, we will prosper: "Give, and it will be given to you: good measure, pressed down, shaken together, and running over will be put into your bosom. For with the same measure that you use, it will be measured back to you."

FAITH HARVEST OFFERING

Our church celebrates an annual free-will "Faith Harvest" offering that provides an opportunity for everyone to liberally sow a financial faith-seed. Each person contributes to this offering according to his or her vision and faith. We teach the Scriptural basis of our financial giving, likening it to the sowing of seed, believing God to water the seed, bless the seed and increase the seed so that there might be a plentiful harvest. We define faith-harvest giving as "an offering given by the believer with the knowledge that this seed is sowed in faith, believing God to water it and enable it to become the full harvest of what God desires to bring into that person's life. A faith-harvest offering is a specific giving with liberality and sacrifice."

The following list of Scriptures encourages faith-harvest giving:

✝ Proverbs 11:24,25: There is one who scatters, yet increases more; and there is one who withholds more than is right, but it leads to poverty. The generous soul will be made rich, and he who waters will also be watered himself.

✝ Genesis 8:22: While the earth remains, seedtime and harvest, cold and heat, winter and summer, and day and night shall not cease.

✝ Genesis 26:12-14: Then Isaac sowed in that land, and reaped in the same year a hundredfold; and the Lord blessed him. The man began to prosper, and continued prospering until he became very prosperous; for he had possessions of flocks and possessions of herds and a great number of servants. So the Philistines envied him.

> "If we can't trust God with our money, how can we trust Him with our lives, our children and the future?"

✝ Deuteronomy 16:17: Every man shall give as he is able, according to the blessing of the LORD your God which He has given you.

✝ Deuteronomy 28:8: The Lord will command the blessing on you in your storehouses and in all to which you set your hand, and He will bless you in the land which the Lord your God is giving you.

✝ Proverbs 10:22: The blessing of the Lord makes one rich, and He adds no sorrow with it.

✝ Ecclesiastes 11:1: Cast your bread upon the waters, for you will find it after many days.

✝ Isaiah 60:5: Then you shall see and become radiant, and your heart shall swell with joy; because the abundance of the sea shall be turned to you, the wealth of the Gentiles shall come to you.

✝ Ezekiel 44:30: The best of all first fruits of any kind, and every sacrifice of any kind from all your sacrifices, shall be the priest's; also you shall give to the priest the first of your ground meal, to cause a blessing to rest on your house.

I learned a lot about giving and receiving from the Lord while I was pastoring in Eugene. We were establishing the church, buying property, building buildings, sending missionaries, creating a budget for our staff—confronting those first financial steps that every new church encounters. One of my greatest lessons occurred when we had a fundraiser in order to purchase the property for our first building. A widow in our church named Mae Ricks approached me during the offering to give me a large sum of money that she had saved. With tears streaming down her face, this dear faithful widow said that she wanted to be the first to plant a faith-seed offering into our vision.

My initial response was, "No, Mae, I can't take this from you. I cannot take that kind of money from a widow." Her words became the basis for a great lesson in how to respond to someone who is walking in faith—which, by the way, I wasn't doing at that point.

She replied, "Please don't rob me of the blessing that I will receive as I sacrificially give, even if you don't fully understand this principle. Please don't rob me." Her pleading with me in that emotional situation left a lifelong impact on my spirit. I realized that as a widow, she had learned to put her faith in God as her provider in a way that I had yet to understand. We received her gift, and

God did not let her down. Mae was taken care of and greatly blessed in the years to come—and so was our church as we learned the principle of sacrificial giving.

✝ A FAITH-HARVEST OFFERING IS GIVEN OUT OF A WILLING HEART

A faith-harvest offering is given out of a willing heart (see Exod. 25:2; Ezra 1:4; Ps. 96:8; 35:5; 110:3). The word "willing" implies "openhanded, to be liberal, to give spontaneously, to give without hesitation." As the Holy Spirit stirs the believers, faith-harvest giving becomes real to every individual as he or she determines in his or her own heart. Exodus 35:21 says, "Then everyone came whose heart was stirred, and everyone whose spirit was willing, and they brought the Lord's offering for the work of the tabernacle of meeting, for all its service, and for the holy garments."

✝ THE FAITH-HARVEST OFFERING IS GIVEN OUT OF A BELIEVER'S SPECIAL TREASURE

The giver gives out of his or her own personal, special treasure. First Chronicles 29:3 says, "Moreover, because I have set my affection on the house of my God, I have given to the house of my God, over and above all that I have prepared for the holy house, my own special treasure of gold and silver." We start with what we have, giving out of our own resources. The Lord honors and responds to sacrificial giving. There are times when our faith is stirred, and we give beyond our normal sacrificial giving—we give beyond our own ability. Second Corinthians 8:3 confirms this kind of giving: "For I bear witness that according to their ability, yes, and beyond their ability, they were freely willing."

Start with a sacrifice of something in your hands; a precious gift is one that means something special to you. Jesus affirmed a poor widow who gave all that she had, everything in this world (see Mark 12:41-44). We would undoubtedly have tried to stop her, to rationalize with her and redirect her thinking. Not Jesus. He simply affirmed her attitude of faith and sacrifice and used it to instruct His own disciples.

If we expect to see a supernatural flow of finances, we must release a supernatural sacrifice. We should encourage liberal and sacrificial giving beyond the tithe. Second Corinthians 9:6 cautions that "He who sows sparingly will also reap sparingly, and he who sows bountifully will also reap bountifully." Let us be encouraged and encourage others to sow seed liberally, not sparingly. Seed must be planted in order to reap a harvest; giving is the seeding for our miracles which God, our source, will multiply.

Move beyond what is in your hand and believe for the blessing of God upon your future. How big of a field do you see? What are you believing God to do with your dreams, your vision, your job, your business and your personal world? How much faith for supernatural growth do you have in that seed? Determine that you will plant the seed and that God will move your mountain. When a farmer scatters seed, it appears as though he is wasting seed as he tosses handfuls in every direction. But the more seed he throws, the more harvest he reaps!

The following is another list of great faith-seed Scriptures to consider:

- ‡ Genesis 8:22: While the earth remains, seedtime and harvest, cold and heat, winter and summer, and day and night shall not cease.
- ‡ Psalm 126:6: He who continually goes forth weeping, bearing seed for sowing, shall doubtless come again with rejoicing, bringing his sheaves with him.
- ‡ Matthew 17:20: So Jesus said to them, "Because of your unbelief; for assuredly, I say to you, if you have faith as a mustard seed, you will say to this mountain, 'Move from here to there,' and it will move; and nothing will be impossible for you."
- ‡ Galatians 6:9: And let us not grow weary while doing good, for in due season we shall reap if we do not lose heart.
- ‡ Hebrews 11:6: But without faith it is impossible to please Him, for he who comes to God must believe that He is, and that He is a rewarder of those who diligently seek Him.

"When a farmer scatters seed, it appears as though he is wasting seed as he tosses handfuls in every direction. But the more seed he throws, the more harvest he reaps!"

Financial giving is a spiritual matter that involves the heart; it shows our spiritual capacity for faith in God and His invisible powers. Giving reflects our value system, our priorities and our disciplines. Seeing God work in the things of the material world will enlarge faith for the invisible world, the kingdom of God.

The following testimonies shared with our congregation by two faith-harvest seed sowers, people who are living a life of liberal giving, will show how God uses our financial giving to increasing our faith-"fullness" in other areas of our lives.

FIRST GIVER

"We need to recognize, develop and honor the gift of giving in our congregation. We need to develop a passion for giving sacrificially with a spirit of faith. Our giving should be done with a childlike faith because we cannot reason it or calculate it, use logic, figure it out like any other investment or humanize it.

"We must give regardless of expected blessings coming our way. God's promises are true, but there needs to come a purity in our giving so that we freely give it all, even if God returns nothing. This is unconditional giving.

"There are times when we will feel the pain of not being able to give and not being in a position to bless liberally. That's okay because there are times and seasons in receiving and giving. Don't wait to give until you have that big lump sum of money. Start small, expecting those seeds to produce more. Start now. Don't put off the spirit of faith."

SECOND GIVER

"My wife and I have always tithed; it's never been an issue with us. We have also given sacrificially, sacrificing something to contribute to a Kingdom purpose. We've emptied our savings account, gone without a vacation, sold or given something of value. It was a sacrifice, but we were glad to do it because of all the Lord has done for us.

"For us, faith giving meant going a step beyond. When we gave sacrificially, we didn't risk anything—we simply did without something we enjoyed. Faith giving took us to a level of giving that impacted our lifestyle. We don't give our rent money or go in debt or risk our child's education, but we have given so deeply that it hurts, and we've put a 'spending freeze' on our personal budget. Faith-harvest offering has impacted our lives, and yet the spiritual impact on our personal lives and on our family has far exceeded any impact on our budget or finances."

SEEDTIME AND HARVEST

Even the largest fruit trees started with the obedient act of planting seed. If we want to see fruitful financial harvests, we must become seed sowers like the famous Johnny Appleseed of old.

Born John Chapman in Massachusetts during the early 1800s, John moved to Pennsylvania as a young man to work at a cider mill. "It was while he was working at that cider mill that John Chapman became possessed with an idea and a vision that gripped his heart and became more influential in preparing the way for the future of a nation than he could ever have dreamed. One obvious by-product of work at the cider mill was seeds—piles and piles of apple seeds, left over from the pressing process. They formed mounds which seemed useless to most. But one man saw their virtue, and these seeds became central to the vision which captivated John Chapman. He filled large bags with the seeds, quit his job and headed west, planting seeds as he went.

"He was gripped with the vision of westward expansion but he knew that as the settlers headed West, they would find little to sustain themselves in their travels, so all along the trails he planted the seeds, some in random places, some in orchards. He did it with the expectation that when the pioneers would follow, fruit would be available—waiting for them. A man of faith, he not only planted seeds in the ground, but he also carried spiritual seeds that he planted in the hearts of men and women. He was a man with a vision for the future, seeing tomorrow's possibilities for a fledgling country and sowing into its future as an act of faith. Some thought him insane, 'But the world will probably always think that those who give their lives to a vision—who plant for the future—are not worthy of society's approval.' Some thought him to be 'one among key men who paved the way to what became a great nation.'" [2]

Gate-Church believers plant the seeds and trust God for the harvest!

NOTES

1. S. R. Hirsch, *The Pentateuch* (Brooklyn, N.Y.: Judaica Press, 1998), p. 43.

2. Jack Hayford, *The Key to Everything* (Orlando, Fla.: Creation House, 1993), pp. 119-121.

"Then he dreamed, and behold, a ladder was set up on the earth, and its top reached to heaven; and there the angels of God were ascending and descending on it." Genesis 28:12

Jesus answered and said to him, "Because I said to you, 'I saw you under the fig tree,' do you believe? You will see greater things than these." And He said to him, "Most assuredly, I say to you, hereafter you shall see heaven open, and the angels of God ascending and descending upon the Son of Man." John 1:50,51

The Gate Church Opens the Gate of Healing and Miracles

It is Jesus who refers to Genesis 28:12. In John 1:50,51, Jesus marks Nathaniel as the first believer by asking, "Do you believe?" And Jesus goes on to tell Nathaniel that he will be given far deeper grounds for his belief than Jesus' foreknowledge of himself as the one who was sitting under the fig tree. Jesus states that as Nathaniel's ministry unfolds, he will see mighty works, "greater things" and wondrous surprises, revealing the glory of God.

Seeing these "greater things" with the physical eye will open the door to eternal realities through Jesus. The language in John 1:50,51 is reminiscent of Jacob's dream of a ladder that reached from earth to heaven with angels ascending and descending as the Lord stood "above it," affirming again that He was the God of Jacob's forefathers and would fulfill all the promises made to them. Jacob called this an "awesome place, the house of God and the gate of heaven."

The time has now come when all the promises are made possible through Christ; all grace is fulfilled in Him. Jesus truly is the Builder of the house of God, the place of divine encounter with the presence of God—not only for Nathaniel and Philip and those first disciples, but for all who believe in Him. To them, He has become the very gate of heaven, for through the life and ministry of the Word made flesh (see John 1:14), all the resources of heaven are available to all believers.

BELIEVING IS SEEING

Nathaniel received a promise: "you shall see greater things than these" (v. 50). The Gate Church is also recipient of this promise. We are living in the age of prophetic fulfillment. Christ as the Ladder connecting heaven and earth has been established by His work on the cross. All of heaven's resources are available to the church through Christ by faith. The "greater things" have a proper fulfillment in the gradual manifestation of Christ's person and character, which lay unrevealed to the world as of yet. The church must believe first and then see the full manifestation of God's power and glory upon the earth today. The world claims that "seeing is believing," which is true in regard to natural things, but in regard to God and spiritual truths, "believing is seeing."

The principles set forth by Christ in this passage from John 1:50,51 are foundational principles of faith and prayer. The principle of seeing and believing for "greater things" encourages us in new pursuits of faith, stretching us and moving us forward. This reaching for the greater things protects the church from the ever-present enemy of stagnation. The promise is that you shall see the ladder again with the angels moving upon it in their errands of mercy. The ladder is Christ with its foot on earth and its top in the heavens. As the Gate Church establishes a clear picture of who Christ is, we see that His power and His authority are for now, His ladder is a now ladder.

> The world claims that "seeing is believing," which is true in regard to natural things, but in regard to God and spiritual truths, "believing is seeing."

THE LADDER RESTORED

Every Gate Church must establish the ladder again—the ladder of open heavens, supernatural activity, the ministry of healing and miracles. Wherever Christ went, the ladder was set up and the heavens were opened so that healings and miracles occurred.

What we commonly call miracles were sometimes in the Scriptures termed "wonders" (see Matt. 24:24; Acts 14:3; Rom. 15:19; Heb. 2:4), "signs" (see John 2:11; Rev. 13:13), "powers" (see Mark 6:14) and "works" (see John 14:12). The miracles did cause astonishment and were believed to be a sign, a token and an indication of the near presence of God. Miracles are signs and pledges of something more than and beyond themselves, valuable not so much for what they are as for what they indicate about the grace and the power of the doer. Often the miracles in Scripture are seals of power attributed to the person who accomplishes them (see Mark 16:20; Acts 14:3; Heb. 2:4), legitimizing that person's claim to be a messenger from God. Miracles are the "wonderful works" or the "mighty works" of Christ, both in the past and in the now (see Matt. 11:20; Mark 6:14; Luke 10:13; Acts 2:22; Gal. 3:5).

The Gate Church believes for "greater works," greater things for today's world. The Gate-Church confession should be the same as Job's in Job 42:2: "I know that You can do everything, and that no purpose of Yours can be withheld from You."

THE MIRACLES OF CHRIST TODAY

Most miracles recorded in the Gospels were miracles of healing and are signs to us of Jesus' power to heal our sin-sick world. Both in Christ's day and today, the needs people have are very different; everyone's body, spirit and soul has been affected differently by the Fall which ushered in the entrance of sin and sickness. When Christ healed people, there were some who required life itself; others needed sight or hearing or power or cleansing. Some needed to be set right internally; others had diseases that ate away their flesh. Still many others suffered from mental conditions. All of these cases were equally simple to the One who created us. And yet, the act of power cost Jesus much: He could feel the "virtue" go out from Him (Mark 5:30; Luke 6:19; 8:46, KJV). The Gate Church must have the virtue in order for the virtue to flow out to a tormented world.

On several occasions, before the Lord Jesus worked the miracle, He commanded those who needed a cure to do something themselves. If they had not done the simple things, He would not have done the greater!

The Gate Church must do the simple things, such as preach the life of Christ in order to show His power to heal, read healing Scriptures to the church, and pray for the sick and diseased in every service. Can we commit to doing the simple things? The man with the withered hand was told to stretch forth his hand (see Mark 3:3-5). He was told to do the very thing that had been impossible. As he obeyed, the healing came. We, the leaders of the church, need to stretch forth our hands. We need to move toward the ministry of releasing healing and miracles. We need to do the simple first: preach, teach, pray.

To move forward, however, we must also understand the past. Let's ask ourselves, *What have been the hindrances to the ladder being built in every church with opened heavens and a "greater than these things" attitude?*

Within the past several decades, healing and miracles as a present-day reality have been sought after by people believing for the release of the supernatural. And yet, during the twentieth century, the church suffered with a faulty theology concerning healing and miracles. Generally speaking, a wide segment of mainline Christianity believed that the age of miracles had ceased with the apostolic period, and that there was no present need for signs, wonders, healing and miracles. They embraced the belief that God no longer heals people as He did in the days of Christ.

What a short, limited and erroneous viewpoint that is! I lament the fact that today's church has seemingly descended to the level of the natural in preaching, in soul winning, in doing church and, more specifically, in believing for healing. The gifts of the Spirit have been supplanted by the arts of logic and rhetoric when God wants the miraculous to function in His church powerfully and consistently. God desires a full release of His power through His people, now, today, in your life and mine, in your church and my church. I seek to promote biblically and righteously a higher interest and a spiritual pursuit of genuine, authentic, biblical and supernatural healings and miracles in the church of the twenty-first century.

"The Gate Church must have the virtue in order for the virtue to flow out to a tormented world."

Healing and gift-based ministry should be a normal and biblical part of the life of faith in Christ. Healing prayer is part of the normal Christian life. It should not be elevated above any other ministry in the community of faith, nor should it be undervalued. Rather, it should be kept in proper balance. Healing is simply a normal aspect of what it means to live under the reign of God.

HINDRANCES TO UNLEASHING THE SUPERNATURAL

Why is today's church experiencing such difficulty in seeing a breakthrough in its healing ministry? Many answers are possible, but let me offer seven basic hindrances to a full release of the supernatural:

1. There has been and remains today a strong academic community of people who resist the healing ministry as an unbiblical, erroneous ministry.

2. There has been and remains today extremists, frauds and charlatans who have caused a reproach to be upon the healing ministry.

3. There has been and remains today many extreme practices within Pentecostal groups that have caused reactions, questions and denial of the healing ministry.

4. There has been very little strong, biblical, theological preaching on healing from the pulpit in most churches, thus a spirit of faith or expectation has not been created for the healing ministry to operate within the church today.

5. There has been and still seems to be a suppressed attitude toward expectation for the supernatural. Perhaps believers are afraid to expect much from God because they have been disappointed so many times in the past. This is the stronghold of no expectation.

6. There has been and remains today a spiritual war fought within the context of natural man, a war that fights against God's will, God's best and God's plan for man—a war over humankind's spirit, soul and body.

7. There has been and remains today a spiritual resistance to healing, signs and wonders because throughout Scripture and history the miraculous was a main gateway to seeing the harvest of souls.

In the years preceding the Civil War, one of America's leading theologians, Horace Bushnell, summed up the spiritual dilemma of his day and, in so doing, seems to describe our own:

Bushnell observed that Christian souls were falling into "a stupor of intellectual fatality....Prayer becomes a kind of dumb-bell exercise, good as exercise, but never to be answered. The Word is good to be exegetically handled, but there is no light of interpretation in souls, more immediate; all truth is to be second-hand truth, never a vital beam of God's own light....Expectation is gone—God is too far off, too much imprisoned by laws, to allow expectation from Him. The Christian world has been gravitating, visibly, more and more, toward this vanishing point of faith, for whole centuries, and especially since the Modern Era began to shape the thoughts of men by only scientific methods. Religion has fallen into the domain of the mere understanding, and so it has become a kind of wisdom to not believe much, therefore to expect as little."[1]

Let Him [God] now break forth in miracle and holy gifts, let it be seen that He is still the living God, in the midst of His dead people, and they will be quickened to a resurrection by the sight. Now they see that God can do something still, and has His liberty. He can hear prayers, He can help them triumph in dark hours, their bosom-sins He can help them master, all His promises in the Scripture He can fulfill, and they go to Him with great expectations. They see, in these gifts, that the Scripture stands, that the graces and works, and holy fruits of the apostolic ages, are also for them. It is as if they had now a proof experimental of the resources embodied in the Christian plan. The living God, immediately revealed, and not historically only, begets a feeling of present life and power, and religion is no more a tradition, a second-hand light, but a grace of God unto salvation, operative now.[2]

BIBLICAL SCHOLARS ON HEALING AND MIRACLES

Other prominent biblical scholars and Early Church fathers have also encouraged a correct biblical theology about healings and miracles. The following quotes deserve careful consideration:

✝ "F. F. Bruce, the well-known evangelical British New Testament scholar, considered Jesus' healing ministry an integral part of the message Jesus preached: 'While the miracles served as signs, they were not performed in order to be signs. They were as much a part and parcel of Jesus' ministry as was his preaching—not...seals affixed to the document to certify its genuineness but an integral element in the very text of the document.'" [3]

✝ "The British New Testament scholar, Alan Richardson, points out that Jesus' healing ministry was a necessary concomitant of His preaching: 'The working of miracles is a part of the proclamation of the kingdom of God, not an end in itself. Similarly, the sin of Chorazin and Bethsaida [Mat. 11:21; Lk. 10:13] is spiritual blindness; they do not accept the preaching of the kingdom of God or understand the miracles were its inevitable concomitants... Can we interpret the remarkable connection which this saying establishes between the miracles and repentance in any other way than by understanding the miracles as the necessary concomitants of the preaching of the kingdom of God?'" [4]

✝ H. van der Loos, Dutch New Testament scholar: "The miracles were therefore not works or signs which happened for the sake of the apostles, but originated in the point at issue, viz. the proclamation of salvation by Jesus Christ and the coming of His Kingdom. They did not accompany the preaching of the gospels as incidentals, but formed an integral part of it; in the healing, as a visible function of the Kingdom of God, something that could be experienced, God's will to heal the whole of man was manifested." [5]

✝ Augustine: "Once I realized how many miracles were occurring in our own day and which were so like the miracles of old and also how wrong it would be to allow the memory of these marvels of divine power to perish from among our people. It is only two years ago that the keeping of records was begun here in Hippo, and already, at this writing, we have nearly seventy attested miracles." [6]

✝ Justin Martyr: "For numberless demoniacs throughout the whole world, and in your city, many of our Christian men exorcising them in the Name of Jesus Christ...have healed and do heal, rendering helpless and driving the possessing devils out of the men, though they could not be cured by all the other exorcists, and those who used incantations and drugs." [7]

We must have a settled conclusion that healings, miracles, signs and wonders are for today's Gate Church. God is unchangeable; He healed the sick in the past, and He will heal the sick today. Malachi 3:6 says, "For I am the Lord, I do not change." And Hebrews 13:8 reminds us that "Jesus Christ is the same yesterday, today, and forever." The Holy Spirit is the same; the same Holy Spirit who worked within Christ and the apostles is the same Holy Spirit who works in you and me.

Christ's last command, the Great Commission to the church, includes healing the sick (see Mark 16:17,18). The balanced ministry of the church is teaching, preaching and healing. Matthew 9:35 reveals, "Then Jesus went about all the cities and villages, teaching in their synagogues, preaching the gospel of the kingdom, and healing every sickness and every disease among the people." Let us be lovers of the Word of God. Let us be lovers of the lost. Let us be hungry for the healing of all people, making them whole in body, soul and spirit. Let us be like Jesus.

SCRIPTURES ON HEALING AND MIRACLES

At this point, I would like to offer some healing Scriptures that encourage us to contend for the ladder to be built in every church:

✝ Isaiah 53:5: But He was wounded for our transgressions, He was bruised for our iniquities; the chastisement for our peace was upon Him, and by His stripes we are healed.

✝ Matthew 8:16,17: When evening had come, they brought to Him many who were demon-possessed. And He cast out the spirits with a word, and healed all who were sick, that it might be fulfilled which was spoken by Isaiah the prophet, saying: "He Himself took our infirmities and bore our sicknesses."

✝ Matthew 9:28-30: And when He had come into the house, the blind men came to Him. And Jesus said to them, "Do you believe that I am able to do this?" They said to Him, "Yes, Lord." Then He touched their eyes, saying, "According to your faith let it be to you." And their eyes were opened. And Jesus sternly warned them, saying, "See that no one knows it."

✝ Mark 5:36: As soon as Jesus heard the word that was spoken, He said to the ruler of the synagogue, "Do not be afraid; only believe."

✝ Mark 5:41,42: Then He took the child by the hand, and said to her, "Talitha, cumi," which is translated, "Little girl, I say to you, arise." Immediately the girl arose and walked, for she was twelve years of age. And they were overcome with great amazement.

✝ Mark 9:23-26: Jesus said to him, "If you can believe, all things are possible to him who believes." Immediately the father of the child cried out and said with tears, "Lord, I believe; help my unbelief!" When Jesus saw that the people came running together, He rebuked the unclean spirit, saying to it, "Deaf and dumb spirit, I command you, come out of him and enter him no more!" Then the spirit cried out, convulsed him greatly, and came out of him. And he became as one dead, so that many said, "He is dead."

✝ Mark 11:24: "Therefore I say to you, whatever things you ask when you pray, believe that you receive them, and you will have them."

✝ Luke 4:18: "The Spirit of the Lord is upon Me, because He has anointed Me to preach the gospel to the poor; he has sent Me to heal the brokenhearted, to proclaim liberty to the captives and recovery of sight to the blind, to set at liberty those who are oppressed."

✝ Luke 8:50: But when Jesus heard it, He answered him, saying, "Do not be afraid; only believe, and she will be made well.

✝ John 4:48-50: Then Jesus said to him, "Unless you people see signs and wonders, you will by no means believe." The nobleman said to Him, "Sir, come down before my child dies!" Jesus said to him, "Go your way; your son lives." So the man believed the word that Jesus spoke to him, and he went his way.

✝ John 11:40-44: Jesus said to her, "Did I not say to you that if you would believe you would see the glory of God?" Then they took away the stone from the place where the dead man was lying. And Jesus lifted up His eyes and said, "Father, I thank You that You have heard Me. And I know that You always hear Me, but because of the people who are standing by I said this, that they may believe that You sent Me." Now when He had said these things, He cried with a loud voice, "Lazarus, come forth!" And he who had died came out bound hand and foot with graveclothes, and his face was wrapped with a cloth. Jesus said to them, "Loose him, and let him go."

✝ Acts 3:1-10: Now Peter and John went up together to the temple at the hour of prayer, the ninth hour. And a certain man lame from his mother's womb was carried, whom they laid daily at the gate of the temple which is called Beautiful, to ask alms from those who entered the temple; who, seeing Peter and John about to go into the temple, asked for alms. And fixing his eyes on him, with John, Peter said, "Look at us." So he gave them his attention, expecting to receive something from them. Then Peter said, "Silver and gold I do not have, but what I do have I give you: In the name of Jesus Christ of Nazareth, rise up and walk." And he took him by the right hand and lifted him up, and immediately his feet and ankle bones received strength. So he, leaping up, stood and walked and entered the temple with them—walking, leaping, and praising God. And all the people saw him walking and praising God. Then they knew that it was he who sat begging alms at the Beautiful Gate of the temple; and they were filled with wonder and amazement at what had happened to him.

✝ Acts 8:6-8: And the multitudes with one accord heeded the things spoken by Philip, hearing and seeing the miracles which he did. For unclean spirits, crying with a loud voice, came out of many who were possessed; and many who were paralyzed and lame were healed. And there was great joy in that city.

✝ Acts 9:32-43: Now it came to pass, as Peter went through all parts of the country, that he also came down to the saints who dwelt in Lydda. There he found a certain man named Aeneas, who had been bedridden eight years and was paralyzed. And Peter said to him, "Aeneas, Jesus the Christ heals you. Arise and make your bed." Then he arose immediately. So all who dwelt at Lydda and Sharon saw him and turned to the Lord. At Joppa there was a certain disciple named Tabitha, which is translated Dorcas. This woman was full of good works and charitable deeds which she did. But it happened in those days that she became sick and died. When they had washed her, they laid her in an upper room. And since Lydda was near Joppa, and the disciples had heard that Peter was there, they sent two men to him, imploring him not to delay in coming to them. Then Peter arose and went with them. When he had come, they brought him to the upper room. And all the widows stood by him weeping, showing the tunics and garments which Dorcas had made while she was with them. But Peter put them all out, and knelt down and prayed. And turning to the body he said, "Tabitha, arise." And she opened her eyes, and when she saw Peter she sat up. Then he gave her his hand and lifted her up; and when he had called the saints and widows, he presented her alive. And it became known throughout all Joppa, and many believed on the Lord. So it was that he stayed many days in Joppa with Simon, a tanner.

‡ Acts 4:12-16: Nor is there salvation in any other, for there is no other name under heaven given among men by which we must be saved. Now when they saw the boldness of Peter and John, and perceived that they were uneducated and untrained men, they marveled. And they realized that they had been with Jesus. And seeing the man who had been healed standing with them, they could say nothing against it. But when they had commanded them to go aside out of the council, they conferred among themselves, saying, "What shall we do to these men? For, indeed, that a notable miracle has been done through them is evident to all who dwell in Jerusalem, and we cannot deny it."

‡ Acts 14:8-12: And in Lystra a certain man without strength in his feet was sitting, a cripple from his mother's womb, who had never walked. This man heard Paul speaking. Paul, observing him intently and seeing that he had faith to be healed, said with a loud

voice, "Stand up straight on your feet!" And he leaped and walked. Now when the people saw what Paul had done, they raised their voices, saying in the Lycaonian language, "The gods have come down to us in the likeness of men!" And Barnabas they called Zeus, and Paul, Hermes, because he was the chief speaker.

✝ Acts 19:11,12: Now God worked unusual miracles by the hands of Paul, so that even handkerchiefs or aprons were brought from his body to the sick, and the diseases left them and the evil spirits went out of them.

✝ Romans 15:18,19: For I will not dare to speak of any of those things which Christ has not accomplished through me, in word and deed, to make the Gentiles obedient—in mighty signs and wonders, by the power of the Spirit of God, so that from Jerusalem and round about to Illyricum I have fully preached the gospel of Christ.

✝ 1 Corinthians 2:4,5: And my speech and my preaching were not with persuasive words of human wisdom, but in demonstration of the Spirit and of power, that your faith should not be in the wisdom of men but in the power of God.

✝ 1 Corinthians 4:20: For the kingdom of God is not in word but in power.

✝ 2 Corinthians 12:12: Truly the signs of an apostle were accomplished among you with all perseverance, in signs and wonders and mighty deeds.

✝ Ephesians 1:19,20: And what is the exceeding greatness of His power toward us who believe, according to the working of His mighty power which He worked in Christ when He raised Him from the dead and seated Him at His right hand in the heavenly places.

✝ 1 Thessalonians 1:5: For our gospel did not come to you in word only, but also in power, and in the Holy Spirit and in much assurance, as you know what kind of men we were among you for your sake.

REMOVING UNBELIEF FROM BELIEVERS IN THE GATE CHURCH

The Gate Church must become a place of faith, believing in the promise of "greater things than these." The church must change the faith level by changing what I call the "unbelieving believers" into "believing believers." Unbelieving believers are believers who have mental unbelief, a wavering doubt influenced by outward circumstances; they rely on feelings, emotions, moods and what they can see and understand. Mark 9:24 echoes the cry of an unbelieving believer: "Lord, I believe; help my unbelief!"

Emotional unbelief is a religious mental rejection of things not seen, understood or experienced. It is a habit of negative response, a "knowledge" faith only (see Matt. 13:53-58; Mark 16:14; Rom. 4:20). This habit of negative response is like a cable: A person weaves a thread every day until it is so strong that he or she cannot break it. The result: hardened unbelief—a settled, deepseated unbelief that has experienced failures and disappointments with wrong responses to God, allowing doubting, questioning, blaming God and ultimately rejecting Him (see Job 17:7; Heb. 3:12,13; 3:15,18,19).

In Scripture, a believer is not a person who holds a certain set of beliefs about God as if they were merely reverential convictions. A true believer has responded to the gospel message by trusting in Jesus, His Word and His work on Calvary. A true believer joins the company of believers in living out the life of believing in the invisible, the unexplainable, and doing the impossible. He or she is convinced; thus, no further proof is needed. The act of examining and weighing has been concluded, and a firm conviction and unshakable certainty has been attained.

The true believer trusts in and relies upon God and His Word with confidence, in spite of the atmosphere, circumstance or crisis. The true believer trusts and believes with complete confidence in the character and motives of God to fulfill His promises, realizing that at times He works mysteriously. The true believer is a person of faith, a person whose faith is fastened on God as One who, by His nature, is the sole certain and sure reality in this life.

God is faithful and unchanging, established in eternity. Because He is who He is, we can commit our-

> *"Unbelieving believers are believers who have mental unbelief, a wavering doubt influenced by outward circumstances; they rely on feelings, emotions, moods and what they can see and understand."*

selves to Him. Our faith has validity because God Himself is utterly faithful and trustworthy (see Ps. 56:11; 62:8; Prov. 3:5; Heb. 11:33-40).

The Gate Church establishes a ladder of faith, faith in God as the One who does the things we humans cannot do—heal the sick, raise the dead, calm the storms. As a Gate Church in the making, we are diligently pursuing the ministry of healing and miracles so that they will be consistently released in our midst. We have established some practical outworkings of our faith in God's ability to heal and perform miracles. They include:

✝ Brass Bowl: Near our altar is a small table with a brass bowl on it. People fill out prayer cards with healing needs and place them in this bowl. During the service, we publicly pray for all healing requests in that brass bowl.

✝ Ministry Prayer Teams: We have ministry prayer teams trained in the area of praying for the sick. These ministry teams pray for the sick at the beginning of each service during our opening-service intercessory-prayer time.

✝ Prayer Center: Our Prayer Center is open seven days a week; there, people pray all hours of the day and night. All healing requests are taken to the Prayer Center so that they receive many hours of interceding prayer. We also have a specific night each week when those in need of healing come to the Prayer Center for prayer.

✝ Day of Healing and Prayer: One Saturday each month is devoted to a day of healing and prayer. From 9:00 A.M. until 4:00 P.M., we pray over individuals who are in need of healing. Our time together includes worship, reading Scripture, asking prayer teams to pray over each person individually, corporate prayer, reading prayers of healing together in unity, and more.

Someone once said that faith is like the bumblebee: dead to doubts, dumb to discouragement and blind to impossibilities. Military leaders during World War II heralded the following message about the bumblebee:

By all known laws that can be proved on paper and in the wind tunnel, the bumblebee cannot fly. The size of its wings in relation to its body, according to aeronautical and mathematical science, simply means that it cannot fly. It is an impossibility. But, of course, the bumblebee doesn't know about these laws so it goes ahead and flies anyway.

The buzz word in the Gate Church is "believe"—with God all things are possible!

NOTES

1. Paul G. Chappell, *Great Things He Hath Done: Origins of the Divine Healing Movement in America,* (taken from the unpublished manuscript), p. 10.

2. Horace Bushnell, *The Nature and the Supernatural as Together Constituting the One System of God* (London: Alexander Strahan, originally published 1858), p. 6.

3. Gary S. Greig, ed., *The Kingdom and the Power* (Ventura, Calif.: Regal Books, 1993), p. 24.

4. Ibid., p. 25.

5. Ibid., p. 26.

6. Michael L. Brown, *Israel's Divine Healer* (Grand Rapids: Zondervan Publishing, 1995), p. 64.

7. Ibid., p. 63.

"So He drove out the man; and He placed cherubim at the east of the garden of Eden, and a flaming sword which turned every way, to guard the way to the tree of life." Genesis 3:24

Gatekeepers: Leaders of Gate Churches

We now move from the making of a Gate Church to the making of a Gate Leader, a gatekeeper, the one who has the responsibility to guard the entryway. As a gatekeeper, the Gate Leader stands at the entrance with a commitment to keep out what God rejects and to guard within all that God has given. Proverbs 8:34 puts it this way: "Blessed is the man who listens to me, watching daily at the gates, waiting at the posts of my doors." The gatekeeper is a watchman for the city, a protector, a leader with discernment and wisdom to act upon what is perceived to be harmful.

The gatekeeper sits among the elders of the city, "known in the gates, when he sits among the elders of the land" (Prov. 31:23). The gatekeeper is a leader with authority, integrity, wisdom, judgment and wise counsel—a just leader whom the whole city trusts (see Deut. 21:19; 22:15,24; 25:7). In the Old Testament, "gates" became a synonym for power because of their supportive strength and importance to the city. Gates represented those who held leadership and government positions, people of significance (see Ruth 4:10,11).

The gates of our churches can be either entry points of life or entry points of destruction (see Matt. 7:13,14). The gatekeeper is the primary leader for keeping the Gate Church pure and powerful, refusing to allow the destructive forces of institutionalism, cultural mixture, compromise, moral decay or spiritual decay. The gatekeeper is committed to keeping the gate with a flaming sword that turns every way to guard the way of life (see Gen. 3:24).

The gatekeeper therefore is the doorkeeper, a keeper of sacred things. The word "keeper" in Hebrew is *shamar* which means to hedge about, guard, to protect, to have charge of something, to keep watch, to observe, to be on one's guard, to take heed, beware. The keepers were stationed at the entry points of the city, the temple or the makeshift camps. They were the guards stationed at guardposts. If necessary, they would give their lives to keep their posts. Their position carried great responsibility and great honor.

RESTORING GATE LEADERS
TO THEIR POSTS

The enemy has overcome and removed many great gatekeepers because he knows that they are of grave importance to the success of the Gate Church. Our enemy is continually strategizing to ensnare and eventually destroy the leaders of Gate Churches. In Judges 16:2, we discover the way that Samson's enemies strategized to ensnare him: "When the Gazites were told, 'Samson has come here!' they surrounded the place and lay in wait for him all night at the gate of the city. They were quiet all night, saying, 'In the morning, when it is daylight, we will kill him.'" The enemy has patience. He will lie in wait all night, waiting for the opportune moment to spiritually wound and kill the gatekeepers of God's church.

Lamentations 5:14 sadly reports that "the elders have ceased gathering at the gate, and the young men from their music." Like the Gate Leaders in Israel, Gate Leaders today have ceased to gather at the gates because of discouragement, pain, frustration, a desire to give up and satanic hindrances. All of these things are used to force the leader to move away from the gate of responsibility.

Lamentations 2:9 says that "her gates have sunk into the ground; he has destroyed and broken her bars. Her king and her princes are among the nations; the Law is no more, and her prophets find no vision from the Lord." Is this a description of some Gate Churches from the past? The gates have sunk into the ground, the bars of the gate have been destroyed, the teaching of the law has ceased, and there is no prophetic vision from the Lord. The Gate Church has ceased to be a place where God's presence and His power are experienced; it has ceased to be a place where His voice is clear and where His promises are fulfilled.

The Lord wants to restore discouraged Gate-Church leaders in the calling upon their lives, back to the place of power and authority found in the Holy Spirit. Are you a Gate-Church leader who is in need of a partial or maybe even full restoration? Have you laid down your weapons of war? Have you given up on the vision God gave and confirmed to you again and again? Has the enemy slowly removed you as the gatekeeper and found easy access into your church? If so, today is the day to stop the destruction and stand your ground, take back your place of authority and leadership. God is in the restoration business!

RESTORING GATE LEADERS WHO HAVE BEEN OVERTHROWN

In Judges 9:40, we read that "Abimelech chased him, and he fled from him; and many fell wounded, to the very entrance of the gate." The Abimelech of our day could be likened to the many snares the leader faces within his own fallen culture. The word "overthrow" means to be overwhelmed, cast down or forced down. The enemy will use many trivial things to overwhelm the heart of the Gate Church.

Financial discouragement is one of the stones our Abimelech hurls at us all the time. Falling short of the budget can become a consistent pressure. We wonder: Where is the money? Why do the people withhold the tithe? Is there something wrong with the church, with me, with our vision? Are you overwhelmed by building payments, staff salaries, missions, youth workers? Overwhelmed by the needs of the poor? Have you lost your faith in God's ability to provide in all seasons for all things? Have you allowed a sense of despair and discouragement? Are you overwhelmed by the moral decay of our culture and the constant war within the church to compromise? Have you become discouraged with the number of young people that are losing the battle of moral purity, with the numerous marriages suffering and losing the battle to maintain their vows, with leaders resigning because the pressure has finally snapped something in their homes? Overwhelmed! Are you feeling overwhelmed with my description of being overwhelmed?

We need the grace of God to visit us right now. When we are in an overwhelmed state of mind, the Holy Spirit desires to overshadow us and fill us again. Remember the words of the apostle Paul when he was overwhelmed:

✝ 2 Cor. 4:8-12: We are hard pressed on every side, yet not crushed; we are perplexed, but not in despair; persecuted, but not forsaken; struck down, but not destroyed—always carrying about in the body the dying of the Lord Jesus, that the life of Jesus also may be manifested in our body. For we who live are always delivered to death for Jesus' sake, that the life of Jesus also may be manifested in our mortal flesh. So then death is working in us, but life in you.

Notice Paul's "come back" statements: yet not crushed, not in despair, not forsaken, not destroyed. Put your life and ministry in a biblical context to gain a biblical perspective. God will never forsake you, never crush you or destroy you. God is for you; God is on your side. God will strengthen your spirit, even in the darkest hours when everything is falling apart. Paul states the Gate Leader's attitude in 2 Corinthians 4:13: "And since we have the same spirit of faith, according to what is written, 'I believed and therefore I spoke,' we also believe and therefore speak."

We have the spirit of faith through the spirit of grace that enables us to be strong in the power of His might. We can draw on God's grace so that "we do not *lose heart.* Even though our outward man is perishing, yet the inward man is being renewed day by day" (2 Cor. 4:16, italics added). Regaining heart is a first step toward regaining your position at the gate. Do you feel a little stirring, a little hope, a little faith, a maybe or a might or a could it be? Allow hope to arise within you. Proverbs 18:14 warns that "the spirit of a man will sustain him in sickness, but who can bear a broken spirit?"

You can choose to allow God to heal your wounded heart and your broken spirit. In Psalms 109:22, we read about the wounded heart: "For I am poor and needy, and my heart is wounded within me." The word "wound" suggests being pierced through as though having been shot by an arrow. Choose to yank out the arrow of hopelessness; fill the wound with words of life. Then, lift your shield of faith to gain your heart for leadership once again. God only allows pressures to teach us about His grace and to release more of His grace upon our lives. Whatever the circumstances, choose now to be restored to your gate. Choose to receive healing for your wounded heart. Choose to confess the confessions of the apostle Paul from 2 Corinthians 4:8-15. Choose life!

RESTORING GATE LEADERS WHO HAVE BEEN SNARED BY DISLOYAL LEADERS

Absalom sits by the gate in many Gate Churches. Second Samuel 15:2 illustrates how "Absalom would rise early and stand beside the way to the gate. So it was, whenever anyone who had a lawsuit came to the king for a decision, that Absalom would call to him and say, 'What city are you from?' And he would say, 'Your servant is from such and such a tribe of Israel.'" Some Gate-Church leaders don't detect this Absalom spirit until it is too late, or after the damage is already done.

Overseeing pastors as well as those who are part of the leadership team will not only be faced with the temptation to be disloyal but also with working with disloyal people. Disloyalty hurts much worse when it comes from someone you have trusted, someone you have been close to and have depended upon. Maybe it's your first disciple or your first staff leader; maybe it's your closest friend, or the one you have loved the most.

The name Absalom has become synonymous with disloyalty in most Christian circles. How many children have you heard of who are named Absalom? It is not a compliment or a name of honor today. Originally it was intended to be an honorable name and meant "father of peace" (see 2 Sam. 3:3). Absalom was to be a peacemaker, a bridge builder, one who brought people together and did not separate them. Absalom was of royal descent on both sides and was the obvious heir apparent, the favorite choice of his father. Gifted with remarkable physical magnetism (see 2 Sam. 14:25), he had a commanding presence, natural dignity and extraordinary graces. He was a winner! He also possessed a charm of eloquence and persuasiveness that easily won him the heart of people and leaders. People felt that in Absalom, they had a God-sent champion and a person who cared about their problems more than the all-too-busy King David who had to run the affairs of the kingdom.

Yet Absalom had a traitorous nature. He murdered his own brother and skillfully planned the dethroning of his own father (see 2 Sam. 13:29; 15:2,3,13,14). Brilliant in his beginnings, Absalom was cunning and crafty in his dealings. A man with so many great gifts, he ended in sorrow and tragedy, buried like a dog in a pit in the woods. Hardly a kingly ending. Disloyalty ruined his life in every way. Disloyalty ruined his love for his father and caused him to use and discard people. Disloyalty drove him to only see and do what was best for himself and no one else.

Have you been wounded by an Absalom? We've all encountered our Absaloms at one time or another. Is it disheartening? Yes. The greater the love, the greater the hurt. The more we have trusted and believed, the more we are bewildered and shamed. You will recover from your Absaloms. You will recover your heart of trust and love for young and old leaders alike. If you are to be a Gate Leader, you cannot stand in the gate by yourself. You must risk loving other leaders, making covenant, allowing your life to be intertwined with theirs. There is no other way. Let your guard down, don't withdraw anymore, confess your need to others.

Moses had his Korah, Dathan and Abiram who influenced 250 of his best leaders to rise up against him by questioning his motives and accusing him of pride and wrong ambitions (see Num. 16:1-10). These were men who had been called to be gatekeepers (see 1 Chron. 9:19), yet they stood in the gate with a wrong spirit and were seduced by the enemy of their souls.

These sowers of discord and disloyalty will be removed by the sovereign hand of God. God loves His church, and God loves his leaders. He will not allow disloyal leaders to continue without His divine intervention. As a Gate Leader, I resist the spirit of disloyalty, and I resist my reaction to distance myself from the leaders and people with whom I serve. People need to belong, not just positionally, but also spiritually and relationally. Gate Leaders must without hesitation and without reserve give their lives to those they serve. The willingness to lay down your life and be open is the bond of love that strengthens the leadership team.

Mark 10: 45 tells us that "even the Son of Man did not come to be served, but to serve, and to give His life a ransom for many." Gate-Church leaders are personal, vulnerable, transparent, relational, real, softhearted, tender, emotionally whole. Someone disloyal cannot destroy anything in you if you don't stoop to that person's character flaw by becoming disloyal in your own spirit. Don't be disloyal to a disloyal person. Don't fight back by spreading rumors, bad reports or half-truths. Keep your own integrity intact. Guard your spirit and let God do the correcting and the judging. God allows tests of this kind to release more grace into our lives. The wounds and hurts of broken relationships are used to work the Cross principle more deeply into our lives and ministries (see Deut. 32:39; Job 24:14).

> *"Someone disloyal cannot destroy anything in you if you don't stoop to that person's character flaw by becoming disloyal in your own spirit. Don't be disloyal to a disloyal person."*

RESTORING GATE LEADERS WHO HAVE
BEEN GREATLY DISCOURAGED

The need to give and receive encouragement is great among all levels of God's leaders and God's people. In 2 Chronicles 32:6, we read: "Then he set military captains over the people, gathered them together to him in the open square of the city gate, and gave them encouragement." As leaders with a responsibility to stand in the gate and continually be alert, spiritually alive, prayerful, bear burdens, give words of counsel, make wise decisions and always be victorious in both attitudes and actions, we will at times need to deal with discouragement.

Discouragement comes in varying degrees: mild, strong and disabling. Most everyone has experienced the first two levels of mild discouragement or strong discouragement. Most, however, do not live in the presence of disabling discouragement. And yet, I have no doubt that the enemy loves to continually beat down the Gate Leaders—to batter, bruise and discourage them.

The word "discouragement" means "to dishearten, to depress the spirit, to lack confidence, that which destroys or abates courage, to lose heart, to be broken in pieces." The scriptural idea of discouragement is revealed in words such as "oppressed" (see 1 Sam. 12:3), "broken" (see Eccles. 12:6), "crushed" (see Amos 4:1), "bruised" (see Isa. 42:3), "struggle" (see Gen. 25:22), "fainthearted" (see Deut. 20:8; Prov. 24:10), "distress" (see 2 Cor. 6:4; 12:10), "weary" (see Gal. 6:9; 2 Thess. 3:13).

The most common causes of discouragement are personal failure, prolonged spiritual battles, continued unanswered prayer, emotional strain, physical illness, satanic fiery darts, a sense of being overwhelmed, disappointments and unconfessed sin. Many Bible characters suffered from bouts of mild or strong discouragement: Joshua (see Deut. 1:21), Gideon (see Judg. 6:11-15), Jonah (see Jonah 4:4-11), David (see Ps. 34), Elijah (see 1 Kings 19:4-18), Peter (see John 21:3) and John Mark (see Acts 15:38). It is not a sin to be discouraged; it is a sin to stay discouraged. God wants to charge your flattened batteries with His Word, His Spirit and His faithfulness. Haggai 2:4 says, "'Yet now be strong, Zerubbabel,' says the Lord; 'and be strong, Joshua, son of Jehozadak, the high priest; and be strong, all you people of the land,' says the Lord, 'and work; for I am with you,' says the Lord of hosts." The word to all leaders of Gate Churches is to be strong! Be encouraged!

Job 4:4 promises, "Your words have upheld him who was stumbling, and you have strengthened the feeble knees." Words are a powerful force. They turn losers into winners, quitters into starters, weary souls into watered gardens. In the Greek language, the word "encouragement" has the idea of one person joining someone else on a journey and speaking words that encourage the traveler to keep pressing on despite the obstacles or the fatigue. Words were the rallying call used in speeches by leaders and by soldiers to urge and motivate them.

Winston Churchill served as Prime Minister in England during a time of great discouragement. The country was under attack and appeared to be losing the war. The most powerful tool he wielded was not his skill at developing battle strategies; it was the power of his words of encouragement. Through his speeches, Churchill challenged the British people to rise to the challenge because they *would* overcome. His words of encouragement to fearful soldiers catapulted them courageously into battle. The power of his encouraging words made ordinary men cope gallantly in their perilous, or dangerous, situations. His words encouraged men in great distress to hold their ground, to keep on their feet while the world collapsed around them. Churchill's words enabled men to pass the breaking point without breaking; they caused a nation that appeared to be losing the war to stir its courage to face overwhelming odds with a victorious spirit.

We need to receive words of encouragement as we stand in the gate, words from Scripture and *rhema* words from the Holy Spirit (see Acts 9:3; Rom. 12:8; 1; 2 Cor. 1:17). We also need words from encouragers (see Acts 4:36; 11:22-26). God places certain people into our lives to minister to us in every way. They are people like Epaphroditus, an encourager to the apostle Paul, who was a fellow worker, a fellow soldier—one whom Paul says ministered to his need (see Phil. 2:25-29; 4:18). There will be those special people who will disregard their own lives in order to pour into ours—people who reflect 1 John 3:16: "By this we know love, because He laid down His life for us. And we also ought to lay down our lives for the brethren." There will be God-ordained people like Onesiphorus who will bring refreshing to our lives such as we read about in 2 Timothy 1:16: "The Lord grant mercy to the household of Onesiphorus, for he often refreshed me, and was not ashamed of my chain." (See also Matt. 3:17; Rom. 12:16; 15:1; Gal. 6:1-4.)

As our approval buckets are filled, our personalities flourish. If, however, those buckets remain empty, our personalities wither and suffer deprivation. Do not let your spirit wither. Be encouraged right now, this moment. Let the

Spirit of God hover over your life as He did over the face of the deep (see Gen. 1:1-10) in order to bring forth in you a new creation.

PERSONAL GATES FOR GATEKEEPERS TO GUARD

The Gate-Church leader is not only responsible to guard the gates of the church, but also his own personal gates. The personal gates of the leader are those areas of his or her personal life that shape and direct life and ministry. Genesis 4:7 warns that "sin is crouching at your door; it desires to have you, but you must master it" (NIV). Exodus 12:23 suggests that "the destroyer" is at the door! The Gate Leader is to take heed of the entry points, or the gates, to his own life which may be likened to the gates around the city.

In Nehemiah's day the city was ruined, the walls were broken down and the gates were destroyed. Nehemiah warns the people, "Do not let the gates of Jerusalem be opened until the sun is hot; and while they stand guard, let them shut and bar the doors; and appoint guards from among the inhabitants of Jerusalem, one at his watch station and another in front of his own house" (Neh. 7:3). Notice that the exhortation to watch the gates ends with a call to the gatekeeper to guard the gates of his own house (see Neh. 4:23; 12:24). Let us be alert to our own houses, our own gates, our own battles, realizing that we have a personal responsibility to repair all broken gates in our own lives and to guard them with all diligence. Now let's look at the kinds of gatekeepers we are to become.

GATEKEEPERS OF OUR COVENANTS

A spirit of "covenant breaking" (see Rom. 1:31) has invaded our culture and especially our nation. Covenants are being broken in the areas of morality, marriage, business, church and personal commitments. True integrity desires to express itself in covenant commitment. The Gate Leader must be a covenant person in all areas of life and ministry, keeping covenant with God and with people.

The word "covenant" speaks of a binding contract, a written agreement of promise under a seal between two or more parties for the performance of some action. Covenants between God and people must originate with God, for He alone has the authority and ability to make covenants effective. God initiates His covenants with people and our responsibility is to respond. God is a covenant-making and covenant-keeping God who expects His leaders to be covenant people. We are to guard the covenant that we have made with God through the cross of Christ and our spiritual birth. Our growth and continual transformation is extremely important (see Ezek. 11:19-21; 36:25-27; Heb. 8:6-13). We are to watch and keep our covenant with people, leadership and the church. A breakdown in covenant keeping in any one area of a covenant person's life will weaken other areas and cause a spiritual decay. Guard the gate of covenant—the covenant of marriage, the covenant with God and the covenant with the church!

GATEKEEPERS OF OUR VINEYARDS

The Gate Leader must pay close attention to the vineyard that God has given and not be guilty of neglecting to guard this gate. The vineyard represents what God has allowed us to be a leader over, whether that be as an influencer and shaper of a particular ministry in a local church or as the overseer of a local church. Isaiah 27:3 exhorts, "I, the Lord, keep it, I water it every moment; lest any hurt it, I keep it night and day." Song of Solomon 1:6 laments that the Lord has made us keepers of the vineyard but our own vineyard we have not kept. The enemy will come in through this open gate and take our vineyards from us. According to 1 Samuel 8:14, "He will take the best of your fields, your vineyards, and your olive groves, and give them to his servants." Make a commitment to guard the vineyard, or garden, that God has given you. I use the word "garden" because Genesis 2:15 says, "Then the Lord God took the man and put him in the garden of Eden to tend and keep it."

GATEKEEPERS OF OUR MOUTHS

Gate Leaders must guard carefully the gate of the mouth, our words, our conversations, and our expressions. Proverbs 13:3 warns, "He who guards his mouth preserves his life, but he who opens wide his lips shall have destruction." And Psalm 34:13 cautions to "keep your tongue from evil, and your lips from speaking deceit." The psalmist exhorts us to place a guard over our mouths: "Set a guard, O Lord, over my mouth; keep watch over the door of my lips" (see Ps. 141:3). God's Word is His bond; our word is our bond. Our words are a measuring rod of our character. We must keep our words of promise. As leaders, follow-through on our word is the integrity factor that others will judge. Psalm 15:4 says the one who will dwell in the holy hill of the Lord is the one "in whose eyes a vile person is despised, but he honors those who fear the LORD; he who swears to his own hurt and does not change." Keep your word at all times to all people in all seasons of life, even if it causes you pain to do so!

GATEKEEPERS OF OUR DREAMS AND VISIONS

The Gate Leader must be a dreamer, a person with God-given vision and the heart to pay the price to fulfill the vision. Proverbs 29:18 reminds us that without a vision, people live without power, without motivation and will ultimately be swayed by every wind that blows upon them. Guard the dream that God has given you. Don't let it shrink; don't let it fall to the ground. At the same time, be realistic about your dreams. Don't allow spiritual foolishness to damage the real thing that God desires to do in and through your life.

I heard a story about Dan O'Brien that illustrates our need to guard our dreams and visions. Dan was trying out for the 1992 Olympic pole-vault team. The bar started at 14 feet 5 1/2 inches, but O'Brien always vaulted far more than that. Instead of wasting his energy on the lower jumps, he decided to wait until the bar was at 15 feet 9 inches, a jump he frequently made. Since he had not warmed up, he missed his first try, then his second and finally his third and final. He did not qualify for the Olympic team. His ambition robbed him. He should have begun with the lower jump at 14 feet 5 1/2 inches and worked his way up to 15 feet 9 inches like he had on many other occasions. His failure to do so destroyed his dream. We are to be real people of faith, taking one step at a time, dreaming with discipline.

THE MISSION OF THE GATE-CHURCH LEADER

I have created an acronym for the word "gate" that helps capture our mission as Gate leaders for the twenty-first century.

G = Guarding faithfully the gates of spiritual life and family values

A = Achieving the God-given dreams and visions with integrity

T = Taking back our city, our culture and our nation with courage

E = Equipping the next generation for Kingdom expansion

Now let's look at some specific gates we are to guard for Gate Churches. We are:

1. Gatekeepers of the vision gate (see Prov. 29:18)
2. Gatekeepers of the harvest gate (see Neh. 3:3)

3. Gatekeepers of the values gate (see Neh. 3:6)

4. Gatekeepers of the river gate (see Neh. 3:15)

5. Gatekeepers of the city gate (see Neh. 2:13; 2 Chron. 35:15)

6. Gatekeepers of the prayer and praise gate (see Ps. 47:7; 111:1; 1 Pet. 2:5)

7. Gatekeepers of the warfare gate (see Gen. 22:17; 2 Kings 11:5-11)

8. Gatekeepers of the miracle gate (see Acts 3:10; 10:17)

9. Gatekeepers of the finance gate (see 2 Chron. 31:14)

10. Gatekeepers of the glory of God gate (see Ezek. 43:4; 44:4; John 17:1-15)

EVERY GUARD SHOULD KEEP THE GATES

The Lord has called some to be kings and others to be priests. No matter what the call, however, everyone of us have gates that we are to guard. The following are the words of a man who was summoned to guard the gates of a nation, President Theodore Roosevelt:

> It is not the critic who counts, not the man who points out how the strong man stumbled, or where the doer of deeds could have done them better. The credit belongs to the man who is actually in the arena; whose face is marred by dust and sweat and blood; who strives valiantly, who errs and comes short again and again; who knows the great enthusiasms, the great devotions, and spends himself in a worthy cause; who, at the best, knows in the end the triumph of high achievement; and who, at the worst, at least fails while daring greatly, so that his place shall never be with those cold and timid souls who know neither victory nor defeat.

If a man will lay down his life for a nation that will one day pass away, how much more should we, God's Gate-Church keepers, be willing to sacrifice in order to guard the gates for a Kingdom that will never end!

APPENDIX

One of our practical applications to this challenge is in our School of Equipping, which we offer as a systematic approach to learning the Word of God. The following is a typical layout of our eight tracks and the different classes offered in each.

TRACK	100 SERIES FOUNDATIONAL	200 SERIES DEVELOPMENTAL	300 SERIES ELECTIVES	400 SERIES LEADERSHIP DEVELOPMENT
CHURCH LIFE	**101** Church Membership	**201** Giving, Receiving, and Prospering	**301** Women's Ministry	**401** Cell Leaders Training
	102 Finding and Developing Your Spiritual Gifts	**202** Building Relationships That Last	**302** Developing Prophetic and Preaching Gifts	**402** Lay Pastor Training
	103 Restoration Theology and the New Testament Church	**203** Worship Power, Principles and Practice	**303** Church Planting	**403** Lay Counselor's Training
	104 Success in Business for Young Leaders	**204** Success in the Marketplace	**304** Building a Successful Business God's Way	**404** Timothy Training Class
	105 Lifetime Financial Strategies	**205** Becoming a Godly Man	**305** Character Qualifications for Leadership	**405** Children's Ministry Training
			306 Becoming a Godly Woman	
FAMILY LIFE	**101** Building a Successful Family	**201** Growing Kids God's Way	**301** Deepening Intimacy in Marriage	**401** Learning to Heal Broken Homes or Marriages
	102 Building a Successful Marriage	**202** Parenting Pre-School Age	**302** Handling Finances in the Home	**402** Leading a Young Marrieds Cell Group
	103 Becoming a Successful Parent	**203** Parenting School Age	**303** Handling Family and Marriage Conflicts	**403** Family and Marriage Counseling Training

TRACK	100 SERIES FOUNDATIONAL	200 SERIES DEVELOPMENTAL	300 SERIES ELECTIVES	400 SERIES LEADERSHIP DEVELOPMENT
FAMILY LIFE CONT.	**104** Being a Successful Single	**204** Parenting Teens		
	105 Family Covenant	**205** Five Stones to Build Your Marriage		
SPIRITUAL GROWTH	**101** Breakthrough to Maturity	**201** Right/Wrong Thinking	**301** Walking in Freedom	**401** Leading and Releasing Others in the HS
	102 Spiritual Disciplines	**202** Spirit-Filled Life	**302** Decision- Making and the Will of God	**402** Helping Others Find Their Freedom in Christ
	103 Principled Living	**203** Character Development	**303** Paul's Basic Theology (Rom 1-8)	**403** Christian Maturity
	104 Growing in Intimacy with God			
BIBLE TRUTHS	**101** How to Get the Most out of Your Bible	**201** An Introduction to the OT	**301** The Life of Christ	**401** How to Study the Bible
	102 What the Bible Teaches	**202** An Introduction to the NT	**302** The Book of Genesis	**402** How to Interpret the Bible
	104 The Truth About the Church	**203** The Truth About God	**303** The Book of Acts	**403** How to Teach the Bible
	103 Living in Blessing	**204** The Truth About Salvation	**304** The Truth About Jesus	
			305 The Truth About the Holy Spirit	
			306 The Truth About the Kingdom of God	

TRACK	100 SERIES FOUNDATIONAL	200 SERIES DEVELOPMENTAL	300 SERIES ELECTIVES	400 SERIES LEADERSHIP DEVELOPMENT
YOUTH ISSUES — COLLEGE AGE	**101** Foundations for Life I	**201** Roots of Character	**301** World Views	**401** Generation Church Leadership Training
	102 Foundations for Life II	**202** Godly Relationships	**302** Apologetics for the University Student	**402** Counseling
	103 Walking in Spiritual Freedom	**203** Life Choices		
YOUTH ISSUES — SENIOR HIGH	**101** Wise Foundations	**201** Roots of character	**301** Ethics	**401** Generation Church Leadership Training
	102 Firm Foundations	**202** Basic Apologetics	**302** Moral Issues	**402** School of Discipleship
	103 Building on the Foundations	**203** Holy Spirit	**303** Confronting Popular Culture	**403** Missions
				404 Worship
YOUTH ISSUES — JUNIOR HIGH	**101** Wise Foundations	**201** Keys to a Happy Life	**301** What is Prayer and How to Pray	**401** Jr High Leadership Training
	102 Firm Foundations	**202** Attitudes: Good and Bad	**302** Youth and the Great Commission	**402** Counseling Junior Highers
	103 Building on the Foundations	**203** Family Relationships	**303** Stomping on Fear	
PRAYER INTER-CESSION	**101** Seven Power Points of Prayer	**201** Becoming a General Intercessor	**301** Principles of Altar Prayer Ministry	**401** Functioning as Prayer Leaders in the Home
	102 Principles of Intercession	**202** Becoming a Personal Intercessor	**302** Principles of Deliverance Prayer Ministry	**402** Functioning as Prayer Leaders in the Church
	103 Spiritual Armor & Weapons of Spiritual Warfare	**203** Informed Intercession	**303** Principles of Healing Prayer Ministry	**403** Functioning as Leaders in the Community

TRACK	100 SERIES FOUNDATIONAL	200 SERIES DEVELOPMENTAL	300 SERIES ELECTIVES	400 SERIES LEADERSHIP DEVELOPMENT
PRAYER INTER-CESSION CONT.	**104** Prayer and Fullfilling Life's Destiny	**204** Becoming a World Intercessor		
HARVEST MINISTRIES	**101** Finding Freedom in Sharing Your Faith	**201** Spirit Empowered Evangelism	**301** Children's Evangelism	**401** Structuring for Assimilation
	102 Learning to Share the Gospel	**202** Care Evangelism	**302** Urban Evangelism	**402** City Care Training
	103 Making Disciples	**203** Prayer Evangelism	**303** Event Evangelism	**403** Ultimate Journey Small Group Evangelism
			304 Apologetics World Religions & Cults Types/Styles of Evangelism	**404** Community Classes
INTERCUL-TURAL MINISTRIES	**101** Great Commission Churches	**201** Bridging Culture	**301** Local Ethnic Ministry	**401** Missions Strategies
	102 Great Stories from the Front Lines		**302** The 10/40 Window: Target-ing Unreached People Groups	**402** Making of a Missionary
	120 Membership (Spanish, Laotian, Russian)		**303** Cross-Cultural Communication	**403** STORM Team Preparation
	121 Turning Points (Spanish, Laotian, Russian)		**304** World Religions and Cults	
	122 Basic Christian living (Spanish, Laotian, Russian)			

TRACK	100 SERIES FOUNDATIONAL	200 SERIES DEVELOPMENTAL	300 SERIES ELECTIVES	400 SERIES LEADERSHIP DEVELOPMENT
SPECIAL ELECTIVES	101 Songwriting